P9-CQI-238

*Literary Circles and
Cultural Communities in
Renaissance England*

Literary Circles and Cultural Communities in Renaissance England

*Edited by Claude J. Summers
and Ted-Larry Pebworth*

University of Missouri Press
Columbia and London

Library of Congress Cataloging-in-Publication Data

Literary circles and cultural communities in Renaissance England / edited by Claude J. Summers and Ted-Larry Pebworth.

   p.   cm.

   Includes index.

   "The original, abbreviated versions of the essays collected here were presented at the thirteenth bienniel Renaissance conference at the University of Michigan—Dearborn, October 15–17, 1998"—P. 3.

   ISBN 0-8262-1317-0 (alk. paper)

   1. English literature—Early modern, 1500–1700—History and criticism—Congresses.   2. Literature and society—England—History—17th century—Congresses. 3. Authors, English—modern, 1500–1700—Biography—Congresses.   4. Social interaction—England—History—17th century—Congresses.   6. Community in literature—Congresses.   7. Social interaction in literature—Congresses.   8. Renaissance—England—Congresses.   9. England—Intellectual life—17th century—Congresses.   I. Summers, Claude J.   II. Pebworth, Ted-Larry.   III. Renaissance Conference (13th : 1998 : University of Michigan—Dearborn)

PR418.S64 L58   2000
820.9'003—dc21   00-064882

Designer: Stephanie Foley
Typesetter: The Composing Room of Michigan, Inc.
Printer and Binder: Thomson-Shore, Inc.
Typeface: ITC Giovanni

For Elnora Ford and Maggie Martin

Contents

Acknowledgments

This book and the scholarly meeting from which it originated have profited from the great effort, wide learning, and scholarly generosity of the conference steering committee: Diana Treviño Benet, Achsah Guibbory, Robert B. Hinman, Judith Scherer Herz, John R. Roberts, and Michael C. Schoenfeldt helped referee the submissions to the conference and offered valuable suggestions for revision. Their contributions have been extensive, and we join the authors of the essays in expressing gratitude for their insights and devotion. It is also our pleasant duty to acknowledge the support of the following administrators at the University of Michigan–Dearborn: Emily L. Spinelli, former chair, Department of Humanities; John W. Presley, former dean, College of Arts, Sciences, and Letters; and Robert L. Simpson, provost and vice chancellor for Academic Affairs.

Literary Circles and
Cultural Communities in
Renaissance England

Claude J. Summers and Ted-Larry Pebworth

Introduction

The literary circle is widely recognized as a significant feature of Renaissance literary culture. Indeed, it is one of the essential material conditions for the production of literature in an era in which patronage relations were crucial and in which manuscripts were frequently circulated among coteries of sympathetic readers. Moreover, literary circles may have helped shape many aspects of an individual writer's work, including his or her distinctive style and subject matter. Arthur Marotti, for example, has argued that all the basic features of Donne's art resulted from its coterie character: "His creation of a sense of familiarity and intimacy, his fondness for dialectic, intellectual complexity, paradox and irony, the appeals to shared attitudes and group interests (if not to private knowledge), the explicit gestures of biographical self-referentiality, the styles he adopted or invented all relate to the coterie circumstances of his verse."[1] Despite the broad consensus as to its importance, however, the literary circle has received remarkably little examination as an element of literary culture worthy of study in its own right. Although literary historians and critics have identified a large number of literary circles and cultural communities in the period—most notable among them, the Sidney-Herbert circle, the School of Donne, Jonson and the Sons of Ben, the group at Little Gidding, the Cavendish or Newcastle network, the Samuel Hartlib circle, and the Great Tew alliance—and nearly every prominent Renaissance writer has been assigned to one or more circles or literary communities, the phenomenon itself nevertheless remains largely unexplored.

Most often, the literary circle is defined as a coterie whose members are linked by shared social, political, philosophical, or aesthetic interests or values, or who vie for the interests and attention of a particular patron, or who are

1. Arthur F. Marotti, *John Donne, Coterie Poet* (Madison: University of Wisconsin Press, 1986), 19.

1

drawn together by bonds of friendship, family, religion, or location. Often writers are members of multiple, sometimes overlapping, coteries and communities, or during the course of their careers, they move from one circle to another. Jonson, for example, was, simultaneously, not only the leader of the famous group of younger poets and wits who identified themselves as Sons of Ben, but also a member of the circle of poets patronized by members of the Sidney family, especially William Herbert, earl of Pembroke, and at various times also associated with such circles as those that revolved around Lucy Harrington, countess of Bedford; Lucius Cary, viscount Falkland of Great Tew; and William Cavendish, earl of Newcastle. Not surprisingly, many critics and historians employ the concept of the circle as a means of explaining the germination, transmission, and revision of ideas and the exertion and extension of influence, as well as a kind of map on which to locate individual writers in relation to each other and to various intellectual, political, and social issues and causes. But in the hands of many literary historians and critics, the exact dimensions and the specific functions of literary circles are often frustratingly vague or suspiciously flexible and shifting. The imprecision with which literary circles are usually demarcated is one indication of their general neglect as a topic.

This volume attempts to understand more precisely the nature and function of literary circles and literary communities in Renaissance England. The essays presented here explore the various ways in which literary circles—both actual and imaginary—are conceived and the manifold needs that they fulfill. While the emphasis is primarily on particular circles (or putative circles), attention is also paid to larger theoretical issues relating to literary circles and to the broader and more general concept of cultural communities. The authors raise important questions about the extent to which literary circles are themselves fictional or historical constructs, about how the concept of a literary circle may be illuminating or limiting, about how the circle metaphor itself might usefully be extended or reformulated, and about how particular groups and communities actually operated. Some authors problematize the very concept of the literary circle, while others attempt to illustrate the varied effects of specific networks on individual writers. For some contributors, the primary interest is the illumination of particular communities, while for others the focus is on how aspects of literary circles can elucidate specific works or the entire literary system. The aim of the volume is not to propagate a single view of the function of literary circles in Renaissance culture, but to explore the various ways in which Renaissance literature may be fruitfully approached via literary circles and cultural communities.

The original, abbreviated versions of the essays collected here were presented at the thirteenth biennial Renaissance conference at the University of Michigan–Dearborn, October 15–17, 1998.[2] The final versions printed here have benefited from the stimulating exchanges and responses afforded by the conference, and they intersect, reinforce, and challenge each other in significant and interesting ways. But the essays were initially written independently of each other and without consultation among the authors. No topics or approaches were assigned, and none were proscribed. All the essays are historically grounded and critically vital, but they vary widely in their historical perspectives, critical techniques and presuppositions, scope, and focus. The only criterion for selection is that each essay contribute to our fuller understanding of the nature and function of literary circles and cultural communities in Renaissance England.

In the provocative opening essay, Judith Scherer Herz ranges from the circles of Dante's *Purgatorio* and the group of friends, writers, and artists who met in Bloomsbury in the early decades of the twentieth century to the Society of Friendship created by Katherine Philips in the mid-seventeenth century. Con-

---

2. Selected papers from the previous Dearborn conferences have also been published: those from the 1974 conference as *"Trust to Good Verses": Herrick Tercentenary Essays,* ed. Roger B. Rollin and J. Max Patrick (Pittsburgh: University of Pittsburgh Press, 1978); those from the 1976 conference on seventeenth-century prose as a special issue of *Studies in the Literary Imagination* (10:2 [1977]), ed. William A. Sessions and James S. Tillman; those from the 1978 conference as *"Too Rich to Clothe the Sunne": Essays on George Herbert,* ed. Claude J. Summers and Ted-Larry Pebworth (Pittsburgh: University of Pittsburgh Press, 1980); those from the 1980 conference as *Classic and Cavalier: Essays on Jonson and the Sons of Ben,* ed. Claude J. Summers and Ted-Larry Pebworth (Pittsburgh: University of Pittsburgh Press, 1982); those from the 1982 conference as *The Eagle and the Dove: Reassessing John Donne,* ed. Claude J. Summers and Ted-Larry Pebworth (Columbia: University of Missouri Press, 1986); those from the 1984 conference as *"Bright Shootes of Everlastingnesse": The Seventeenth-Century Religious Lyric,* ed. Claude J. Summers and Ted-Larry Pebworth (Columbia: University of Missouri Press, 1987); those from the 1986 conference as *"The Muses Common-Weale": Poetry and Politics in the Seventeenth Century,* ed. Claude J. Summers and Ted-Larry Pebworth (Columbia: University of Missouri Press, 1988); those from the 1988 conference as *On the Celebrated and Neglected Poems of Andrew Marvell,* ed. Claude J. Summers and Ted-Larry Pebworth (Columbia: University of Missouri Press, 1992); those from the 1990 conference as *Renaissance Discourses of Desire,* ed. Claude J. Summers and Ted-Larry Pebworth (Columbia: University of Missouri Press, 1993); those from the 1992 conference as *The Wit of Seventeenth-Century Poetry,* ed. Claude J. Summers and Ted-Larry Pebworth (Columbia: University of Missouri Press, 1995); those from the 1994 conference as *Representing Women in Renaissance England,* ed. Claude J. Summers and Ted-Larry Pebworth (Columbia: University of Missouri Press, 1997); and those from the 1996 conference as *The English Civil Wars in the Literary Imagination,* ed. Claude J. Summers and Ted-Larry Pebworth (Columbia: University of Missouri Press, 1999).

tending that insofar as circles are drawn by literary historians, "they are less found objects than artifacts of the discovery process, constructed to serve varied critical, theoretical, and historical ends." When we talk about literary circles, Herz argues, "we are primarily talking about . . . the construction of an archive where the circle functions as a cataloging mechanism and as a heuristic, that is, as a way to pose questions about textual production and reception, and about the subtle and not always predictable intellectual, political, and literary affiliations that connect families, friends, and colleagues." She examines a number of Renaissance and seventeenth-century groupings, including the Sidney and Hartlib circles, to illustrate her point that, depending on how the lens is focused, "either circles do not exist or there are only circles, there are either fewer than you can count on one hand or more than you can possibly enumerate, all rotating ceaselessly through and around one another." Concluding with a discussion of Philips's fictive Society of Friendship, she observes that among the uses of circles—even mystical ones—is an increased understanding of the "construction of the idea and practice of friendship and of the codings of erotic desire as well."

In his study of the complex relationship of Donne's "Baite" and Marlowe's "Passionate Shepheard to his love," M. Thomas Hester raises intriguing questions about the nature of literary circles in the period, especially the ways in which the membership and circumferences of those circles expanded and contracted depending on the authors' employment of particular lexicons. He argues that the possibility that Donne's "own literary circle might hear or read 'The Baite' differently from another group of readers or even from another of the circle of readers for whom the poem was intended is borne out by recollection of the various contexts and lexicons of the poem." More pointedly, Hester contends that the presence within "The Baite" of words suggestive of the lexicon of late-Elizabethan political and religious discourse points toward a literary circle that includes, in addition to the members of the Inns of Court traditionally associated with Donne in the 1590s, a readership especially sympathetic to the poet's Catholicism. "It also suggests that Donne's literary circle would have been not just attuned to the young recusant poet's witty parody of current courtly literary fashions and debates, but also responsive to the implications of the satirical poet's verses."

Sharon Cadman Seelig is concerned with "circles that were not, of failures of connection and of isolation, of circles that existed in longing and imagination," in her study of Aemelia Lanyer, a woman who stands outside a social group yet vividly imagines such a community and seeks to create it in her work. Concentrating on "The Description of Cooke-ham" and the dedications prefaced to *Salve Deus Rex Judaeorum*, Seelig finds that Lanyer constructs a fictive circle of strong women "that functions as an alternative to the patriarchal structure." Lanyer, Seelig contends, finds in Margaret Russell, Anne Clifford, and the women to whom she dedicated *Salve Deus*, "a virtue that is strength rather than merely endurance," and she depicts these women as "distinctly heroic and independent, as dominant." Although she is denied presence and contact with them, she imaginatively creates of these women "a cohort of female Worthies worthy of the name of virtue, a circle calculated to elicit—even in the absence of historical documentation—admiration and assent." Out of her marginality and weakness, Lanyer constructs a remarkable community "present more powerfully and enduringly in her fiction than in life itself."

John Considine also examines an imagined circle, though one created for reasons far different from Lanyer's construct. In a careful bibliographical analysis of the collection of prose and verse ascribed by the publisher Lawrence Lisle to Sir Thomas Overbury and his literary circle, Considine convincingly demonstrates that the so-called Overbury circle never actually existed. As he concludes, "Sir Thomas Overbury's *Wife* does not record the literary exchanges of Overbury and his friends. It is the document not of a literary circle but of an invented literary circle." Lisle created the "Overbury circle" as an opportunity to issue enlarged editions of *A Wife* without appearing to include extraneous material in it, while also feeding his readers' desire to look into the private transactions of the court, as encapsulated in what are ostensibly passages of wit shared by Overbury and his friends. Rather than courtiers, the contributors to Lisle's editions are actually educated but not particularly successful minor writers with little or no connection to Overbury. In inventing the Overbury literary circle, Lisle probably also sought to appeal to middle-class readers' increasing awareness of a system of manuscript transmission of texts from which they were largely excluded.

Focusing on the responses by the members of Jonson's circle to his famous failure of 1629, *The New Inn*, Robert Evans finds that the episode raises a number of intriguing questions about the role of literary circles and cultural communities in the period. He concludes that the *New Inn* controversy suggests that members of Jonson's circle could exercise independent judgment, but their judgments would inevitably also be affected by social pressures from within and outside their circle. Membership in a circle could help an individual cope with the frustrations of social isolation, but embarrassing behavior, especially by the circle's leader, might also cause greater isolation. Membership in a circle, especially one that is in constant flux, "meant acquiring both a group of (temporary) allies and a collection of (potential) rivals, and rivalry might especially become an issue when the leader of a circle seemed to be losing influence both within and outside his own group." Evans concludes that the evidence provided by the *New Inn* controversy suggests that ideology played far less of a role in determining Jonson's standing within and without his circle than micropolitical considerations and his artistic ability.

Timothy Raylor begins his essay by remarking on the wide range of alliances that is designated by the term *circle* and by observing that the image is also problematic because "it describes only two dimensions. As such, it has a leveling effect, reducing all participants in an activity to the same size or, in social terms, to the same rank and status." His study of the group that revolved around the figures of William Cavendish—successively earl, marquess, and duke of Newcastle, probably the most powerful nobleman in northern England—and his brother Charles emphasizes not only the issue of collaborative authorship but its hierarchical nature as well. "When we reconceive the relationships among the Cavendish brothers and their associates in terms of patronage, rather than in terms of a circle drawing together men with a shared interest in science, our picture of the group becomes a little more supple and inclusive," he asserts. In a fascinating analysis of the collaboration between William Cavendish and his assistant Robert Payne on an elegy for Ben Jonson, Raylor finds that Cavendish's reliance on Payne and other members of his household in literary matters was analogous to the reliance of scientific gentlemen of the day on "invisible assistants." He concludes that "the so-called Cavendish, Newcastle, or Welbeck circle is really best understood as an extension of the aristocratic household."

The question of influence is a vital concern in Paul Parrish's study. Finding the circle metaphor inadequate to describe the rich cultural community in and around Cambridge in the 1630s and 1640s, Parrish depicts instead a "literary ellipse, with the two foci being Herbert and Crashaw," and including among others Nicholas Ferrar, Joseph Beaumont, and Abraham Cowley. Acknowledging the supremacy of Herbert as a poet and an influence during the century, Parrish argues that for a while the positions of Herbert and Crashaw were regarded with equal attention by Beaumont, Ferrar, and Cowley. The latter, however, eventually escapes the shadow of his early mentors: "[A]s we progress beyond the immediacy of the lives and art of Herbert and Crashaw, their influence is less controlling, particularly on a poet such as Cowley who establishes a more independent voice shaped by diverse antecedents and contemporary associations." Although even the figure of the ellipse may be problematic for a poet such as Cowley, it at least acknowledges the continuing, though sometimes subtle and complicated, presence of Herbert and Crashaw in his work.

Anna Nardo is, like Seelig and Considine, also concerned with circles that were not actually realized, in this case Milton's proposal in *The Reason of Church-government* that English magistrates "create literary academies, associations more formally structured than the 'circles' surrounding Sir Philip Sidney or Ben Jonson." Contrasting the situation in England, where "literary circles were fluid—forming, dissipating, then reforming around a charismatic figure or a generous patron," with that in Italy, where "literary academies were civic institutions," Nardo explores the nature and function of the Italian academies that Milton remembered so fondly from his Italian journey and sought to transplant to English soil. As Nardo points out, by classifying these academies as a form of "'recreating intermission of labour, and serious things,'" Milton "locates these gatherings in a space set apart from the tumult of political discourse"; by describing their learned meetings as "affable," he "emphasizes the easy conversation among friends that he found so congenial"; and by identifying their goals as the attempt to "'civilize, adorn and make discreet our minds,'" he makes clear their importance and his reason for recommending them. Although the poet's recommendation never yielded fruit, in his later poetry, including his epics as well as his sonnets, Milton continued to depict scenes that recall the cultured leisure of the Italian academies.

Stella Revard investigates the group of scholar-poets patronized by the young royalist poet Thomas Stanley during the 1640s and later memorialized in his lengthy poem "A Register of Friends." The circle included, among others, the dramatist James Shirley and the poets Alexander Brome, Robert Herrick, and Richard Lovelace. This group, most of whose members were associated with the Middle Temple, was linked by friendship and devotion to scholarly and poetic endeavors, especially translations of classical texts, but also by the hard political times that many in the circle endured. Not all the members shared the same political allegiances—the young poet-essayist John Hall, for instance, was anti-royalist—but in their original compositions and translations, all were united in seeking to preserve classical and neoclassical virtues in an era that they regarded as inhospitable. The turbulent times in which the Stanley circle was born may have made it especially valuable for its participants, but the fact that some members, such as Edward Sherburne, lived on to become part of other poetic circles after the Restoration suggests that the functions performed by the Stanley group transcended the necessities of its era.

In complementary essays, Paul G. Stanwood and M. L. Donnelly discuss two aspects of the circle that surrounded Lucius Cary, viscount Falkland, in the 1630s. Drawn to Cary's estate of Great Tew, a few miles from Oxford, that group consisted of such future luminaries in church, state, and letters as Edward Hyde, George Morley, Henry Hammond, William Chillingworth, Thomas Hobbes, George Sandys, Edmund Waller, Sidney Godolphin, and John Hales. Stanwood explores the influence of Richard Hooker's *Of the Lawes of Ecclesiastical Polity* on the religious and political thinking of the circle, especially notable in the works of Chillingworth, Hammond, and Hyde. He finds in Hooker's emphasis upon "natural law, reason, design, harmony, and the desire to uncover the divine order in human affairs" the intellectual source for the ideals of tolerance, irenicism, independence, critical reason, humanist scholarship, and active virtue espoused by the members of the circle. Looking forward, Donnelly sees the Tevians as contributing significantly to the construction of the neoclassical aesthetic that was to dominate the Restoration and the earlier eighteenth century. Concentrating on Davenant and Hobbes and the critical papers prefacing *Gondibert*, he finds in the Tew circle crucial elements of the neoclassical mode: a sophisticated critical historicism, a sense of propriety and graceful simplicity, an irenic attitude toward theological controversy and political theory, and the elevation of judgment and reason as the only genuine arbiters of truth and expression.

As Achsah Guibbory points out in the final contribution to the volume, not all seventeenth-century cultural communities were conservative, uniting individuals of shared ideals and opinions, nor were all devoted primarily to manuscript circulation. Some were radical in their agendas, seeking to persuade rather than to confirm, and their medium was print. Such was the attempt of the millenarian Quaker preacher and prophet Margaret Fell to construct a new kind of circle, one concerned with bringing about the messianic ideal of a unified humanity. Through her published pleas and responses to the writings of the Amsterdam rabbi Menasseh ben Israel, who in the 1650s sought to have Jews readmitted into England, Fell worked to convert ben Israel and European Jews in general to Christianity. Most interestingly, in the spiritual community she attempts to construct, "she is its messianic center," as she presents herself as the instrument through whom God has called the Jews. But her "'loving' approach" was compromised by her deep hostility to Judaism and her erasure of Jewish difference. Not surprisingly, her attempt to convert the Jews failed, and the circle she sought to construct never materialized. Still, as Guibbory suggests, Fell's "dream of a more inclusive community," her model of diversity, could be seen as admirable if her goal of conversion had not turned it after all into a model of sameness.

As these brief summaries suggest, in their varied approaches and imaginative analyses, the essays collected here not only explore the dynamics of long-recognized literary circles, but also expand and problematize our concept of the literary circle in Renaissance England. Some contributors illuminate groups defined in the familiar terms of friendship, family ties, shared political and aesthetic sensibilities, influence, and patronage relations, but others discover and trace the circumferences of less obvious circles and communities. Among the latter groupings are those that attempt linkage across the boundaries of time and place, that are constructed in the imaginations of isolated or excluded individuals, and even those manufactured out of whole cloth by unscrupulous publishers. Other contributors explore the nature of the relationship between a literary lion and his circle of disciples, expose hidden agendas that lie behind related works, and clarify the unacknowledged collaboration of paid employees in the works of their employers. Although literary historians have rather promiscuously identified a number of interlocking and overlapping literary circles in Renaissance England, the topic itself has been curiously neglected as a worthy subject of study. But as this volume demonstrates, careful scrutiny of literary circles—in their many and varied forms—enriches our understanding and appreciation of early modern literature by elucidating some of the crucial social transactions, intellectual networks, and material conditions that helped shape it.

Judith Scherer Herz

Of Circles, Friendship, and the Imperatives of Literary History

Circlings

The first circle on this journey is really a circular terrace, the fifth in Purgatory. There Dante and Virgil appear, followed by a third figure, just "as Christ new risen from the sepulchral cave appeared to the two who were in the way."[1] That third is Statius, for whom the *Aeneid*, when he was composing his *Thebaid*, was mother to him, was nurse *(mamma e nutrice)*. "To have lived yonder when Virgil lived"—for that, he says, he would have extended his exile from Paradise by another year. He does not know, when he says this, that he is addressing Virgil, for Virgil had silenced the pilgrim with a glance, but now, allowed to speak, Dante identifies his companion as his guide, "the same Virgil from whom you derived the power to sing of men and of the gods." Furthermore, in Statius's account, speaking back to Virgil his words from the fourth Eclogue, Virgil made him both poet and Christian ("per te poeta fui, per te cristiano"). Now as the three poets mount the sixth terrace, their places are reversed and it is Dante who follows behind, listening to a conversation that gives him "understanding in the making of poetry" (Italian has a nice verb for that act—*poetare*). They speak from within their shared literary culture ("where is Terence, Cecilius, Plautus, Varius?" recalling that earlier literary circle in canto 4 of the *Inferno* where poets talk together for eternity), and they talk, as well, from within their texts, for their characters are also figures in this literary conversation. Dante is outside their circle, but he turns it to his own use; he has, after all, created it. In the fiction of conversion, instanced here in the figure of Statius, Dante plays out the

---

1. Dante, *The Divine Comedy*, vol. 2, *Purgatorio*, canto 21, ed. and trans. John Sinclair (London: John Lane, the Bodley Head, 1948), 271.

encounter between writer and writer, writer and reader, that constitutes both his literary and his redemptive project.

Interestingly, immediately afterward, moving through the sixth and seventh terraces, he meets a series of poets who are in a more obvious sense of his own literary circle—first his friend Forese Donati with whom he had once exchanged several edgy, angry sonnets, and then Bonagiunta, possibly an acquaintance but certainly a literary adversary, now made to see the limitations of his earlier views of poetry. Then appear the two poets behind the "stil nuovo" of both Cavalcanti and Dante—Guido Guinizelli and Arnault Daniel, "fu miglior fabbro." In their conversations an aesthetic is debated in terms that are at once literary, political, and doctrinal. Dante is here both literary historian and the subject of his own literary history. Less self-fashioning than soul-fashioning, he draws a circle around his own literary and spiritual enterprise and makes his literary past and present speak together (Statius remains present, having delayed his own ascent)—not exactly voices in a room, but voices conversing in a textual space—my first literary circle.

And now to do something about which Euclidean geometers can only dream . . . squaring the circle, that is, Gordon Square, or Fitzroy Square, or Tavistock Square, haute Bloomsbury by any other name. But was the Bloomsbury group a circle? Was there a Bloomsbury group? Why discuss it at all when the subject is literary circles in Renaissance England? To work back from the last question, I want to suggest that Bloomsbury provides a useful model for looking backward to the formation of the groups, sets, circles, coteries, conversations, schools, tribes, and sons of the early modern period, especially in terms of the problems it presents to literary history. As with many of the seventeenth-century groupings, Bloomsbury, despite its high name-recognition value, gets harder and harder to see the more closely you examine it. Leonard Woolf, from the half-century retrospect of his autobiographies, says outright, "Bloomsbury never existed in the form given to it by the outside world. . . . [It] is a term . . . applied to a largely imaginary group of persons with largely imaginary objects and characteristics." Yet, most assuredly, a group of friends, mostly from various overlapping Cambridge circles—the Midnight Society, the Apostles—did meet in and around those squares in the southern portions of the borough of Camden, beginning around 1905 and continuing into the First World War. And they had their Thursday evenings and their Friday club and their play-reading club, their Aristotelian club, their 1917 club, and then later, in the '20s, their memoir club where all those earlier clubs and groupings were retrospectively and nostalgically examined and debated. And, too, there might be something overdetermined and defensive in their insistence that they were, in Leonard Woolf's words, "primarily and fundamentally a group of friends . . . [and] there was no more a communal connection between Roger Fry's *Critical and Specula-tive Essays on Art*, Maynard Keynes's *The General Theory of Employment, Interest, and Money*, and Virginia Woolf's *Orlando* than there was between Bentham's *Theory of Legislation*, Hazlitt's *Principal Picture Galleries of England* and Byron's *Don Juan*" (that *Orlando–Don Juan* pairing is worth some investigation on its own).[2] But friends they were, if not "just friends," and the ways they entered into their friendships, how they understood them, valued them, discussed them, structured them both publicly and privately, and sometimes even be-trayed them, can tell us a great deal about the social structures of Edwardian and Georgian England, and about the concept of friendship as a historical phe-nomenon and a philosophical and psychological idea, more indeed than about the specific literary or artistic production of any of the members of this pre-sumed circle.

Raymond Williams's essay "The Significance of 'Bloomsbury' as a Social and Cultural Group" is useful here as it provides terms for thinking about the rela-tion between a group and the world around it and for his reminder of the ways in which such circles keep alive a cultural memory of those who might other-wise be barely remembered save for their association with those whose reputa-tions and accomplishments are quite independent of the group.[3] This is true even if the group is an artifact of literary history, constructed after the fact to frame otherwise heterogenous materials. Further, his emphasis on "the struc-ture of feeling of the group" has direct applicability to our understanding of seventeenth-century groupings, such as Great Tew or Katherine Philips's Soci-ety of Friendship. Finally, his emphasis on the importance for Bloomsbury of "the supreme value of the civilized individual" helps identify an important element of these Renaissance circles, sets, and conversations, although for Williams it forms part of his critique of the Bloomsbury group insofar as he identifies this value with the bourgeois Enlightenment.

"The civilized individual" as a social value, however, certainly has roots old-er than the eighteenth century. Montaigne, for example, evokes it in his discus-sion of conversation in the essay "On Three Types of Relationship." If we keep the word *conversation* in mind and think of Steven Shapin's excellent examina-

2. Woolf, *Beginning Again: An Autobiography of the Years 1911 to 1918* (New York: Har-court, Brace, and World, 1964), 21, 26.

3. Williams, "The Significance of 'Bloomsbury,'" in *Keynes and the Bloomsbury Group*, ed. Derek Crabtree and A. P. Thirwell (London: Macmillan, 1980), 40–67.

tion of that concept and practice in *A Social History of Truth* as more than a discursive practice, as rather "civically living together," we can qualify the Williams analysis in useful ways. For Montaigne, conversation is both the practice of and the textual space for friendship. In conversation "there is a truce to ceremony. . . . Here everyone behaves as he pleases, and communes with his thoughts if he likes. . . . The purpose of our intercourse is simply intimacy, familiarity and talk; the exercise of the mind is our sole gain." Indeed, one definition of *conversation* in the *Oxford English Dictionary* makes it even more than *circle* the salient term for the seventeenth century: "The act of consorting or having dealings with others, living together, commerce, society, intimacy; or circle of acquaintance, company." To this we can add Colin Morris's discussion of *amicitia* and *fin'amors* in *The Discovery of the Individual, 1050–1200*, particularly his argument that "both systems [monastic friendship and troubadour *cortezia*] rest on a desire to make personal experience and personal relations the focus of life," a claim for the twelfth century that clearly anticipates the Bloomsbury refrain and has important resonances for those social formations of the Renaissance that were founded on friendship inflected by literary, intellectual, and political affinities. As Donald Dickson extensively documents in his study of Johan Valentin Andreae, Samuel Hartlib, and utopian brotherhoods, "one of the distinctive features of the learned classes in early modern Europe was the circle of literary friends." Andreae, he asserts, "loved a sociable house and 'visited' with his friends often through his correspondence."[4]

Taking as a noncontestable, and certainly obvious, assumption that like-minded people cluster together, we can find circles wherever we look. They will often have political, religious, ideological, and class coherence, but with the exception of groupings such as the Pre-Raphaelite brotherhood, not necessarily significant literary or artistic interrelationships. To study the concept and functioning of the circle is to gain access to "the texture of social relations," in Shapin's phrase, and to the conditions of intellectual, literary, artistic production. An interesting example of such a use of the circle in the writing of intellectual history is the recently published first volume of the life of the late-nineteenth-, early-twentieth-century American architect Ralph Adams Cram by Douglas Shand-Tucci, a study that is also architectural history, urban history,

---

4. Shapin, *A Social History of Truth, Civility, and Science in Seventeenth-Century England* (Chicago: University of Chicago Press, 1994), 115; Montaigne, *Essays*, trans. J. M. Cohen (Harmondsworth: Penguin, 1959), 257; Morris, *Discovery of the Individual* (Toronto: University of Toronto Press, 1972), 118; Dickson, *The Tessera of Antilia Utopian Brotherhoods and Secret Societies in the Early Seventeenth Century* (Leiden: Brill, 1998), 30.

and gay history. He focuses closely on the circles in which Cram moved, the Boston and Harvard bohemians, the Dwight-Sullivan set, and Cram's own Pinkney Street circle, as "the three leading of several not yet fully documented Bohemian circles of the period," linked by Isabella Stewart Gardner, George Santayana, and Bernard Berenson, among others.[5] Cram's Pinkney Street is placed alongside Wilde's and Whistler's Chelsea, city spaces of interlocking circles. Studying these spaces and the circles located there allows for a more densely nuanced reconstruction of gay history than can be deduced from police reports and public documents that have often provided the materials for such reconstructions. As with both Bloomsbury and the early modern groupings, the concept of the circle helps frame a set of questions and offers ways of answering them.

Bloomsbury itself rotated around and through several other overlapping circles, and two in particular help focus this issue: one around Lady Ottoline Violet Ann Cavendish Bentinck Morrell (I include all the names to give some sense of the family ramifications of this topic) and another around Sybil Colefax. Colefax as hostess brought together, and in some cases helped, a range of writers, including Thornton Wilder, H. G. Wells, Virginia Woolf, Noel Coward, and Aldous Huxley. Were they a circle? Probably in her eyes, but not necessarily in theirs. A precursor of these social formations was the late-nineteenth-century grouping the Souls, made up of Wyndhams and Charterises, Tennants, Custs, Windsors, and Grenfells. They played parlor games and talked, weaving texts, however gossamer, and in this sense they created something closer to the French salon of the seventeenth century, where fictions were created communally and where authorship was more a social than an individual function, than to the somewhat different social formation of the English coteries and conversations of the early modern period.[6] In the words of the daughter of a Soul, "they were merely a group of very intelligent, articulate people who happened to be friends and to share a love of good talk; and . . . insofar as they were a charmed circle, the line was drawn by those outside, not inside the circle."[7]

Identifying the hand that draws the circle, however, can lead to Escher-like

---

5. Shapin, *Social History of Truth*, 124; Shand-Tucci, *Boston Bohemia, 1881–1900: Life and Architecture* (Amherst: University of Massachusetts Press, 1995), 220.

6. See Joan de Jean, *Tender Geographies: Women and the Origins of the Novel in France* (New York: Columbia University Press, 1991); Caroline C. Lougee, *Le Paradis des Femmes: Women, Salons, and Social Stratification in Seventeenth-Century France* (Princeton: Princeton University Press, 1976); and Elizabeth Goldsmith, *Exclusive Conversation: The Art of Interaction in Seventeenth-Century France* (Philadelphia: University of Pennsylvania Press, 1988).

7. Jane Abdy and Charlotte Gere, *The Souls* (London: Sidgwick and Jackson, 1984), 13.

bafflement. Lady Elcho's daughter suggests that it is drawn by those excluded, which is not entirely true. As a group takes shape, it is ordered by affinities both elective and inherited, and those within know themselves there and often cast a wary eye on those outside. Thus, as Vanessa Bell of Bloomsbury declared: "Any kind of clique is sneered at by those outside it . . . and no doubt our ways of behaviour in our own surroundings were sufficiently odd, according to the customs of the day, to stir criticism." However, insofar as circles become a topic in literary history, they are often drawn by literary historians; they are less found objects than artifacts of the discovery process, constructed to serve varied critical, theoretical, and historical ends. Are the contributors to the 1593 *Phoenix Nest*—among them, Roydon, Raleigh, Dyer, Breton, Lodge, and Peele—a circle? The answer may be yes in terms of Protestant politics, but not necessarily in any specifically literary sense. And because Peele, Breton, and Lodge were friends of Marlowe, can we speak through them of a Marlowe circle? In each instance, when we speak, for example, of the Sidney circle, Great Tew, the Sons of Ben, the Inns of Court circles, the Lawes circle, or Katherine Philips's Society of Friendship, we mean something different. Sometimes we are talking of lived spaces—houses, taverns, universities, Inns of Court, theaters—at other times, of the structure of social relations and gender relations; of brothers, sisters, cousins; of friendship, love, and conversation (in its sexual sense, as well); of patronage and politics; and of intellectual networks and religious affiliations. We are, too, talking of textual spaces: of title pages, of dedicatory poems and epistles, of circles and circulation, and of issues of genre, both those genres that derive from the circle (the country house poem, the pastoral and masque, or, in France, the salon novel) and those genres from which we constitute the circle after the fact—dedications, records of conversations (Drummond and Jonson, for example), letters, and diaries. Thus, what we are primarily talking about is the construction of an archive where the circle functions as a cataloging mechanism and as a heuristic, that is, as a way to pose questions about textual production and reception, and about the subtle and not always predictable intellectual, political, and literary affiliations that connect families, friends, and colleagues. As Arthur Marotti has shown, the circle was an important mechanism for manuscript circulation, and, too, for the social textuality of manuscript formation as texts were revised, corrected, and supplemented in the process of transmission.[8] It is, as well, and has been from the first campfire to the *ruelle* alongside Madeleine de Scudéry's bed, a space for talk and friendship.

8. Bell, "Notes on Bloomsbury," in *The Bloomsbury Group*, ed. S. P. Rosenbaum, rev. ed. (Toronto: University of Toronto Press, 1995), 105; see Marotti, *Manuscript, Print, and the English Renaissance Lyric* (Ithaca: Cornell University Press, 1995), and "Patronage, Po-

Some Seventeenth-Century Circles

A survey of a few of these circles may illustrate the point that, depending on how you focus the lens, either circles do not exist or there are only circles, there are either fewer than you can count on one hand or more than you can possibly enumerate, all rotating ceaselessly through and around one another. The Sidney circle is in many ways the most interesting example of the circle that is and is not. Indeed, line or lineage or double helix may possibly be a more pertinent figure (there is certainly enough Sidney DNA to go around). There are the writing siblings: Robert, Philip, and Mary. But they do not really construct a circle among themselves, although *The Arcadia*, apparently written during Philip's visits to his sister at Wilton and Ivychurch, speaks to a shared literary sensibility and experience, epitomizing their writer-reader-writer relationship. Then there is Mary Sidney's revision and massive completion of the Psalm translations that Philip had begun, which further merges their literary projects, as do her translations of Petrarch, Mornay, and Garnier. But the figure of the circle does little to elucidate this relationship.

Philip certainly had friends, and, possibly, he, Greville, Spenser, and Dyer made a circle in those gatherings at Leicester House, which Spenser apparently referred to as "the Areopagus." One catches glimpses of this in Gabriel Harvey's *Letter Book* where he quotes a letter from Spenser, another strand in the reweaving of the "texture of social relations": "The twoe worthy gentlemen, Mr. Sidney and Mr. Dyer [wrote Immerito, that is, Spenser, to Harvey] have me, I thanke them, in sum use of familiaritye."[9] But save for keeping Dyer's name "alive," one does not learn much more than that around 1579–1580 a group of friends met and talked together. One could almost say that Sidney belonged to more circles after his death than during his life. Rendered instantly mythic, he became a figure in the circulation of his reputation—as radical Protestant, as literary model, as someone to complete, continue, or echo. Circles were drawn around his memory, in the first instance by Spenser and Mary Sidney, and then, some quarter century later, by Greville. His niece Mary Wroth circulated her own fictions, both romance and sonnet sequences, through his writings, circling his Arcadia with her Urania, and, too, circling her aunt's authorship in their shared custody of the name Mary Sidney.

---

etry, and Print," in *Patronage, Politics, and Literary Traditions in England, 1558–1658*, ed. Cedric Brown (Detroit: Wayne State University Press, 1991), 21–46.

9. Spenser to Harvey, *The Letter-Book of Gabriel Harvey, 1573–1580*, ed. E. J. L. Scott (London: Camden Society, 1884), 101.

Of course, it is the first Mary Sidney whose place in literary history was secured as the center of a circle of her own, although, possibly, "patronage machine" is a more apt description. Certainly, when literary historians talk of the Sidney circle they are referring primarily to the countess and her clients, chiefly at Wilton House, her little court, college, nursery, or university as dedications to her variously describe it, during a period starting in the mid-1580s and continuing for ten or more years. Yet, as Mary Ellen Lamb has demonstrated in a study that renders problematic a key term in her title, *Gender and Authorship in the Sidney Circle*, "decades of literary historians have gathered writers into her group on the slimmest of pretexts: a dedication to her of one work also dedicated to thirty-four other people; a writer's friendship with another writer she may have patronized; patronage of a writer by her son William after the period of her own residence at Wilton." Lamb includes in this list Henry Lok, Richard Barnfield, Gabriel Harvey, Ben Jonson, John Florio, Philip Massinger, as well as Barnabe Barnes, John Taylor, and Aemilia Lanyer. That Mary Sidney gave patronage and support, bed and board, attentive listening and comfortable surroundings to several writers is without question. The least contestable list of Wilton visitors includes, besides Spenser, Abraham Fraunce, Thomas Moffett, Nicholas Breton, Samuel Daniel, and Nathaniel Baxter. They wrote poems and plays, and Gervase Babington preached his sermons there. Some no doubt knew each other; others did not. There is a link, as well, to Raleigh, and, possibly, as Margaret Hannay suggests, following Alice Luce, Shakespeare, too, "c[a]me within the circle of her patronage."[10] But the phrase "circle of patronage" is more a geometric figure than a lived space. This data bank of names is useful as a way to locate Mary Sidney in literary history, and many of its bearers circulate in other sets and circles, but they do not, as a group, form a circle.

However, the concept of the circle still remains a convenient way to construct the spaces of literary history. Sandra Burner, for example, subtitles her study of James Shirley *A Study of Literary Coteries and Patronage in Seventeenth-Century England*, and traces Shirley's career via his circular associations: for example, how his friend the poet William Habington provided "the connection for [him] between the early Gray's Inn circle and the later Catholic Court coterie" around Sir Kenelm Digby and Endymion Porter. Her description of the Gray's Inn circle nicely connects the personal and the institutional. This group was "familiar with each other's literary work and presumably serv[ed] as critics and advocates

10. Lamb, *Gender and Authorship* (Madison: University of Wisconsin Press, 1990), 68, 251; Hannay, *Philip's Phoenix: Mary Sidney, Countess of Pembroke* (New York: Oxford University Press, 1990), 125.

for one another. The Gray's Inn circle worked much like a merchant guild, functioning to protect and support its members, seeking to advance their careers."
This is somewhat different from the social formation that Burner labels "the
Newcastle Circle," not here referring to Cavendish's patronage relations with
Jonson and Davenant or to his own theater connections, but rather to his
friendship with several Nottinghamshire Catholic families, "a small group of
literati who used poetry and drama as solace during the war."[11] But these
Markhams, Goldings, and Coopers were apparently more the audience for
Shirley and Newcastle than literary participants themselves. And this grouping
is different still from the group around Thomas Stanley, which included
Lovelace (Stanley's cousin) and Robert Herrick, as well as Shirley. Stanley not
only was a patron of Shirley but also addressed him as "dearest friend" in his
poem accompanying Shirley's 1646 *Poems*. That poem enacts a subtle blend of
patronage and friendship, insofar as Stanley reverses the patronage relation
there, calling Shirley poetry's patron.

Through Stanley, the wheels within wheels within circles rotate even more
dizzyingly, for it was during this same period that Stanley helped support John
Hall when Hall was writing the poetry that he published in 1647 and when he
was beginning his translation, at the behest of Samuel Hartlib, of the utopian
writings of Johan Valentin Andreae, a publication that brought Robert Boyle
into contact with Hartlib.[12] With Boyle and the Hartlib circle and their plans
for, among other groupings and brotherhoods, the "Invisible College," the
"Christian Learned Society," and the "Chymical Club," one is moving toward
the formation of the Royal Society. These friends, fellow utopians, and religious
reformers connect a variety of political, social, and literary coteries, which, with
their overlapping "memberships," nicely illustrates how the social, in some
measure based on theories of Christian brotherhood as well as on family ties,
the intellectual, the scientific, and the literary are in many ways inseparable at
this period. Boyle's sister Katherine Lady Ranelagh was connected to the Hartlib
circle; indeed, she was the center of several "scientific and political groups
which crystallised around [her] during 1646," and was in contact with many
important intellectual figures, such as Henry Oldenburg.[13] She employed Milton as tutor for her son, and she was, as well, an active presence in many of her

11. Burner, *James Shirley* (Lanham, Md.: University Press of America, 1988), 52, 54,
148.
12. Dickson, *Utopian Brotherhoods and Secret Societies*, 172–77.
13. Charles Webster, *The Great Instauration: Science, Medicine, and Reform, 1626–1660*
(New York: Holmes and Meier, 1975), 64.

brother's intellectual and scientific activities. She was also a friend of Lucius Cary, the "irenic aristocrat" in Shapin's phrase, and of Clarendon, and so connects all these circles with the one at Great Tew.[14]

That circle probably comes closest to the generally received idea of a literary or intellectual circle, especially one viewed through the Bloomsbury lens, even if tracing it chronologically spins the circle into a spiral in order to accommodate Cowley and Boyle within its circumference (Boyle was ten years old when Suckling wrote "A Sessions of the Poets" or "The Wits," the roll book for the poets' corner, circa 1637). The group is best characterized as friends sharing similar, although by no means identical, beliefs and interests, brought together not by a patron but by one who, in Hugh Trevor-Roper's apt phrase, "found a way of avoiding the tedium of rural life: he had his friends to stay." It is a curious experience for one who has Bloomsbury texts ringing in her ears to read descriptions of Falkland. In Clarendon's portrait, for example, Falkland is described as one whose "disposition and nature was so gentle and obliging, so much delighted in courtesy, kindness and generosity, that all mankind could not but admire and love him." This encomium sounds much like those recalling Thoby Stephen, Vanessa and Virginia's brother who was the Cambridge friend of all the friends, with whom they were all in some degree or fashion in love ("he had greater personal charm than anyone I have ever known," wrote Leonard Woolf), and who first brought them together in 1905 in Gordon Square, and to the degree that this group was a circle, it was his gift for friendship that made it so.[15]

It is friendship that provides the overarching theme in the writing of Katherine Philips, the Orinda of her own and others' acclaim, particularly her Society of Friendship, offered here as the last example of the circle that is and is not. Just what this society was, indeed whether it ever existed beyond the title of one poem and allusions in a few others, has been much debated. It was certainly an idea that ordered Katherine Philips's affective relations even if this society might never have had more than two members at any one moment ("so friends are such by destiny, / And no third can the place supply"). Of course, it depends what one is referring to with the label Society of Friendship. Philips gave members of her immediate social and domestic circle pastoral names in the French fashion that had been popularized by Henrietta Maria and that she had read

14. Shapin, *Social History of Truth*, 144.
15. Trevor-Roper, *Catholics, Anglicans, and Puritans: Seventeenth-Century Essays* (Chicago: University of Chicago Press, 1988), 168, 171; Woolf, *Sowing: An Autobiography of the Years 1880 to 1904* (New York: Harcourt, Brace, 1960), 137.

about in *précieuse* fiction. One of them, Edward Dering (called Silvander), husband of her friend Mary Harvey (pastoral name unknown, possibly Ardelia or Philocleia), described her undertaking as her "most generous design . . . to unite all those of her acquaintance, which she found worthy, or desired to make so, (among which later number she was pleased to give me a place) into one societie, and by bands of friendship to make an alliance more firme then what nature, our countrey or equall education can produce."[16] Thus, these fanciful names scattered among her friends and relations do suggest some sort of social formation even if this grouping, both chronologically and geographically dispersed, is not identical with the largely abstract and nearly entirely textual Society of Friendship.

One can certainly place Philips near or within various identifiable circles. She was directly connected to the circle around Henry Lawes. He provided settings for "A Dialogue between Lucasia and Orinda," "Friendship's Mysterys, to my dearest Lucasia," "To Mrs. M. A. Upon absence. 12 Decemb. 1650," and "On the death of my first and dearest childe." She wrote a dedicatory poem for *The Second Book of Ayres.* She also has a prefatory poem (her first poem to appear in print) among the fifty-four in the 1651 edition of William Cartwright's *Comedies, Tragicomedies with Other Poems* (she is the only woman in the group, but her Cratander, Silvander, and Poliarchus are also there), and many of the contributors to this volume also have poems in Lawes's *Second Book of Ayres,* which contains a compliment to Philips's friend and Lawes's pupil Lady Dering, Silvander's wife, in its dedication. Furthermore, the network of acquaintances within which she moved crisscrossed, through filament and filiation, many of the major circles and coteries of the midcentury. By one degree of separation, Philips can be connected to Milton, Hartlib, John Wilkins, all the Great Tew figures, and, of course, the Boyle family. The Boyle connection helps place her post-Restoration activities in Dublin and links back to the interregnum abstraction, the Society of Friendship.

In a 1659 letter "To the Honourable Berenice," generally assumed to be Lady Elizabeth Ker, Philips thanks Lady Elizabeth for her "promise of Mr. Boyle's Book, which indeed merits a publick, not view only, but Universal Applause." The book, *Seraphick Love,* is Robert Boyle's first published tract (there had been

16. Philips, "Friendship in Emblem, or the Seale, to my dearest Lucasia," in *The Collected Works of Katherine Philips,* ed. Patrick Thomas, 2 vols. (Essex: Stump Cross Books, 1990), 1:108; Dering quoted in Patrick Thomas, *Katherine Philips* (Cardiff: University of Wales Press, 1988), 13–14.

an earlier scientific essay in a Hartlib volume), treating a subject of immense interest to Philips, although in an even more abstractly Neoplatonic idiom than her own musings. The work, according to John Evelyn, displayed "divine incli-nations, as are only competent to angels and yourself."[17] But Philips's more di-rect Boyle connections in the 1660s were in Dublin with Robert Boyle's broth-er, Roger, earl of Orrery, and his sisters Lady Elizabeth Boyle, the Celimene of several of Philips's poems, and Lady Ann Boyle. Through them she entered the circle of John Butler, duke of Ormond, and with her translation of Corneille's *Pompey*, encouraged and supported by Roger Boyle, she entered a world where she might have gained a quite different position in literary history had small-pox not intervened.

Yet, it is the essentially fictional Society of Friendship, the largely female, ide-alized community created under the sign of the warrior women of the Fronde, that offers the greater provocation to literary history. The poems are the society, and along with the prefatory poems they constitute a social text, but they do not draw a social circle. The abstract entity that is her society is nearly entirely a function of the text. In this circle Philips is both center and circumference. It is a circle of the self in the Montaigne manner ("because it was he, because it was I"), where the other, first Rosania, then, after Mary Aubrey's apostasy, Lu-casia (Anne Owen), becomes the speaker's second self:

> I did not live untill this time
> Crown'd my felicity,
> When I could say without a crime,
> I am not Thine, but Thee.

Its activity was the creation of friendship and its study: "Friendship's a science, and we knowe / There Contemplation's most employ'd."[18]

How does one read this friendship motif whose textual traces are everywhere in her poetry, as the constant, sometimes only, note? For Philips, friendship seems to have meant same-sex erotic desire transformed in the very act of ex-pressing it to a less embodied Neoplatonism, married domesticity, and politi-cal alliances and their negotiation. It meant, too, a set of literary and intellec-

17. Philips, *Collected Works*, 2:2. Boyle's *Seraphick Love* was written in 1648 in the form of a letter to his sister Mary, but was not published until 1659. Evelyn quoted in Shapin, *Social History of Truth*, 188.

18. Philips, "To my Excellent Lucasia, on our Friendship," *Collected Works*, 1:121; Philips, "A Dialogue between Lucasia and Orinda," ibid., 94.

tual traditions, from Cicero's *De Amicitia* to the salon writings and rituals of her contemporaries across the Channel to treatises on the subject of friendship that she elicited from her friend Francis Finch, the faithful Palaemon, and later from Jeremy Taylor. Carol Barash understands the Society of Friendship as "part of a discourse about literary and political alliances during the interregnum. . . . A friend is an ally, one who understands secret, subversive meanings of poems that are, overtly, apolitical," and she develops a reading that sets up a homology between the absent Anne Owen, that is, Lucasia, and the absent king: "[T]o approach Lucasia imaginatively was to recreate the moment when Philips's mystical Society of Friendship protected the endangered Stuart monarchy and maintained hopes of its return to English soil."[19] The political coding changes over the decade, and, given her husband's political alliances, her royalism was always a difficult, although during the Restoration a useful, allegiance. But what prompted her ardent royalism in the first place? It was more, certainly, than Mrs. Salmon's school for girls in Hackney, often evoked as both locus and cause. Indeed, one of the fascinating unanswered questions, which a study of Philips's circlings highlights, is why she so elaborately constructed a royalist ideology given the parliamentary leanings of her entire family. Possibly, the Society of Friendship was a necessary fiction for Philips, one in which erotic and political discourses not only could merge but also need not even be distinguished (her objects of poetic adoration were all supporters of the monarchy in exile). Although courting Lucasia may well imply an idealized political courtiership, the homology that Barash proposes should also allow space for the first term, for Lucasia herself.

Circles have their uses. Whether the Society of Friendship ever existed in other than its "mystical" form is an open question. Nonetheless, the process of deducing affiliations and coteries, even circles, in London, Cardigan, and later in Dublin allows for the study not only of Cavalier culture during the interregnum, of elective affinities in Wales, of the domestic life in a household of split political loyalties, but of the construction of the idea and practice of friendship and of the codings of erotic desire as well.

Writer and writer—past, present, and to come—writer and friend, friend and friend, writer and lover, writer and reader, writer and patron, and writer and God probably sum up the circle of circles: "How summed a circle dost thou

---

19. Barash, *English Women's Poetry, 1649–1714* (Oxford: Clarendon Press, 1996), 56, 63, 99.

leave mankind . . . could we the center find," as Jonson wrote in his praise of the "irenic" Falkland's friendship with Henry Morison. Or, as Dante acknowledges on leaving the circle of poets and philosophers in Limbo: "I cannot give a full account of them all, for the length of my theme so drives me on that many times my words come short of the fact."

M. Thomas Hester

"Like a spyed Spie"
Donne's Baiting of Marlowe

SPIES, you are lights in state, but of base stuffe,
Who, when you'have burnt your selves downe to snuffe,
Stinke, and are throwne away. End faire enough.
—Ben Jonson, Epigram 59

Is any kinde subject to rape like a fish?
. . . To kill them is an occupation,
And lawes make fasts, and lents for their destruction.
—John Donne, Metempsychosis

In his essay "John Donne, Coterie Poetry, and the Text as Performance ," Ted-Larry Pebworth observes that "Donne's motivation for writing poetry was undoubtedly various, responding to intimately personal and intellectual impulses as well as to professional advancement. His poetry is not merely careerist in intent."[1] The following pages aim to modify and expand somewhat his statement about Donne's "various . . . personal and intellectual impulses" by applying his statement about Donne's "motivation" and audience not to Donne's poetry overall, but to only one poem—his late-Elizabethan response in "The Baite" to

---

1. Pebworth, "John Donne," *Studies in English Literature* 29 (1989): 63. My title is taken from the satirist's description of his fearful leaving of the Elizabethan Presence Chamber at the conclusion of Donne's *Satyre IV*: "being among . . . men that doe know / No token of worth, but Queenes man, . . . I shooke like a spyed Spie" (ll. 232–37). All citations of Donne's poems are according to John T. Shawcross, ed., *The Complete Poetry of John Donne* (Garden City, N.Y.: Anchor Books, 1967). All citations of Marlowe's poems are according to Roma Gill, ed., *The Complete Works of Christopher Marlowe*, vol. 1 (Oxford: Clarendon Press, 1987). Raleigh's poem is according to Agnes M. C. Latham, ed., *The Poems of Sir Walter Raleigh* (Cambridge: Harvard University Press, 1951).

Christopher Marlowe's "Passionate Shepheard to his love." The following attempt to read Donne's "various intent[ions]" in "The Baite" in the light of late-Elizabethan generic and religio-political lexicons aims not only to discern some of the "personal and intellectual impulses" of the poem, but also to raise some questions about the character of literary circles during the period—especially the ways in which the membership and circumferences of those circles expanded, contracted, and overlapped as the authors transcribed their own "various . . . impulses" in the lexicons of those reading circles.[2] That Donne's own literary circle might hear or read "The Baite" differently from another group of readers or even from another of the circle of readers for whom the poem was intended is borne out by recollection of the various contexts and lexicons of the poem.

First, a few observations about the ostensible *literary* subjects of Donne's "Baite"—what Izaak Walton in *The Compleat Angler* later called "that smooth song . . . made by Kit Marlowe" and what several manuscripts call "The Aunswere" by Sir Walter Raleigh. Marlowe's poem was probably composed as early as 1588, for Greene borrows from it in his *Menaphon*, published in 1589: R. S. Forsythe finds "fourteen passages in Marlowe's plays in which 'The Passionate Shepherd' is suggested, in material, in purpose, and, at times, in metre," and surmises that "Greene no doubt knew the poem in MS., or perhaps from recitation by its author himself." (Marlowe was dead, of course, in 1593.) The artifacts of these two poems suggest that they circulated together during the last decade of Elizabeth's rule. The earliest extant copies are a four-stanza version of "Shepheard" and a five-stanza version of Raleigh's poem titled "The Aunswere" in that curious mixture of papers bound together in a series of volumes by the seventeenth-century antiquarian astrologer Elias Ashmole (1617–1692). The two poems appear there together in a volume of alchemical papers compiled around 1598 by Simon Forman, as they do in the Rawlinson manuscript and in "most of the texts of [these two] poems." Marlowe's four-stanza version and a one-stanza reply by Raleigh were first published together in 1599 in *The Pas-*

---

2. For important studies of Donne's early audiences, see also A. Alvarez, "Donne and His Circle," *Listener* 57 (1957): 827–28; Pebworth, "The Early Audiences of Donne's Poetic Performances," *John Donne Journal* 15 (1996): 127–37; Achsah Guibbory, "A Sense of the Future: Projected Audiences of Donne and Jonson," *John Donne Journal* 2:2 (1983): 11–21; Dennis Flynn, "Donne and a *Female* Coterie," *LIT: Literature Interpretation Theory* 1 (1989): 127–36; and Arthur F. Marotti, *John Donne, Coterie Poet* (Madison: University of Wisconsin Press, 1986). The seminal study of Donne's subsequent audiences is Ernest W. Sullivan II, *The Influence of John Donne: His Uncollected Seventeenth-Century Printed Verse* (Columbia: University of Missouri Press, 1993).

sionate Pilgrim, and again (in longer versions) in that 1600 collection that begins with Sir Philip Sidney's "Shepherd to his chosen Nimph," *Englands Helicon,* where "The Nimphs reply" of Raleigh is attributed to "Ignoto." As Arthur Marotti says, they seem to have "circulated widely in polite circles."[3] Here is the four-stanza version of Marlowe's poem (as printed by Roma Gill):

The Passionate Shepherd to His Love

Come live with mee, and be my love,
And we will all the pleasure prove,
That Vallies, groves, hills and fieldes,
Woods, or steepie mountaine yeeldes.

And wee will sit upon the Rocks,
Seeing the Sheepheards feed theyr flocks,
By shallow Rivers, to whose falls,
Melodious byrds sing Madrigalls.

And I will make thee beds of Roses,
And a thousand fragrant posies,
A cap of flowers, and a kirtle,
Imbroydred all with leaves of Mirtle.

A belt of straw, and Ivie buds,
With Corall clasps and Amber studs,
And if these things thy mind may move,
Then live with mee, and be my love.

The 1600 printed version of the poem, in *Englands Helicon,* adds the following two as the fourth and sixth stanzas (as printed by Gill):

A gowne made of the finest wooll,
Which from our pretty Lambes we pull,
Fayre lined slippers for the cold:
With buckles of the purest gold.

The Sheepheardes Swaines shall daunce and sing,
For thy delight each May-morning.
If these delights thy minde may move;
Then live with mee, and be my love.

---

3. Forsythe, *"The Passionate Shepherd* and English Poetry," *PMLA* 40 (1925): 692–742; Peter Beal, *Index of English Literary Manuscripts* (London and New York: R. R. Bowker, 1980), vol. 1, pt. 2: 326–27; Marotti, *John Donne,* 84. Evidence concerning the artifacts of these poems is indebted to Beal's five-volume work.

Donne's "Baite" also appears in the Ashmole manuscript, but in a different compilation of the gathering, "in a different hand," Peter Beal informs me. It does not appear with the poems of Marlowe in *Englands Helicon*. Its first appearance in print is in William Corkine's *Second Book of Ayres* (1612). In the Dolau Cothi manuscript (circa 1620–1625)—and in three Group II manuscripts of Donne's poems—it is grouped with several other poems as "Songs which were made to certaine Airs that were made before," but no evidence has been uncovered that it circulated with either Marlowe's or Raleigh's poems in manuscript. Here is Donne's poem (as printed by John T. Shawcross; copy text Donne's *Poems* [1633]):

The Baite.

Come live with mee, and bee my love,
And wee will some new pleasures prove
Of golden sands, and christall brookes:
With silken lines, and silver hookes.

There will the river whispering runne
Warm'd by thy eyes, more than the Sunne.
And there the'inamor'd fish will stay,
Begging themselves they may betray.

When thou wilt swimme in that live bath,
Each fish, which every channell hath,
Will amorously to thee swimme,
Gladder to catch thee, then thou him.

If thou, to be so seene, beest loath,
By Sunne, or Moone, thou darknest both,
And if my selfe have leave to see,
I need not their light, having thee.

Let others freeze with angling reeds,
And cut their legges, with shells and weeds,
Or treacherously poor fishe beset,
With strangling snare, or windowie net:

Let coarse bold hands, from slimy nest
The bedded fish in banks out-wrest,
Or curious traitors, sleavesilke flies
Bewitch poore fishes wandring eyes.

For thee, thou needst no such deceit,
For thou thy selfe art thine owne bait;
That fish, that is not catch'd thereby,
Alas, is wiser farre then I.

The extant evidence about the circulation and printing of the poems suggests that Donne's poem seems to be more of a *response to* those poems than part of a literary game in which he directly participated with the two "court" poets, more in keeping with what Anthony Low aptly calls Donne's "literary . . . revisionism." My own understanding of what Pebworth calls Donne's "personal and intellectual impulses" in this poem is greatly indebted to Low's keen reading of the ways in which "pastoralism is exaggerated, then twisted, depersonified, mocked, and rejected" in the poem in order to discredit both "pastoral poets and the pastoral mode itself . . . as texts divorced from the real world of real events."[4] What I wish to add to his reading of the poem and to Pebworth's perceptions about the poet's "intent" is a consideration of how and why Donne in "The Baite" offers a critique of Marlowe framed in language that responds to "real events" quite significant to him and some of his readers, and that would have been more readily received by members of a different audience from that of Marlowe and Raleigh.

In this sense, most important to an understanding of Donne's "impulses" in response to the poems of Marlowe and Raleigh—but especially to Marlowe's "Passionate Shepheard"—is their ideological center. "The Baite" is typical of Donne's poetry not only for its literary "revisionism" but equally for the wit of an equivocally phrased political incorrectness that would have been most appealing to his fellow recusant readers. Donne may have been following the lead of Sannazaro when he displaces the diction and setting of his lyric from the pastoral pasture to the piscatorial "channell" (l. 10), but his application of the subgenre places an innovative stress on political themes; Donne in "The Baite" not only relies on the imagery of fishing to mock both the pastoral mode and Petrarchan conventions but also revises the diction of that subgenre in order to insinuate a parodic critique of Marlowe and his religio-political associates.

---

4. Low, "The Compleat Angler's 'Baite'; or, The Subverter Subverted," *John Donne Journal* 4 (1985): 10, 7. Other useful commentaries on Donne's and Marlowe's works and lives cited frequently in the following pages include Dennis Flynn, *John Donne and the Ancient Catholic Nobility* (Bloomington: Indiana University Press, 1995); Charles Nicholl, *The Reckoning: The Murder of Christopher Marlowe* (Chicago: University of Chicago Press, 1992); and James V. Mirollo, *Mannerism and Renaissance Poetry: Concept, Mode, Inner Design* (New Haven: Yale University Press, 1984). Other helpful readings of these poems include Eugene R. Cunnar's study of the sacred traditions of the fishing trope in Donne's poem, "Donne's Witty Theory of Atonement in 'The Baite,'" *Studies in English Literature* 29 (1989): 77–98; S. K. Heninger, "The Passionate Shepherd and the Philosophical Nymph," *Renaissance Papers* (1962): 63–70; and Frank Manley, "Formal Wit in the *Songs and Sonnets*," in *That Subtle Wreath*, ed. Margaret Pepperdine (Atlanta: Agnes Scott College, 1973), 8–9.

Patrick Cheney's persuasive study of "the maze of classical and Renaissance sources from which Marlowe [and Raleigh] drew" in composing "The passionate Shepheard" and "The Aunswere" helps to clarify Donne's "multiple intents." Both, Cheney illustrates, belong to that group of Sidneyan poetic "careerists" who were vying with Edmund Spenser about "the question of the poet's voice — his cultural authority, [and above all] his credentials for the job of England's national poet." Marlowe's poem especially, as Douglas Bruster phrases it, "functioned as a particularly Elizabethan reservoir of cultural energy and ambition." The complex intertextual goundplot and lexical synecdoches of these poems, that is, engage what Cheney calls "the writing of Elizabethan England, with its vision of the poet as an elitist figure of cultural authority penning the aristocratic genres of pastoral epic, and [especially] its service to a virgin queen and her [Protestant] regime's imperialist projects."[5] Such an understanding of the intertextual and cultural resonances of Marlowe's "smooth song" goes a long way toward explaining the degree of witty parodic satire with which Donne responds in "The Baite" to the project of that literary circle. In this vein, one might profitably compare, in fact, the ways in which Donne's Holy Sonnets offer a severe interrogation of the dominant soteriological and anti-Catholic polemics endemic to Marlowe's *Dr. Faustus* and, by extension, the sort of Protestant poetics that Cheney and others have shown to be central to the "culturally encoded" pastoral debate of Marlowe's and Raleigh's two poems.[6] Donne's Holy Sonnets, I have suggested, can be used to establish some of the same *doctrinal* basis for Donne's direct assault on Marlowe's work in "The Baite," and to offer some insight into the grounds of the satirical animus, genre, and imagery of Donne's poem.

5. Cheney, *Marlowe's Counterfeit Profession: Ovid, Spenser, Counter-Nationhood* (Toronto: University of Toronto Press, 1997), 68, 76. Cheney sees Marlowe as "instrumental in inaugurating a counter-Spenserian movement that reaches its most immediate achievement in Donne and Jonson. . . . Marlowe invites us to read [his lyric] as a self-reflexive amatory subversion of both the state and the state genre, Virgilian epic, with its Ovidian *cursus*" (18, 71). Marlowe and Donne may indeed be engaged in the same critique of the Elizabethan models, but that does not lessen Donne's disagreements with or his own view of Marlowe's contributions to that critique. Bruster, "'Come to Tent Again': 'The Passionate Shepherd,' Dramatic Rape, and Lyric Time," *Criticism* 33 (1991): 68; Cheney, *Marlowe's Counterfeit Profession*, 87.

6. See, for instance, R. V. Young, "Donne's Holy Sonnets and the Theology of Grace," in *"Bright Shootes of Everlastingnesse": The Seventeenth-Century Religious Lyric*, edited by Claude J. Summers and Ted-Larry Pebworth (Columbia: University of Missouri Press, 1987), 20–39; and M. Thomas Hester, "The 'troubled wit' of John Donne's 'blacke Soule,'" *Cithara* 31 (1991): 16–27. In another version of the present essay, presented before the Renaissance Society of America, March 1998, I undertook such a comparison.

Another specific instance of the relations between Donne and Marlowe offers a similar insight into Donne's "personal impulses" in "The Baite." For the purposes of understanding Donne's "response" to Marlowe's pastoral, in fact, the most significant of Marlowe's writings may well be that poem generally accepted as his most insignificant, his 1592 Latin epitaph on Sir Roger Manwood:

In obitum honoratissimi viri
Rogeri Manwood militis,
quaestorii Reginalis Capitalis Baronis
Noctivagi terror, ganeonis triste flagellum,
Et Jovis Alcides, rigido vulturque latroni
Urna subtegitur. Scelerum gaudete Nepotes.
Insons luctifica sparsis cervice capillis
Plange, fori lumen, venerandae gloria legis
Occidit. Heu secum effoetas Acherontis ad oras
Multa abiit virtus. Pro tot virtutibus uni
Livor parce viro: non audacissimus esto
Illius in cineres, cuius tot milia vultus
Mortalium attonuit; sic cum te nuncia Ditis
Famaque marmorei superet monumenta sepulchri.

On the Death of the Most Honourable Gentleman, Roger Manwood,
Knight, Lord Chief Baron of the Queen's Exchequer
Night-wanderer's terror, glutton's harshest scourge,
Reborn Alcides, vengeance on brigands due,
An urn now covers. Sons of crime, rejoice.
But, guiltless one, with hair spread o'er your neck,
Weep for the forum's light, the court's bright glow
Now set: with him to Acheron's waste shores
Great goodness has departed. He, one man,
Shewed many virtues; Envy, spare him now
And be not wanton where his ashes lie,
Whose face astonished thousands. So when Death
Strikes his last blow, may your bones gently lie
And fame outlast your marble monuments.[7]

A relative of Marlowe by marriage, Sir Roger Manwood was chief baron of the Queen's Exchequer, longtime associate of Marlowe's patrons, the Walsing-

---

7. Translated by Angus Hulton, in Gill, *Complete Works of Marlowe*, 1: 220–21.

hams, and one of the judges who acquitted the poet-dramatist of the murder of William Bradley in 1589. He is figured in Marlowe's epitaph as the *honoratissimi viri*, the enemy of the "Night-wanderer," the "glutton," and the "brigand," terms that upon discovery of the manuscript of the epitaph ironically were thought to be descriptions of Marlowe instead of the "Reborn Alcides" and the "guiltless one" his poem commemorates. They are also terms that many of the age thought equally applicable to Manwood, for he had been "accused of various malpractices and arraigned before the privy council" just before his death.[8] In Marlowe's poem, however, he is that "Most Honourable Gentleman" whose "fame" will "outlast [his] marble monuments." Ironically, his "fame" (or infamy) did last, in one version at least, until 1650—when John Donne Jr. added to the edition of his father's poems that Rabelaisian jeu d'esprit titled *Catalogus Librorum* (The courtier's library of rare books). Among its thirty-four imaginary books—which offer the poet's sassy ridicule of famous and contemporary topics and figures from Luther's curious scriptural emendations to the nefarious activities of spies and informers such as Topcliffe and Phillips—is the following entry concerning the subject of Marlowe's encomium:

> 21. *Manuale justiciariorum*, continens plurimas confessiones veneficarum Manwoodo judici exhibitas, et ab illo abstergendis postea natibus, et evacutionibus adhibitas; nunc à servulis suis redempta, et in usum suum collecta sunt à Io. Helo.
>
> 21. *A Manual for Justices of the Peace*, comprising many confessions of poisoners tendered to Justice Manwood, and employed by him in wiping his posterior; these have now been purchased from his inferior servants and collected for his own use by John Hele.[9]

A participant in the special inquiry that examined Mary, queen of Scots, and one of the interrogators of Father Campion, Justice Manwood was also the Privy Council's commissioner who had investigated the holdings of fugitive Catholics such as Donne's grandfather John Heywood; he was also suspected of having collaborated for a while with Donne's father in shielding the family holdings from forfeiture to the Crown before the elder Donne's sudden death in 1576, most likely from poison. The poet himself, R. C. Bald urges, obviously regarded Manwood "with a degree of contempt that may well have been based on a sense of family injury." Manwood was known as "a proud and cruel man" who may indeed, as Dennis Flynn has illustrated, "have been embarrassed suf-

8. Ibid., 217.
9. Edited and translated by M. Thomas Hester and R. V. Young, *John Donne: Select Prose* (forthcoming). John Hele was a notoriously corrupt and successful lawyer.

ficiently by his dealings with Donne's father to have exacted a fierce revenge."
(At least the poet Donne seems to have thought so anyhow.) John Donne's
"Baite," in its response to Marlowe's "Passionate Shepheard," then, may well be
but one of two direct *responses* to one of Marlowe's writings. Whatever the origins of *The Courtier's Library*, I rehearse once again this data in order to suggest
a vantage point from which to view "The Baite"—not only, that is, as a contribution or response to a playful and ideologically resonant academic game
Donne played with Raleigh and Marlowe, but also as a parodic satire that carries literary competition and innovation to the level of personal and ideological assault. Donne had more than aesthetic and generic disagreements (or
grudges) with Kit Marlowe that are discernible in his spirited response to
Marlowe's quintessentially "Elizabethan" lyric.[10] The Holy Sonnets and *The
Courtier's Library* both suggest, then, grounds for Donne's choosing Marlowe as
the object of satire in "The Baite."

In his response in "The Baite" to the fashionable coterie poem of Marlowe,
Low points out, Donne "takes a tack quite different from Ralegh." Raleigh's
"philosophical nymph, . . . tak[ing] her cue from the love-smitten Thomalin in
The Shepherdes Calendar, . . . grim[ly] rejected both the literary nature and basis" of the Marlovian shepherd's bucolic invitation with a naturalistic "litany of
decadence and disintegration," according to Heninger and Mirollo, respectively. But "instead of joining Marlowe in his pastoral paradise and arguing with
him there, as Ralegh had done, Donne reduces not only Marlowe but all his fellow pastoralists from human adversaries to the impersonal status of anonymous writings. Donne attacks his poetic and amatory rivals on grounds not
[only] of morality but of comparative reality. His, he implicitly claims, is the
real world, the one that truly exists." The "new pleasures" (l. 2) promised by his
witty speaker will "prove" to be that of a "live [—a living—] bath" (ll. 2, 9).
"Marlowe's and Ralegh's is only an imagined world—indeed, nothing but a fic-

10. Bald, *John Donne: A Life* (Oxford: Oxford University Press, 1970), 34; Flynn, *John
Donne*, 72–73. Whether Donne's poem offers any sort of response or even rejection of
Raleigh's own response to Marlowe's poem is not at issue in this essay. I consider it likely that Donne did not find himself among the Raleigh coterie at the time, but his
differences with Raleigh do not seem to play a role in "The Baite." I have treated in a limited fashion the relationships between Donne and Raleigh elsewhere: "Donne's Epigrams: A Little World Made Cunningly," in *The Eagle and the Dove: Reassessing John Donne*,
edited by Claude J. Summers and Ted-Larry Pebworth (Columbia: University of Missouri
Press, 1986), 80–91; and "Donne's (Re)Annunciation of the Virgin(ia Colony) in *Elegy
XIX*," *South Central Review* 4 (1987): 49–64. See also Ernest A. Strathmann, "Ralegh and
the Catholic Polemicists," *Huntington Library Quarterly* 4 (1945): 337–58. For a different view of the Donne-Raleigh relationship, see Dennis Flynn, "Donne, Henry Wotton,
and the Earl of Essex," *John Donne Journal* 14 (1995): 185–218.

tion," Low continues, a fiction, I believe Donne would have urged, created to appeal to popular Elizabethan standards, to qualify these poets for the school of Sidney and Spenser (or even to seize the laureate mantle from them, as Cheney has suggested). Donne "does not belong to this community," and "re-pudiate[s] song for speech, . . . dialogue for monologue."[11]

Even as he seems to follow the rhetorical outlines and Petrarchan tropes of Marlowe's lyric in the first two stanzas, for example, Donne's witty speaker baits the reader with promises of "golden sands," the suggestively wondrous allure of "christall brookes," and the softly luxuriant sibilants that enact the offer of "silken lines" (ll. 3–4) of poetry, only to set the hook suddenly, even while lur-ing our senses with one last sibilant in the final image of "silver hookes" (l. 4). The second stanza offers the same inventive bait. Donne's speaker displaces Marlowe's "Rocks . . . and flocks, . . . shallow Rivers [and] Melodious" Philome-las with a "whispering" river that shuns the glow of poetical artifice for the "warm[th of] thy eyes" (ll. 4–5), but then, once again, he rudely concludes the stanza with the startling final rhyme of "stay" with "betray" (ll. 7, 8). Indeed, Donne's "new pleasures" counter the artificial lures and artifice of pastoral song with a diction that is alive with life and multiple meanings, an unstable poetic world of alluring, suggestive eroticism that is sharply countered by sudden re-versals of tone and diction, a world that shares more with the world of Wyatt's dramatic, satirical admonitions about the "wild" misdirections and pernicious intrigues of the court than with the pastoral artifice of Marlowe's courtly lyric. It is yet a world in which "inamor'd" phallic fish "amorously swimme" to "channell[s]" in that "live bath" of love (ll. 7, 9–10), but "beneath the appar-ently limpid surface of the poetic style," Low points out, the reader can hear "a more characteristically Donnean voice" that is gradually to emerge in order to mock openly the conventions of Marlowe's idyllic world that (like Wyatt's, Donne would claim) only "seem[s] tame." The Marlovian pastoral world of rose beds, "fragrant posies," "kirtle, Mirtle," lamb's-wool gowns, and slippers with "buckles of the purest gold"—with all its elegant allegorical sophistication and luxuriant mythic suggestiveness—is rejected by Donne's speaker for the liq-uid embrace of a beloved who can "command nature":[12]

> When thou wilt swimme in that live bath,
> Each fish, which every channell hath,

11. Low, "Compleat Angler's 'Baite,'" 9; Heninger, "Passionate Shepherd," 66; Mirol-lo, *Mannerism and Renaissance Poetry*, 167; Low, "Compleat Angler's 'Baite,'" 9, 10.
12. Mirollo, *Mannerism and Renaissance Poetry*, 170.

> Will amorously to thee swimme,
> Gladder to catch thee, then thou him.
>
> (ll. 9–12)

Here is a sort of *real goddess* whose beauty and love "darknest both . . . Sunne, or Moone" (l. 14), and who, unlike those sunny-eyed fastidious Petrarchan mistresses of conventional lyrics whose "channell[s]" the "courtly pastoral amorists" would only guiltily dream of "having," provides the only "light" Donne's passionate (and bawdy) fisherman needs: "I need not their light, having thee" (l. 16).[13]

Through the first four stanzas of "The Baite," then, Donne's poem, imaginatively "affirms its status as a participant in a poetic tournament" or circle, contends Mirollo. "It dutifully echoes Marlowe's opening line, follows the formal model of the octosyllabic stanzas and their rhyme scheme," and, instead of the complementary philosophical nymph's response offered by Raleigh, seems to be offering a witty, even bawdy, "realistic" counter to Marlowe's poem that is within the politically correct "rules of the game." Even what seems "new" here, in the move from the pastoral to the piscatorial (from "meadow to stream"), as Low notes, had already been "thoroughly legitimized" by Sannazaro.[14] But unlike Sannazaro's strictly apolitical modification of the pastoral, Donne uses language that increasingly serves to "betray" the political dimensions of the pastoral conventions. In addition to the possibly risqué figure of the fish and the "channell" and the potentially sexual pun on "have," phrases such as "loath," "darknest," "have leave," and "need not their light" (ll. 13–16), Low points out, have already begun to undercut severely the first two stanzas' promise of another smooth pastoral song suited for aristocratic public performance. Like the speaker of the poem, readers have figuratively been given "leave to see" more clearly the satirical "intents" of "The Baite," however much

13. If Cheney's claim that the mistress of Marlowe's poem intends to resemble Queen Elizabeth is right, then, given the association of her with the topography of England, the image of the lover "amorously" moving the Channel to "catch" her certainly offers a bold (and insulting) counter to Marlowe's quite proper court song. But again, as I have suggested elsewhere, such boldness is "characteristically Donnean," as evident from his daring exploitation of the iconography of Queen Elizabeth in *Elegy XIX* (see n. 10 above).

14. Mirollo, *Mannerism and Renaissance Poetry,* 169; Low, "Compleat Angler's 'Baite,'" 6. But unlike Donne's poem, the apolitical *piscatoriae* of Sannazaro, in the words of Wayne Rebhorn, are "Divorced from the realities of the contemporary, historical world, [in] a realm of art and poetry, a dream of life as it ideally should be" (*Courtly Performances: Making and Festivity in Castiglione's "The Book of the Courtier"* [Detroit: Wayne State University Press, 1978], 105).

the real object of its mockery may "beest loath . . . to be so seene" (l. 13). The "darknes[s]" underlying the pretenses of Marlowe's pastoral, and the world it so falsely portrays, becomes more evident in the radical change of tone and diction in stanzas 5 and 6 of "The Baite." Just when we have begun to read it as a witty variation on the poetic game, the poet makes clear that he is rejecting the grounds on which that game was ostensibly being played. By changing the trope of the piscatorial as well as that of "The passionate Shepheard," that is, Donne rejects the benign—and fictional—relationship of protecting shepherd and protected sheep to that of *deceptive* fishermen and *betrayed* fish. The pastoral guise of gentle love and idealized human interrelations by which singing shepherds with their protective crooks save the innocent sheep from the devouring wolves is displaced by the more credible courtly (and political) trope of "sleavesilke" lures (l. 23), of "strangling snare, or windowie net" (l. 20). Now the playful phallic fish "which every channell hath" (l. 10) are pursued with the trickery and false allure of "angling reeds" (l. 17) that are used to "catch" (l. 27) and now really to "betray" (l. 8) and "treacherously" (l. 19) to use "curious traitors" (l. 23) to "Bewitch" (l. 24) with "deceit" (l. 25) the "poore fishes" (l. 24). Having taken the bait of the poetic game proffered in the first four stanzas (and it may be to the 1590s four-stanza form of Marlowe's poem that Donne is responding), the readers are introduced to a world in which "others freeze" (l. 17).

In the world of Donne's poem, in which men come armed with hooks that only resemble shepherds' crooks, the Petrarchan nymph needs no such tropical artifice—"no such deceit" (l. 25). Having "hooked" the readers into an alternative, more realistic vision than Marlowe's fictive, pastoral artifice, that is, after the first four stanzas, Donne's speaker rejects—or insists that we consider specifically—the "physically ugly and painful" (indeed, the "morally suspect") alternative lure, asserts Mirollo. Having "prove[d]" (l. 2) its realistic superiority he now insists that we consider its ramifications as a perspective on the character of devotion in the real world. The point, as Low spiritedly phrases it, is that "Donne has wider intentions than to insult fishermen, . . . that it belongs to the very nature of things, in real life as opposed to books, for fishermen to freeze and to lacerate themselves while they engage in an occupation that, when viewed closely, proves filthy and treacherous." But, at the same time, the highly charged political language of these stanzas—"treacherously . . . strangling . . . curious traitors" (ll. 19, 20, 23)—intimates that Donne's poem has even "wider intentions" than just the riddling exposure of the bookish unreality of "pastoral poets and the pastoral mode itself."[15] As Donne moves from a playfully suggestive parody of pastoral "pleasure" to a harshly dismissive characterization of the "coarse" nature of piscatorial pastoralism, literalizing the tropes of the mode, so "The Baite" moves also from being merely a response to the Marlowe literary game in order to invoke terms more familiar to that literary circle to which Donne's poems were more frequently addressed.

The terms by which Donne's speaker rejects the genre and the "deceit" of the poems of the Marlowe-Raleigh coterie—by which the "coarse" piscatorial trope displaces the artificial and deceptive trope of the pastoral shepherds only to have its "angling reeds" rejected by Donne's "wiser" lover (ll. 17, 28)—recall one of the central analogies of Donne's elegies, satires, and love lyrics. In the world of those poems, the true "lover" is constantly beset by the snares, anglings, lures, and tricks of "priviledg'd spie[s]," "spyed Spie[s]":[16] traitors and self-traitors lie anxious and poised to "snare" the "poore fishes wandring eyes" (l. 24). It is a world literally full of "angling reeds" that always requires (as Donne might be suggesting) survivors to perform "angling reads" (as in "artful and wily means" of interpretation, according to the *Oxford English Dictionary*). It is also the language of Donne's family and coreligionists, those Catholics that were the precise targets of Walsingham's secret police and its wide "net" of spies and traitors that were employed to "catch" English recusants.[17] And most important to a reading of "The Baite," this is also that world well traveled by Christopher Marlowe, that "atheist" projector in Rheims and Walsingham's informant in the households of both Northumberland and Lord Strange (recusants with whom Donne had been frequently associated). One needs only to peruse Harrison's *Elizabethan Journals* or Erasmus's *Colloquies* to hear English Catholics associated with fish, or to peruse the Public Record Office correspondence of Walsingham's network to hear of the "angling" after "big fish" upon discovery or capture of a Catholic "traytor." Catholic records use the same terms. In one of the major presentations of the English Catholic position, *An*

15. Mirollo, *Mannerism and Renaissance Poetry,* 170; Low, "Compleat Angler's 'Baite,'" 8, 7.

16. *Satyre IV* 1, ll. 119, 237.

17. For fuller documentation of Donne's Catholic origins and attitudes, see especially Flynn, *John Donne,* and "Donne's Catholicism," *Recusant History* 13 (1975): 1–17, 178–95. I have more fully unfolded the Catholic dimensions of Donne's *Satyres* in *Kinde Pitty and Brave Scorn: John Donne's Satyres* (Durham: Duke University Press, 1982), and "'Ask thy father': Rereading Donne's *Satyre III,*" *Ben Jonson Journal* 1 (1994): 201–18. Evidence of Marlowe's activities as a government agent is examined in Charles Nicholl's *Reckoning,* to which I am greatly indebted.

Humble Supplication to Her Maiestie, Father Robert Southwell described the "deceit[ful]" Babington plot (which relied on projectors and ambidexters like Marlowe to entrap men such as Donne's Kentish kinsman Harry Dunne, for instance) as "a snare to entrap them, then any devise of their owne, sith it was both plotted, furthered and finished by Sir *Francis Walsingham* and his Complices." Robert Poolie (one of Marlowe's associates), asserts Southwell,

> was the chiefe Instrument to contrive and prosecute that matter, and *to draw into the nett* such greene witts, as (partly fearing the generall oppression, partly angled with golden hookes) might easily be ouerwrought by Master Secretaries subtill and shifting witt. For *Poolie* masking his secrett Intentions vnder the face of Religion, and abusing with irreligious hypocrasie all Rites and Sacraments, to borrow the false opinion of a Catholique still fedd the poore gentlemen with his Masters baytes, and he holding the lyne in his hand, suffered them like silly fish to play themselues vpon the hooke, till it were thoroughly fastened, that then he might strike at his owne pleasure, and be sure to drawe them to a Certaine destruction.[18]

(Indeed, it is in precisely such activity as an agent provocateur that Marlowe has been suspected in those "matters touching the benefits of his country" in Rheims in approximately the same time period, according to Nicholls.) In the same vein, contends Flynn, incremental to the many letters of Father William Allen, Robert Persons, Alfonzo Agazzari, and Donne's uncle Jasper Heywood are the many descriptions of the ancient Catholic nobility of the realm as *"magnos pisces."* In the argot of Walsingham's secret service, pursuivants such as Topcliffe and Young were customarily referred to as "catchers" (there was even a pursuivant known only as "Catcher"), the pursuits of seminary priests were often called "fish-days," and the transportation of fugitives for the Continent was implemented in "fisher-boats." Sir Edward Stafford wrote Walsingham that he was "fishing for one that is daily among them," meaning the fugitive Catholics Charles Paget and Charles Arundel.[19] One should add also Donne's own verse epistle to Sir Henry Wotton ("Sir, more then kisses") where he bemoans the lack of "refuge" in the court in these same terms:

18. R. C. Bald, ed., *An Humble Supplication to Her Maiestie* (Cambridge: Cambridge University Press, 1953), 17–18. Italics added.

19. Nicholl, *The Reckoning,* 91–101; Flynn, *John Donne,* 107 n. 26; on "Catcher" and "fish-days," *HMC Salisbury* 3:366, 12:48; on "fisher-boats," Birch, *Memoirs of the Reign of Queen Elizabeth,* 2 vols. (London: A. Miller, 1754), 1:41; on Stafford, *CSPForeign. Eliz.* 18:269. I am indebted once again to the generosity of Dennis Flynn for these examples.

> And in the worlds sea, do not like corke sleepe
>
> . . . .
>
> Upon the waters face; nor in the deepe
> Sinke like a lead without a line: but as
> Fishes glide, leaving no print where they passe,
> Nor making sound; so, closely thy course goe.
>
> (ll. 14, 53–57)

Perhaps one should not make much of "leaving no print"—especially in combination with the suggestive "Fishes" simile—in treating the manuscripts of a poet with Donne's recusant Catholic associations, but its major usefulness to "The Baite" is the suggestion that he saw "Fishes" as an endangered species in the English court. The "secret theatre" of Walsingham's secret police force—with its "veiled agenda of hooks and baits," reminds Nicholl, with its use of magi (such as Bruno and Faustus) to "Bewitch" and beguile the Catholic "self-betrayers," with its secret ciphers and codes, in which unsuspecting Catholics, said Michael Moody (another of Marlowe's governmental cohorts), are "ready to be hooked, though 'it must be no small bait that [they] will bite at'"—is the world recalled and derided by Donne's speaker in "The Baite." And it is also the world of Christopher Marlowe, the world of Marlowe the apparent Catholic sympathizer who was "in reality the government's man, working in some way against the Catholics," and who was awarded the M.A. after the authorities at Cambridge were told in a Privy Council letter that "he had done Her Majesty good service, & deserved to be rewarded for his faithful dealing . . . in matters touching the benefit of his country . . . beyond the sea [at] Reames" in 1585 (ironically the very time that Donne's uncle Jasper Heywood arrived at the college to discuss the society's future plans). This is the language of the (fisher)men who caught Donne's younger brother with a Catholic priest in 1593, which led to his death, about whom Donne wrote in his second *Satyre,* where he contrasts those "poore [poets,] disarm'd, like Papists," who still manage "Ridlingly [to] catch men" with those poets and lawyers protected by a corrupt legal system who, "Like a Kings favourite, . . . throw . . . Like nets" abused forms of language in order to "drawe [men] Within the vast reach of th'huge statute lawes" (ll. 8–10, 70, 45–46, 111–12).[20]

20. Nicholl, *The Reckoning,* 256; Moody, PRO SP 12/239, No. 140, quoted in ibid., 254; ibid., 93; summary of Privy Council meeting, 29 June 1587, cited in ibid., 92. On Henry Donne's death see Fr. John Morris, "The Martyrdom of William Harrington," *Month* 20 (1874): 411–23. I have rehearsed the facts of Henry Donne's death and its importance to his elder brother's *Satyre II* in *Kinde Pitty,* ch. 2, and in "Henry Donne, John Donne, and the Date of *Satyre II*," *Notes and Queries,* n.s., 24 (1977): 524–27.

The ramifications of Donne's reliance on this imagery are suggested in the final stanza of "The Baite":

> For thee, thou needst no such deceit,
> For thou thy selfe art thine owne bait,
> That fish, that is not catch'd thereby,
> Alas, is wiser farre then I.

As a witty response to the amatory invitation central to Marlowe's pastoralism, Low points out, this "mock retraction" identifies the deadly artificiality of the court poetic, as well as the philosophical melancholy of Raleigh's "realistic" response, but it also repudiates the "treasonous violence of direct, naked sexuality": his mistress's sexuality is "so powerful that she need neither conceal nor idealize it."[21] She is her "owne bait" (l. 26)—and had obviously already "catch'd" (l. 27) the speaker. Of course, the poem at the same time serves as a complimentary "baite" to her also—the "fish" that he wishes to "catch," however, only if she is "wise" enough not to be seduced by the poem herself. His mistress, that is, embodies (literally and figuratively) the wisdom that the speaker desires only in her being "wiser farre" than those who might be "catch'd" by the witty turns of amatory poetry—his own included.

From the perspective of the recusant readers the final stanza also focuses attention on the "wisdom" of the good reader who can resist the allure of the court and its poetic defenders. Its suggestion that the only "fair" bait is beauty itself might easily have been read as Donne's oblique mockery of the extravagant and far-fetched panegyrics of "Gloriana" by the Protestant court poets (much like that of his dangerous elegies, where he mocks the "beauty" of an old redheaded woman whose "will must be done"). But as a satirical response to Marlowe, Donne's poem insinuates that Marlowe is a wolf in shepherd's clothing. His courtly pastoral with its idyllic Protestant Platonism is a sham, an ambidextrous "play" through which the poet has seen. Donne's speaker may playfully submit that "That fish, that is not catch'd" by the beauty of his beloved "Alas, is wiser farre than" he—but the poetic creator of them all "is wiser farre than" those fooled by the courtly, "sleavesilke flies" of Kit Marlowe. But even more so, even "wiser farre" than the speaker himself, is the "fish" who does not respond to the "baite" of courtly "fishermen"—which, ironically, Donne himself had done in the poem itself. The model for response suggested by the witty "mock retraction" is a resolve not to play the Petrarchan or the courtly

21. Low, "Compleat Angler's 'Baite,'" 9.

game.[22] The "fishe" that is "wiser farre" than Donne, then, may well be the Donne who not only did not participate in the literary debate of Marlowe and Raleigh but also did not circulate this poem beyond his circle of manuscript readers—who, "leaving no print . . . Nor making sound," did not, that is, reveal himself to be a recusant "fish" by responding publicly to Marlowe's "bait." Such a response recalls again the final lines of Donne's *Satyre II*, where he submits that his "words none drawes / Within the vast reach of th'huge statute lawes" (ll. 111–12). In "The Baite"—as in his radical, sarcastic reaction to Marlowe's Manwood epitaph, as in those Holy Sonnets that "Ridlingly" question the approach to the truth affirmed by Marlowe's *Dr. Faustus*—Donne is more radical than Marlowe. Donne's radicalism derives from his own situation in the "real world" of English Catholicism, in which the "new pleasures" of Protestantism created a dangerous world in which his own family had "betray[ed] themselves" for their true love, a world in which all "fish" were sought and "caught" and butchered, in which "others" did "treacherously poor fishe beset." Donne— like the Catholic readers of his poems—lived in a world full (like his poems) of "curious traitors" anxious to "Bewitch [the] wandring eyes" of recusants such as John Donne and his younger brother Henry, who died in prison after he was "catch'd" by Topcliffe's, Pooley's, Richard Young's—and Marlowe's—governmental associates.

What I wish to suggest about the larger significance of this poem, then, is the questions it raises about some of our current descriptions of the coterie or literary circle of Donne's poems. From one perspective—as a witty literary *response* to the poems of the Marlowe-Raleigh circle—"The Baite" does "deromanticize the pastoral fantasy" central to that circle, asserts Arthur Marotti. In this sense, through its mock affectation and ultimate rejection of courtly Petrarchan language and stances, its hyperbolic, "bawdy burlesque of the two songs of Marlowe and Ralegh," says Patricia Pinka, and even in its cynically facetious final reversal in which the "seducer is seduced," the fisherman caught by the fish, Donne's poem might well be located within the Inns of Court literary circle among a competitive group of cosmopolitan position-seekers anxious to advertise their novelty, intellectual acuity, and sexual daring.[23] Clearly, the affectation of an ostentatious cynicism and naturalism, the hyperbolic blasphemies and bawdy suggestiveness, and the libidinous candor of the poem might well endorse the common and popular view of "Jack" Donne in the 1590s as a

22. Ibid.
23. Marotti, *John Donne,* 85; Pinka, *This Dialogue of One: Donne's Songs and Sonnets* (University: University of Alabama Press, 1982), 42.

wiseacre amateur manuscript poet anxious to please, tease, and appease such an academic audience. Much of the mockery of poetic conventions with suggestive sexual insinuations reinforces the image of Donne the smart-ass mocking the gravitas of the Elizabethan court poets, much as Ovid had mocked Augustus's poets, Horace and Virgil. However enticing and provocative (and however fashionable in its Foucauldian view of the poet as the mere production—né victim—of fated socioeconomic powers) such a view of the poem (and of the elegies to which this view is most frequently attached),[24] it yet fails to intimate fully enough the "multiple personal and intellectual intents" of this and other Donne poems. As William Kerrigan has aptly phrased it, "When the magic word 'power' appears in Donne studies we almost always find a cruelly emptied out, vitiated Donne, . . . who has nothing in him except simplistic ambitions and an immense appetite for exhibiting his wretched plight before a coterie of self-pitying no-accounts, . . . or the Donne of Goldberg, cringing self-interestedly before the absolutist pretensions of King James."[25] Rather, or, more accurately, in addition to its "analytic examination of fashionable love conventions of which Donne and his readers were fond," and its "iconoclastic" repudiation of Marlowe's poem as "no more than an appealing but empty dream,"[26] when read within the lexicon of late-Elizabethan political and religious discourse, "The Baite" points toward a group of readers, another literary circle, that would include not just the usual suspects but also liminal characters more sympathetic to the young poet's situation, readers such as Henry Goodyer, Tobie Mathew, members of the Stanley family, and other "fish." The recognition of such readers offers a fuller perspective on the "multiple intents" of Donne's early satirical poetry. It also suggests that Donne's literary circle would have been not just attuned to the young recusant poet's witty parody of current courtly literary fashions and debates, but also responsive to the implications of the satirical poet's verses in what van Wyck Smith has shown to be Donne's *satirical* allegory of the late-Elizabethan court in poems such as his provocative mock-epic *Metempsychosis*.[27] In that late-Elizabethan Menippean satire, Donne asks:

24. I have broached this subject more fully in "'Over rekoning' the 'undertones': A Preface to 'some elegies' by Donne," *Renaissance Papers 2000*, ed. T. H. Howard-Hill and P. B. Rollinson (Rochester, N.Y.: Camden House Press, forthcoming).

25. Kerrigan, "What Was Donne Doing?" *South Central Review* 4:2 (1989): 7. For an illuminating treatment of these topics, see especially Richard B. Wollman, "The 'Press and the Fire': Print and Manuscript Culture in Donne's Circle," *Studies in English Literature* 33 (1993): 85–97.

26. Marotti, *John Donne*, 85; Low, "Compleat Angler's 'Baite,'" 10, 9.

27. M. van Wyk Smith, "John Donne's *Metempsychosis*," *Review of English Studies*, n.s., 24 (1973): 17–25, 141–52.

> Is any kinde subject to rape like fish?
>
> . . . .
>
> . . . them all these unkinde kinds feed upon,
> To kill them is an occupation,
> And lawes make fasts, and lents for their destruction."
>
> (ll. 281, 288–90)

The "disputing" fish (l. 276) of *Metempsychosis,* which is "Spied through traiterous . . . spectacle . . . , oft retarded . . . with hidden net, . . . in a prison put" (ll.
274, 253, 241) and finally—because its "weakness [and] silence . . . invite oppression"—"borne away" (ll. 251, 277),[28] might also point toward the membership of that Donne *literary circle* of *sympathetic* readers he so aptly described
in the preface to *Metempsychosis* as "no such Readers as I can teach." Such readers would indeed have been keen to *the recusant lexicon* of the inventive poet's
"multiple intents" in "The Baite." I say "might point toward" at the advice of
the final stanza of this poem. Just as Donne in the last stanza finally urges his
reader to dismiss both Marlowe's pastoral fictionality and his own piscatorial
realism, so I must submit that I cannot "catch" Donne the recusant wit in "The
Baite." Having "spied" the *equivocal* nature of the recusant tenor of the poem,
"no such [self-]deceit" is possible for me. One of the "new pleasures" of the poetry of Donne, after all, is the realization (and the fond hope) that readers of
Donne who think themselves "a little wise, the best fooles bee."[29]

With this warning in mind, one might reasonably conclude that, among
Donne's "undoubtedly various, . . . intimately personal and intellectual impulses," "The Baite" might best reflect the spirited response of an independent-
minded genius whose poems are "In cipher writ" ("A Valediction: of the booke,"
l. 21). While appealing to both a (public) coterie audience of court wits and a
(private) coterie of recusant readers, some of whom may have been in both

---

28. In *Metempsychosis* the "sea Pie"—who "For game and not for hunger / . . . Spied
through this traiterous spectacle, from high, / The seely fish where it disputing lay, / And
t'end her doubts and her, beares her away, / Exalted she is, but to the exalters good, / As
are by great ones, men which lowly stood. / It's rais'd, to be the Raisers instrument and
food" (Shawcross, *Complete Poetry of Donne,* st. xxviii, ll. 274–80)—sounds especially
like Topcliffe. Again, the predicament of the fish in that political allegory resembles that
of the English Catholic recusants' being pursued by the government-made *new men:* the
Soul that is the subject of the poem inhabits a fish that is then eaten by a swan so that
the Soul "Now swome a prison in a prison put" (241) and then is exhaled into another
fish—because the fish can make no resistance: its "weakness" and "silence" invite "oppression." The fish swims on, "oft retarded, once with hidden net"; she keeps her "faith"
and finally makes it to the sea where the sea Pie catches her and "beares her away."
29. "The Triple Foole," l. 21.

groups, it finally indicates most fully not Donne's enthrallment to any religio-political audience as much as it attests to the brilliant wit of an independent-minded genius adept at reframing the norms and forms of coterie poetics to express his own "personal and intellectual" criticisms and positions. If such an equivocal note offers a surprising conclusion to this essay, it yet intends to respect Donne's own early definition of the essence of wit (in his *Juvenilia*), where he suggests that our "wit [is] pleas'd with those iests, which coozen [our] expectation" (sig. A1v). Central to the wit of "The Baite" is Donne's revision of those duels between literary circles endemic to the Elizabethan social and political scene into a witty—and, finally, a personal—assault. That both "Protestant" readers interested in the literary debate initiated by Marlowe and Raleigh would have found much "delight" in Donne's poem and that "Catholic" readers would have found much "teaching" in it should not distract from our recognition of the brilliant wit that lies at the heart of Donne's transformation of his "personal and intellectual impulses" into enduring poetic achievement.

Sharon Cadman Seelig

"To all vertuous Ladies in generall"
Aemilia Lanyer's Community of Strong Women

Pondering the question of literary circles in Renaissance England and attracted by the thought of a literary circle in Dearborn, I began to wonder, with Joan Kelly-Gadol, whether women had literary circles. They did, of course: one thinks of the circle of patronage created by the countess of Pembroke at Wilton, of the notables attracted by the light of Lucy, countess of Bedford, whom Donne and Jonson found the "brightness of our sphere"[1] (though I note that both these circles were inhabited chiefly by male poets); one thinks of Katherine Philips, who re-created herself as Orinda, supplied her husband and friends with literary names to suit, and thereby became known as "the matchless Orinda," center of a fictive as well as an actual circle. I thought even of the much humbler An Collins who, in writing her strongly biblical poetry, seems to have addressed a circle of like-minded believers, a community of the faithful. Or one might recall Margaret Cavendish, who, though not particularly adept at relations with other women, was able, by multiplying images of herself in *The Blazing World*, to create a little circle of her own. But I was also conscious of the circles that were not, of failures of connection and of isolation, of circles that existed in longing and imagination, in particular those of Aemilia Lanyer and the woman who figures strongly in Lanyer's elegiac vision of Cookham, Anne Clifford.

Lady Anne Clifford's diary from the years 1616–1619, for all that it represents a woman of remarkable determination and pluck and for all its connections with wealth and power, includes many striking moments of frustration

---

1. I refer, of course, to Kelly-Gadol's essay, "Did Women Have a Renaissance?" in *Becoming Visible: Women in European History,* ed. Renate Bridenthal and Claudia Koontz (Boston: Houghton Mifflin, 1977), 137–64; Jonson's epigram, "To Lucy, Countess of Bedford, with Mr. Donne's Satires," in *Poems,* ed. Ian Donaldson (Oxford: Oxford University Press, 1975).

and exclusion. Prominent, of course, is Anne Clifford's long-standing battle with her husband, Richard Sackville, earl of Dorset, over her inheritance, which she wanted established in her name and he wanted to trade for cash. Besides enlisting the power of the king, the Church, and the patriarchy, Dorset also used the weapon of isolation: Anne Clifford's diary records his frequent journeys, the time he spent at court, in gambling and cockfighting, while she remained alone at Knole. For example, in May 1616 she wrote:

> All this time my Lord was in London where he had all and infinite great re-sort coming to him. He went much abroad to Cocking, to Bowling Alleys, to Plays and Horse Races, & [was] commended by all the World. I stayed in the Countrey having many times a sorrowful & heavy Heart & being con-demned by most folks because I would not consent to the Agreement, so as I may truly say, I am like an Owl in the Desert.[2]

Perhaps even more poignant is the instance of the following year, when a good many of Anne Clifford's friends and acquaintances were assembled at Pens-hurst, a mere seven miles away, and she, the countess of Dorset, the daughter of George Clifford, third earl of Cumberland, and Margaret Russell, dowager countess of Cumberland, was not allowed to join them. Her entry for August 4, 1617, reads: "In the morning my Lord went to Penshurst but would not suffer me to go with him although My Lord & Lady Lisle sent a man on purpose to desire me to come. He hunted, & lay there all night, there being my Lord of Montgomery, my Lord Hay, my Lady Lucy & and a great deal of other Compa-ny."[3] The next few entries record her depression: "I kept my Chamber, being very troubled & sad in mind" on both the eighth and the tenth of the month; "the 12th and 13th I spent most of the time in playing Glecko & hearing Moll Neville reading the *Arcadia.*" While Anne Clifford's husband enjoyed the life of a courtier, with its manly sports and forms of dissipation, visiting the home of the Sidneys and moving at will and in splendor through the countryside, she could participate only vicariously, finding her chief entertainment in the pas-toral romance that originated with the most notable members of that family.

This image of a woman standing outside a social group, vividly imagining it even as she is denied access, re-creating it in a work of fiction, is for me one of the strongest impressions of Aemilia Lanyer's work, in which, not coinciden-

2. D. J. H. Clifford, ed., *The Diaries of Lady Anne Clifford* (Wolfeboro Falls, N.H.: Alan Sutton, 1990), 33. The image of the owl in the desert, a reference to Ps. 102:6, is also used by Lady Arabella Stuart to convey desolation.

3. Ibid., 60.

tally, Anne Clifford and her strong and pious mother, Margaret Russell, figure prominently. That impression is created by the elegiac representation of "The Description of Cooke-ham" and is also pertinent to the circle of good and powerful women constructed by the dedications to *Salve Deus Rex Judaeorum.* The circle I describe is literary in a particular sense, that is, it is created by the text itself, as Aemilia Lanyer represents a group of powerful women and places herself in relation to them, sometimes as supplicant, as admirer, and even as instructor, though her own circumstances were far humbler than theirs.

As Judith Scherer Herz has provocatively argued, Lanyer might well be seen as outside the literary tradition altogether, as it is not at all clear that her work, despite its numerous dedications, was read, or that it intersected with or influenced subsequent work. Indeed, one might find an emblem of that exclusion in the fact that "The Description of Cooke-ham," unlike its near contemporary "To Penshurst," is restricted to the grounds of the great house; it never penetrates to the warmth of the table and fireside celebrated by Ben Jonson.[4] Yet, I suggest that while Anne Clifford succeeded in life—she was at last able to join the fellowship at Penshurst and through long life and tenacity to reclaim her lands—Aemilia Lanyer succeeds in an imaginative vision: out of marginality, out "of absence, darkness . . . , things which are not," indeed out of weakness, Lanyer creates in *Salve Deus* a remarkable community of strength, present more powerfully and enduringly in her fiction than in life itself. In looking at these poems I shall begin at the end with "The Description of Cooke-ham" and then proceed to the initial dedications, leaving *Salve Deus* itself for another occasion.

"The Description of Cooke-ham" records the loss of the very place and circle it honors. In "Farewell (sweet Place) where Virtue then did rest / And all delights did harbour in her breast" (ll. 7–8), Lanyer bids farewell to something she will never again experience, something that is itself passing away: even Margaret Russell, called "(great lady) Mistris of that Place" (l. 11), is forced to leave

---

4. Herz, "Aemilia Lanyer and the Pathos of Literary History," in *Representing Women in Renaissance England,* ed. Claude J. Summers and Ted-Larry Pebworth (Columbia: University of Missouri Press, 1997), 121–35. Herz raises important questions about "the prior claim the text makes upon us" in distinction to the "things we can do to the text," the "theoretical and critical moves" that we can make in response to it (127).

On the relationship between Lanyer's and Jonson's poems, see Lynette McGrath, "'Let Us Have Our Libertie Againe': Amelia Lanier's Seventeenth-Century Feminist Voice," *Women's Studies* 20 (1992): 331–48; and Ann Baynes Coiro, "Writing in Service: Sexual Politics and Class Position in the Poetry of Aemilia Lanyer and Ben Jonson," *Criticism* 35 (1993): 357–76.

Cookham, a royal country estate that was not in her possession but leased by her brother from the Crown.[5] Cookham thus becomes an emblem of all that is transitory, even as it persists as an image of the eternal bliss and stability the author longs for:

> As fleeting worldly Joyes that could not last:
> Or, as dimme shadowes of celestiall pleasures,
> Which are desir'd above all earthly treasures.
> (ll. 14–16)

Not only the poet but all nature mourns the loss of the countess and her daughter; the same trees and winds that celebrated their coming now lament their departure in a thoroughgoing and dramatic act of pathos:

> The trees that were so glorious in our view,
> Forsooke both flowres and fruit, when once they knew
> Of your depart, their very leaves did wither,
> Changing their colours as they grewe together.
> (ll. 133–36)

Even more striking is Lanyer's relation to the society she depicts, for she stands tentatively on the margins, claiming relationship even as she acknowledges difficulties. Although she describes Margaret Russell as the source of "Grace" (that is, favor) (l. 2) and attributes to her the impulse of authorship—"From whose desires did spring this worke of Grace" (l. 12)—Lanyer laments the effect of

> Unconstant Fortune . . .
> Who casts us downe into so lowe a frame:
> Where our great friends we cannot dayly see,
> So great a diffrence is there in degree.
> (ll. 103–6)

The difference in rank that makes "The Description of Cooke-ham" something like a dream vision also makes Lanyer's connection with the family so tenuous

5. Susanne Woods, ed., *The Poems of Aemilia Lanyer* (New York: Oxford University Press, 1993), 130 n. All references to Lanyer's poetry are to this edition. As Barbara Kiefer Lewalski notes in *Writing Women in Jacobean England* (Cambridge: Harvard University Press, 1993), this poem must have been composed after the death of George Clifford in October 1605; it refers to a time before the marriage of Anne Clifford ("noble *Dorset*, then a virgin faire") in February 1609, a reference that itself indicates a subsequent date (216–17, 396 nn. 21, 28).

that she claims her parting kiss not from Anne Clifford ("noble *Dorset*, then a virgin faire" [l. 160]) but secondhand, from the tree from which Anne Clifford "with a chaste, yet loving kisse tooke leave" (l. 165). This line may, unfortunately, bring to mind another image of indirection—the kiss that Thisbe bestows on the wall that separates her from Pyramus—a sign that Lanyer has not found an altogether satisfactory way to represent her connection with the Cliffords, a connection clearly less intimate than she desires.[6]

Lanyer's claim of relationship has been variously interpreted: Barbara Lewalski asserts that Lanyer's dedications, "though hyperbolical like most of their kind," nevertheless "reveal something about Lanyer's actual associations," whereas Kari Boyd McBride argues that Lanyer's portraits subvert "the realities of social position and power to construct her own authority." Similarly, Lisa Schnell sees considerable ambivalence in Lanyer's attitude toward her patrons and argues that in the act of praising them, she in effect exercises control over them.[7] In any case, such control as Lanyer exercises is authorial and textual: she constructs in her texts relationships that include her, even as she laments their limitations in fact.

Yet, Lanyer, who struggles from the margins to earn a place in the story, also establishes a powerful image of community, not just, as has been rightly suggested by Barbara Lewalski, a community of good women, but also a community of strong women, a constellation of heroic virtue.[8] In this exclusively female society, the male associates are purely religious or mythological figures; whatever is done is done by women who (as in the argument for women's colleges or cities of ladies) assume all the roles themselves. Margaret Russell sits on a "Prospect fit to please the eyes of Kings" (l. 72), where "Hills, vales, and woods, as if on bended knee / They had appeard, your honour to salute" (ll.

---

6. "I kiss the wall's hole, not your lips at all" (*A Midsummer Night's Dream* 5.1.201). Michael Morgan Holmes sees the kissing of the tree as part of a pattern of homoerotic expression ("The Love of Other Women: Rich Chains and Sweet Kisses," in *Aemilia Lanyer: Gender, Genre, and the Canon*, ed. Marshall Grossman [Lexington: University Press of Kentucky, 1998], 182).

7. Lewalski, *Writing Women*, 220; McBride, "Sacred Celebration: The Patronage Poems," in *Aemilia Lanyer*, ed. Grossman, 71; Schnell, "So Great a Difference Is There in Degree," *Modern Language Quarterly* 57 (1996): 23–35; and "Breaking 'the rule of *Cortezia*': Aemelia Lanyer's Dedications to *Salve Deus Rex Judaeorum*," *Journal of Medieval and Early Modern Studies* 27 (1997): 77–101.

8. It is Enobarbus in *Antony and Cleopatra* who hopes for a place in the story (3.13.46). Lewalski speaks of "a contemporary community of good women who are spiritual heirs to the biblical and historical good women her title poem celebrates" (*Writing Women*, 220).

68–69). Margaret's religious devotion brings her into male company on functionally equal terms, as she joins a society drawn from biblical texts:

> In these sweet woods how often did you walke,
> With Christ and his Apostles there to talke;
>
> . . . .
>
> With *Moyses* you did mount his holy Hill,
> To know his pleasure, and performe his Will.
> With lovely *David* you did often sing,
> His holy Hymnes to Heavens Eternall King.
>
> . . . .
>
> With blessed *Joseph* you did often feed
> Your pined brethren, when they stood in need.
>   (ll. 81–82, 85–88, 91–92)

Although engaged in activities that might be gendered feminine—walking in the woods and groves, meditating on scripture, praying and singing psalms, and nurturing the hungry—Margaret Russell is associated with prophets, apostles, patriarchs, and monarchs, and represented as joining in actions analogous to theirs. She is not simply a pious woman but an influential and effective one. Her daughter likewise is depicted in the strong terms suitable to the (male) heir of a great family, as "that sweet Lady sprung from *Cliffords* race, / Of noble *Bedfords* blood, faire steame of Grace" (ll. 93–94).[9]

This presentation of women as strong and in some sense masculine, clearly evident in "The Description of Cooke-ham," is even more prominent in the dedications to *Salve Deus Rex Judaeorum*. These perhaps extravagantly numerous dedications—nine to particular figures and two more general ones ("To all vertuous Ladies in generall" and "To the Vertuous Reader")—have occasioned some comment. But as Lewalski notes, citing the seventeen dedications to *The Faerie Queene*, multiple dedications were not uncommon. Most readers put the number of Lanyer's dedications down to her straitened economic circumstances: she addresses the most prominent female members of the Jacobean

---

9. "Streame," the reading silently adopted by A. L. Rowse, might seem the more likely, as in a stream of blood (*The Poems of Shakespeare's Dark Lady* [New York: Clarkson N. Potter, 1978]). But Lanyer's printed text clearly reads "steame," which the *Oxford English Dictionary* gives as an alternate spelling for *stem*, as in the scion of a family, a reading also quite plausible in its context. (My thanks to Susanne Woods for alerting me to this point.)

court, some of them apparently well known to her, others clearly not.[10] But while financial and social support were clearly objectives, more striking to me is the way in which these dedications construct a fictive community that functions as an alternative to the patriarchal structure. Both in number (nine to particular individuals) and in emphasis—on strength of character, intellect, and accomplishment—the dedications suggest a group of female worthies in a sense I will explore later. They are, as Achsah Guibbory suggests, "a female alternative to the male nexus of power, both secular and sacred."[11]

While Louise Schleiner sees the dedications as an image of "a lady's circle busy with readings, music, and devotions," thus emphasizing the feminine activities of this group, and Elaine Beilin stresses the spiritual accomplishments of these women, Lanyer's use of the words *virtue* (or *virtuous*), which appears fifty times in the dedications, and *worthy* (or a variant), which occurs twenty-three times, carries a sense lost to modern readers.[12] The most obvious sense of *virtue*, to us, is goodness, as in the *Oxford English Dictionary*'s definition: "conformity of life and conduct with the principles of morality." But in the years between Lanyer and ourselves, *virtue* has become an increasingly narrow concept, associated with that peculiarly female virtue chastity (perhaps even silence and obedience). The first recorded use of *virtue* in the sense of chastity is, interestingly, from *Much Ado about Nothing* (1598–1599). But this meaning does not seem to be precisely what Lanyer has in mind, and the subsequent shadings of meaning may make us misread her text. To be sure, the women she celebrates are virtuous in the narrower sense thought particularly appropriate to women, but they are also considerably more powerful figures. They remind us that from the fourteenth through the nineteenth centuries *virtue* also meant "the posses-

---

10. Lewalski, *Writing Women*, 220. Herz, however, finds the effect entirely different from Spenser's dedications, noting that "in Lanyer's text the margins, crowded with noble readers, take up almost as much space as the text itself" ("Aemilia Lanyer," 129).

Rowse cavalierly dismisses Lanyer's "too obviously sycophantic poems" (*Shakespeare's Dark Lady*, 33). Elaine Beilin offers substantive descriptions of the dedicatees and suggests connections to the Nine Worthies and the seven spiritual virtues (*Redeeming Eve* [Princeton: Princeton University Press, 1987], 182–91).

11. Guibbory, "The Gospel according to Aemilia," in *Sacred and Profane: Secular and Devotional Interplay in Early Modern British Literature,* ed. Helen Wilcox, Richard Todd, and Alasdair MacDonald (Amsterdam: VU University Press, 1996), 107.

12. Schleiner, *Tudor and Stuart Women Writers* (Bloomington: Indiana University Press, 1994), 24; Beilin, *Redeeming Eve,* 177–207. Jonathan Goldberg speaks of the tradition of good women, a tradition whose dangers he also notes (*Desiring Women Writing: English Renaissance Examples* [Stanford: Stanford University Press, 1997], 9).

sion or display of manly qualities; manly excellence . . . courage, valour," and that the root of the English word *virtue* is the Latin *vir,* man (Middle English *vertu* from Old French, from Latin *virtus,* manliness). Some of this meaning persists in the phrase "by virtue of the authority . . ."; it may also be seen in the language of the Authorized Version of the Bible: when Jesus, having been touched by a woman with an infirmity, senses that "virtue has gone out of him" (Mark 5:30), he means that he has imparted strength, not that he has declined in goodness.

The nine noble women celebrated in Lanyer's dedications are preeminently figures of influence and power: they are associated with goddesses and with masculine, martial virtues, and even their traditionally female qualities are recast in terms of strength. The dedications are arranged, at least at the beginning, in order of rank, proceeding from Queen Anne to her daughter Princess Elizabeth and thence to Lady Arabella Stuart; they are addressed to particular prominent individuals as well as to those who, like "the Vertuous Reader" and "all vertuous Ladies," aspire to the standard of perfection here outlined.[13] Lanyer represents Queen Anne as an imperial figure who recalls Queen Elizabeth I; Anne combines the qualities of the three goddesses judged by Paris—Juno, Athena, and Venus—listed in an order that emphasizes queenly supremacy ("from *Juno* you have State and Dignities") and wisdom ("From warlike *Pallas,* Wisdome, Fortitude") over the more vaguely represented beauty and love ("And from faire *Venus* all her Excellencies").[14] Like those who follow, Queen Anne is a pattern or compendium of virtue ("all royall virtues are in you, / The Naturall, the Morall, and Divine" [ll. 67–68]), the embodiment of a quality that is also recognized by other good women, a mirror of virtue, a book of instruction

13. The complete order is: Queen Anne; her daughter Princess Elizabeth; "To all vertuous Ladies in generall"; Arabella Stuart; Susan, countess dowager of Kent; Mary Sidney, countess of Pembroke; Lucy, countess of Bedford; Margaret Russell, countess dowager of Cumberland; Katherine, countess of Suffolk; Anne Clifford, countess of Dorset; and "To the Vertuous Reader." See Woods, *Poems of Aemilia Lanyer,* for an account of apparently intentional omissions in several copies (xlvii–li). Schleiner argues interestingly about the decentering that ultimately makes Margaret Russell, rather than the monarch, the focal point (*Tudor and Stuart Women Writers,* 25). Leeds Barroll sees a considerable error in Lanyer's placing Lucy, countess of Bedford, after the countess of Pembroke ("Looking for Patrons," in *Aemilia Lanyer,* ed. Grossman, 40).
14. Lewalski notes that Pallas was "Queen Anne's chosen personification in masques and addresses," but the qualities of that goddess are particularly appropriate for Lanyer's list of strong women (*Writing Women,* 220). In fact, Minerva is the first figure in the list of "Nine worthie women almost equivalent, / With those nine worthie men so *valient*" given by Robert Chester in *Loves Martyr; or, Rosalins Complaint* (1601).

as well as praise, and a figure powerful enough to "grace" Lanyer's "rude un-pollisht lines" (l. 35).[15]

In the second poem, Anne's daughter Princess Elizabeth is addressed in terms that summon up the memory of her famous predecessor, whose quali-ties she is said to possess:

> Most gratious Ladie, faire ELIZABETH,
> Whose Name and Virtues puts us still in mind,
> Of her, of whom we are depriv'd by death;
> The *Phoenix* of her age, whose worth did bind
> All worthy minds so long as they have breath. . . .
>
> (ll. 1–5)

In this dedication, Lanyer offers two kinds of lineage—the mother-daughter link between Anne of Denmark and her daughter Elizabeth and the connection of a powerful name, from Queen Elizabeth to her namesake, the princess—both of which disregard the male heirs to the throne. And she uses two crucial terms, *virtues* and *worthy*, that underscore the notion of models of female strength.[16]

The seven remaining dedications to specific women are framed by a ninety-one-line poem, "To all vertuous Ladies in generall," and a final prose address, "To the Vertuous Reader." In this third dedicatory poem, the most prominent figure is not a member of the royal family but virtue itself, a figure whom Lan-yer constructs as a queen waited on by all virtuous women. Lanyer adapts the biblical parable of the wise and foolish virgins waiting for the bridegroom (Christ) to give particular prominence to this female figure; the other emi-nences of this poem, also female, are the muses "whose Virtues with the purest minds agree," the "nine Worthies" to whom "all faire mindes resort" (ll. 31, 35).

15. The predecessor one might think of here is Boccaccio's *De mulieribus claris*, which, as Pamela Joseph Benson notes, "praised many women for acting with strength, valor, fortitude, and intelligence, that is, for exercising 'manly' virtues in traditionally male fields" (*The Invention of the Renaissance Woman* [University Park: Pennsylvania State Uni-versity Press, 1992], xxxvii). But as Benson goes on to argue, Boccaccio's text is actually deeply contradictory in its mixing of kinds of women, in its aims and effects. Janel Mueller, though she does not argue for a direct influence, appropriately creates a "cross-cultural and transhistorical perspective" by citing Christine de Pizan ("The Feminist Po-etics of Aemilia Lanyer's *Salve Deus Rex Judaeorum*," in *Feminist Measures: Soundings in Po-etry and Theory*, ed. Lynn Keller and Cristanne Miller [Ann Arbor: University of Michigan Press, 1994], 211). See also Natalie Zemon Davis, "'Women's History' in Transition: The European Case," *Feminist Studies* 3 (1976): 83–103.

16. In contrast to McBride, who argues that Lanyer emphasizes the childbearing abil-ity of the queen, thus undermining her independent authority ("Sacred Celebration," 68), I see Lanyer constructing a female line based on names and qualities.

While the primary reference of the phrase "nine Worthies" (l. 35; reinforced by "worthy ladies," l. 71) here may be the muses, the use of the term with its specifying number also suggests an alternate female power structure, a counterbalance to those male figures of primarily military accomplishment, the nine Worthies drawn from classical, Judaic, and Christian history. Caxton, in his preface to *Le Morte d'Arthur,* lists Hector, Alexander, and Julius Caesar; Joshua, David, and Judas Maccabaeus; and Arthur, Charlemagne, and Godfrey of Bouillon. Shakespeare's list in *Love's Labour's Lost* includes Pompey, Hector, Alexander, and Hercules (5.2). The example of "Those sacred sisters that on *Pallas* wait" (l. 30) is for Lanyer as powerful as that of military conquerors but "free / From sword, from violence, and from ill report" (ll. 33 – 34); they are capable of "godly labours" (l. 32) and able to avoid the temptations into which their male counterparts may fall.

There was in fact a tradition of classical female Worthies that arose in the late thirteenth century in the visual arts and persisted into the seventeenth century in written texts.[17] The cast of characters varies somewhat, and the division into three eras of history was not universally observed. But in a poem that Lanyer might well have known, Robert Chester's *Loves Martyr* (published together with Shakespeare's "Phoenix and the Turtle"), Chester sets out a group of "Nine worthie women," arranged into classical, Hebrew, and Christian.[18] Chester's list (Minerva, Semiramis, and Tomyris; Jahel, Deborah, and Judith; and Maude, Elizabeth of Aragon, and Johane of Naples) is not identical with Lanyer's, but it does include four of the same figures, and it stresses the warlike qualities of several of them. Of Minerva we hear that she "many manlike battailes manly fought"; of Tomyris that "From forth her eyes she lightned Honors Brand, / And brandished a Sword, a sword of Fame, / That to her weake Sexe yeelded Hectors name"; Jahel's "uncomprehensible valour in the end, / Did free and set at large her captiv'd Countrie, / . . . By killing hand to hand her foe great Sisar"; and Judith, "Bringing in triumph Holofernes head, / . . . got a great and greater Victorie, / Then thousand Souldiers in their maiestie."[19]

---

17. Brigitte Buettner, *Boccaccio's Des Cleres et Nobles Femmes: Systems of Signification in an Illuminated Manuscript* (Seattle: College Art Association, in association with the University of Washington Press, 1996), 35–36. For a more comprehensive discussion, see Horst Schroeder, *Der Topos der Nine Worthies in Literatur und Bildender Kunst* (Göttingen: Vandenhoeck and Ruprecht, 1971); and Glenda McLeod, *Virtue and Venom: Catalogues of Women from Antiquity to the Renaissance* (Ann Arbor: University of Michigan Press, 1991).

18. Beilin notes this instance of the female Worthies (*Redeeming Eve,* 188).

19. Chester, *Loves Martyr; or, Rosalins Complaint,* ed. Alexander B. Grosart (1601; reprint, London: New Shakespeare Society, 1878), 29–32.

While Chester's worthies are an important reference point for Lanyer's text, one should note that the women of "To all vertuous Ladies in generall," though heroic, are not specifically warriors. Although triumphant, urged to "bring your palmes of vict'ry in your hands" (l. 37) to celebrate the ultimate victory of virtue, they have a kind of priestly function similar to that of the women of Cookham; they are urged to "Annoynt your haire with *Aarons* pretious oyle" (l. 36). And, riding in a chariot drawn by "simple Doves" and "subtill serpents" (l. 49), they are associated with innocence and wisdom: Lanyer's iconography turns away from images appropriate simply to Venus—the doves signifying love—to recall the command of Christ to be "wise as serpents and innocent as doves" (Matt. 10:16), that is, to fulfill the duties of Christians in a dangerous world. One might say that the muses are to women what the Worthies are to men, providing alternate, more feminine models. But Lanyer's dedications, which foreground bold and transcendent behavior coupled with a refusal of violence, create in effect the nine Worthies of a female hierarchy.

In the dedications that follow, which vary in length and in the degree of intimacy or acquaintance asserted, Lanyer emphasizes qualities of strength, learning, and heroism. Arabella Stuart, cousin to King James and potential heir to the throne, is praised as a learned lady, associated with Pallas Athena. Susan Bertie, countess dowager of Kent, described as a bold voyager, a veteran who has "delighted in Gods truth" (l. 3), is depicted as making a heroic and dangerous journey:

> Whose Faith did undertake in Infancie,
> All dang'rous travells by devouring Seas
> To flie to Christ from vaine Idolatry.
> (ll. 19–21)

In fact it was the countess's mother, the duchess of Suffolk, who initiated the journey: she fled England during the reign of the Catholic Queen Mary, taking her child with her. Lanyer represents this action as both a virtuous imitation of Christ and a manifestation of principled courage:

> Leaving here her lands, her state, dignitie;
> Nay more, vouchsaft disguised weedes to weare:
>> When with Christ Jesus she did meane to goe,
>> From sweet delights to taste part of his woe.
> (ll. 27–30)

There is also a kind of architecture to these dedications, conveying and implying worth. The longest of them (224 lines, arranged in quatrains) and the one that occupies a central place is that to the countess of Pembroke, with whom, as a poet, Lanyer wishes to be linked.[20] In a dream vision that places the poet in the *"Edalyan* Groves" in search of "a Lady whom *Minerva* chose" (ll. 1, 3), Lanyer depicts Mary Sidney as associated with the muses and crowned by Fame. But she calls up a more vigorous figure, Bellona, goddess of war and wisdom, "a manly mayd which was both faire and tall" (l. 35), to honor this woman whose behavior is such that "a Sister well shee may be deemd, / To him that liv'd and di'd so nobly" (ll. 149–50), her warrior and courtier brother, "valiant *Sidney.*" Mary, according to Lanyer, even surpasses Sir Philip in qualities in which men and women may join: "And farre before him is to be esteemd / For virtue, wisedome, learning, dignity" (ll. 151–52). Both in the degree of praise and in the qualities emphasized, the countess emerges as a figure of strength, honored by Minerva and crowned by Fame, a powerful foremother to whom, when the dream vanishes, Aemilia Lanyer intends to present her poems.

The last specific dedication is to Anne Clifford, daughter of the chief dedicatee of these poems, Margaret Russell. The younger woman is celebrated as a defender of a proud heritage that combines traditional masculine and feminine qualities:

> You are the Heire apparant of this Crowne
> Of goodnesse, bountie, grace, love, pietie,
> By birth its yours, then keepe it as your owne,
> Defend it from all base indignitie.
>
> (ll. 65–68)

But this heritage has a kind of double valence: to be "Gods Steward" (l. 57), as instructed "by your most worthy mother" (l. 59), and to honor her ancestors, Anne must perform the most traditional acts of Christian charity:

> And as your Ancestors at first possest
> Their honours, for their honourable deeds,

---

20. The other long poems are the first, to Queen Anne (162 lines arranged in six-line stanzas), and the last two, to Katherine, countess of Suffolk (108 lines, also *ababcc*), and to Anne Clifford (144 lines in ottava rima). In fact, what Barroll sees as a misstep on Lanyer's part (see n. 13 above) may be a deliberate placing of Mary Sidney, whom Lanyer would like to see as a mentoring poet, in the architectural center of these dedications.

> Let their faire virtues never be transgrest,
> Bind up the broken, stop the wounds that bleeds,
> Succour the poore, comfort the comfortlesse,
> Cherish faire plants, suppresse unwholsom weeds.
>
> (ll. 73–78)[21]

Virtue here is active, not passive, certainly not limited to female chastity, but Lanyer significantly makes of actions often associated with women the chief acts of the virtuous Christian, valorizing them in a new way. Like Christ and like Peter before her, Anne Clifford is a master builder and a shepherd of the flock.[22]

> He [Christ] is the stone the builders did refuse,
> Which you, sweet Lady, are to build upon;
> He is the rocke that holy Church did chuse,
> Among which number, you must needs be one;
> Faire Shepheardesse, tis you that he will use
> To feed his flocke, that trust in him alone.
>
> (ll. 129–34)

In acting as builder, shepherd, and guardian, Anne Clifford will, according to Lanyer, "shew from whence you are descended"—in other words, Christ, Peter, and Margaret Russell—"And leave to all posterities your fame" (ll. 81–82).

Concluding the dedications is the prose address "To the Vertuous Reader." In contrast to the initial "To all vertuous Ladies in generall," which depicts Queen Virtue served by virtuous women, the latter warns against women slandering women. Yet, this warning prefaces a highly rhetorical elevation of women on the grounds that all men are "begotten of a woman, borne of a woman, nourished of a woman," and that Christ was even "obedient to a woman" (p. 49, ll. 43–44, 45). The women Lanyer praises are not only those who have passively "indured most cruel martyrdome for their faith" (l. 53) but also the more active "wise and virtuous women" appointed by God to "bring downe [the] pride and arrogancie" (ll. 32–33) of wicked men; their accomplishments range from violence to cunning to determined resistance. "[C]ruell *Cesarus* [was brought down] by the discreet counsell of noble *Deborah,* Judge and Prophetesse of Israel: and resolution of *Jael* wife of *Heber* the Kenite: wicked

---

21. The references to "Bind up the broken, stop the wounds that bleeds," recall Isa. 61:1 ("To bind up the broken hearted") and Ezek. 34:16 ("I will . . . bind up that which was broken") as well as Luke 10:34, the parable of the good Samaritan.

22. The charge to Simon Peter to "Feed my Lambs" and "Feed my sheep" occurs in John 21:15–17. "The stone the builders did refuse" is that of Luke 20:17.

Haman, by the divine prayers and prudent proceedings of beautifull *Hester:* blasphemous *Holofernes,* by the invincible courage, rare wisdome, and confident carriage of *Judeth:* & the unjust Judges, by the innocency of chast *Susanna"* (p. 49, ll. 33 – 39). These are the powerful women who will be celebrated in the body of *Salve Deus* itself, as "famous women . . . / Whose glorious actions" overthrew "powrefull men" (ll. 1465 – 67).[23]

While the powerful and sometimes violent women of this list, like the women of Lanyer's dedications, are notably chaste, Lanyer's treatment strongly emphasizes their boldness and initiative, virtues that are strength rather than merely endurance. In fact, there is some testing of gender roles as several of Lanyer's worthy contemporaries are set against the suffering Christ who is the subject of the longer poem, and whose passivity and subjugation complement their strength and active engagement. As several critics have argued, *Salve Deus* presents a Christ who is feminized and women who are by contrast masculinized; in that process Lanyer, putting Christ in the position usually occupied by a female subject, makes him the object of the female gaze.[24] Arabella Stuart is urged to

> spare one looke
> Upon this humbled King, who all forsooke,
> That in his dying armes he might imbrace
> Your beauteous Soule, and fill it with his grace.
> (p. 17, ll. 11 – 14)

Lucy, countess of Bedford, is enjoined to "entertaine this dying lover," "the truelove of your soule, your hearts delight" (pp. 32 – 33, ll. 16, 6). To Margaret Russell, countess of Cumberland, Lanyer offers Christ as a jewel surpassing all jew-

23. The list also resembles that found in Henry Cornelius Agrippa's *Declamation on the Nobility and Preeminence of the Female Sex,* which suggests, perhaps paradoxically, the very reversal of values at the heart of Lanyer's poems.

24. Jacqueline Pearson, "Women Writers and Women Readers: The Case of Aemelia Lanier," in *Voicing Women: Gender and Sexuality in Early Writing,* ed. Kate Chedgzoy, Melanie Hansen, and Suzanne Trill (Pittsburgh: Duquesne University Press, 1997), 45 – 54; Michael Schoenfeldt, "The Gender of Religious Devotion: Amelia Lanyer and John Donne," in *Religion and Culture in Renaissance England,* ed. Claire McEachern and Debora Shuger (Cambridge: Cambridge University Press, 1997), 209 – 33; Catherine Keohane, "'That Blindest Weakenesse Be Not Over-Bold': Aemilia Lanyer's Radical Unfolding of the Passion," *ELH* 64 (1997): 359 – 89. Wendy Wall says "the eroticized other, . . . Christ, occupies the same position of powerlessness as the speaker" ("Our Bodies/Our Texts? Renaissance Women and the Trials of Authorship," in *Anxious Power: Reading, Writing, and Ambivalence in Narrative by Women,* ed. Carol J. Singley and Susan E. Sweeney [Albany: State University of New York Press, 1993], 67).

els. To Katherine, countess of Suffolk, and her daughters, Christ is presented as "a Lover much more true / Than ever was since first the world began" (pp. 38–39, ll. 52–53), "In whom is all that Ladies can desire" (l. 85). Later, in *Salve Deus* proper, Lanyer emphasizes Margaret Russell's having no earthly lover but only a heavenly one, Christ, as "the Husband of thy Soule" (l. 253), who "dying made her Dowager of all" (l. 257). Lanyer depicts women as distinctly heroic and independent, as dominant, placed in relationship to a Christ who is suffering rather than triumphant. Although they may sometimes imitate that suffering, more often they are distinguished by valuing Christ's passion, acting as strong partners to this bridegroom.

In short, the dedications to Lanyer's *Salve Deus* are not only, as has been thought, a bid for patronage, or simply a circle of reading women, or merely an assertion of female goodness, or simply a collection of the most prominent women of Lanyer's day. Lanyer does bring together a group of women who were powerful at court, distinguished for learning, for endurance and independence, for religious faith and action. But the virtuous ladies she praises are not good merely in our dilute modern sense; rather, they are powerful and exemplary figures. Lanyer's circle of good women is drawn from life: its characters are historical yet fictive in that the associations she forms by placing them together are stronger than those that actually existed. And she reaches beyond these women to address "all vertuous Ladies in generall," a circle that all her female readers are encouraged to join, a community in part created by Lanyer herself, in part joined and concluded by her readers.

Our search for a literary circle then has led from life into texts, from fact to fiction, and perhaps from fiction back into life. Literary circles in Renaissance England, I suggest, are created not only by presence and contact but also by absence, longing, and imagination. They exist as vividly in texts as in reality. Anne Clifford had difficulty reaching the circle at Penshurst to which by birth and inclination she belonged, yet she created it in her diary; Margaret Cavendish, although she could not be Henry V or Charles II, announced her determination to be Margaret the First, in a world of her own construction; Katherine Philips, through naming, poetry, and letters, created a salon of largely absent friends; and Aemilia Lanyer, even as she lost touch with Anne Clifford, Margaret Russell, and Cookham, created a vivid and enduring image of the circle of virtue and strength assembled there. Her dedications represent a community of powerful women, a cohort of female Worthies worthy of the name of virtue, a circle calculated to elicit—even in the absence of historical documentation—admiration and assent.

John Considine

The Invention of the Literary Circle of Sir Thomas Overbury

One of the most spectacular publishing successes of Jacobean England was a collection of prose and verse ascribed by its publisher to Sir Thomas Overbury and his literary circle. At its heart was a poem by Overbury called *A Wife*, which comprises forty-seven verses in the *Venus and Adonis* meter, discussing the origins and benefits of marriage, and the qualities of the ideal wife. It was published in 1614 by Lawrence Lisle. The second edition of the poem, also published by Lisle in 1614, announced some additions on its title page: *A Wife Now The Widdow of Sir Thomas Overburye. Being A most exquisite and singular Poem of the choice of a Wife. Whereunto are added many witty Characters, and conceited Newes, written by himselfe and other learned Gentlemen his friends.* This claim that the second edition of Overbury's poem was augmented with texts from a literary circle of which Overbury himself was a member, if not the center, is an important one, and has been widely accepted. Nine more progressively augmented editions, all published by Lisle, followed in rapid succession. The last of them—the eleventh edition of Overbury's poem—appeared in 1622. By this stage the collection was made up of numerous liminary poems, *A Wife*, eighty-one "Characters," twenty items of "Newes," and several miscellaneous poems and prose pieces (one later edition was even further augmented, with the first printed text of Bacon's poem "The World's a Bubble").[1]

1. The best bibliographical survey is still Gwendolen Murphy, *A Bibliography of English Character-Books, 1608–1700*, Supplement to the Bibliographical Society's Transactions No. 4 (Oxford: University Press for the Bibliographical Society, 1925), 15–25. There were eighty-two prose "Characters" in all; "A Purueior of Tobacco" appeared in only the sixth and eighth editions. Bacon's poem, of which Peter Beal records fifty-four early manuscripts (*Index of English Literary Manuscripts, 1450–1625*, 2 vols. [London: Mansell, 1980], BcF 1–53 and addenda), appeared in the twelfth edition (Dublin: Company of Stationers, 1626), sig. N4v–5; its first printing has previously been supposed to be in Thomas Farnaby, *Florilegium Epigrammatum Graecorum* (1629).

If all of these texts were indeed exchanged within a literary circle composed of Thomas Overbury "and other learned Gentlemen his friends," then the successive editions of *A Wife* would constitute a full and attractive record of the activities of that circle. The example of *The Odcombian Banquet* and Thomas Coryate's letters from India shows that writings from a Jacobean literary circle could be documented in print; can we take *A Wife* to be the monument of a group like the "Sireniacal Gentlemen"? In order to answer that question, I shall first provide contexts for *A Wife* in the other writings of Thomas Overbury, and the other publications of Lawrence Lisle. Then I shall discuss the constituents of the collection separately, under five headings: first, liminary verses and miscellaneous poems and prose pieces added to the seventh and subsequent editions of *A Wife*; second, the "Characters"; third, the "Newes"; fourth, the poem *A Wife* itself; and, fifth, the liminary verses printed in the first edition.

A Wife is the only poem that can be ascribed to Overbury on the basis of external evidence. John Owen congratulated him on it in an epigram, and Ben Jonson mentioned it as his in the "Conversations with Drummond." Owen must have seen it in manuscript before November 1612, because his epigram on it was printed in 1612, in a collection that included an epigram promising Prince Henry good fortune in that year and must therefore antedate the prince's death in November. Jonson must have seen it in manuscript before August 1612, if his recollection of reading it to the countess of Rutland is to be trusted.[2] Before writing it, Overbury had made a series of notes about France and the Low Countries, the *Observations in His Travailes,* of which at least twelve manuscript copies are extant. A number of letters signed by him also survive.[3]

---

2. John Owen, *Epigrammatum libri tres* (Nicholas Okes for Simon Waterson, 1612), sig. A8, "Thomæ Ouerbury equitis poëma ingeniosum, de Vxore perfecta"; there is an unpublished translation by Joseph Sylvester in Bodleian MS Don. c. 54, fol. 4, where it precedes a manuscript copy of *A Wife.* Benjamin Jonson, "Conversations," in *Works,* ed. C. H. Herford, Percy Simpson, and Evelyn Simpson, 11 vols. (Oxford: Clarendon Press, 1925–1952), 1:138.

3. The *Observations* are copied separately as Bodleian MS Tanner 434, BL MSS Add. 2143, and Lansdowne 722, and a manuscript in the Buffalo Public Library, Buffalo, N.Y. (De Ricci). They are included in the collections and composites Lambeth MS 841; BL MSS Add. 34218, fol. 129ff, and Stowe 279, fol. 15ff; Bodleian MS Tanner 93, fols. 70–79; Bradford MS Hopkinson 14 (HMC *3rd Report* 295); and manuscripts in the duke of Northumberland's collection at Alnwick (ibid., 119), Lord Jersey's collection (HMC *8th Report* 94a), and the Pole-Gell collection, now in the Derbyshire Record Office (HMC *9th Report* 386). Several of the letters are transcribed in BL MS Harl. 7002, fols. 281–91; a separate transcript of one is in BL MS Stowe 180, fols. 34–35; two are at the Public Record Office (PRO SP 14, lxxii, fol. 83, and lxxxii, fol. 29, copied fol. 30); letters to Salisbury are reported in HMC *3rd Report* 177 and HMC *Salisbury (Cecil)* 21:250; and to William Trumbull in HMC *Downshire* 2:103, 3:369, 4:83.

He had also, apparently, written letters in the name of his patron at court, the earl of Somerset, to whom he wrote in 1613 that "you fell in Love with that Woman, as soon as you had wonne her by my Letters"; in the same year, Viscount Fenton told the earl of Mar, "I think his Majestie will let the world see that yet for a tyme Rotchester can make his Majesties dispatchis vithout the helpe of Overberrye."[4] These writings are the products of a short career: Overbury died unpleasantly in the Tower of London on September 15, 1613, when he was thirty-two. A series of highly scandalous trials in 1615 and 1616 concluded, rightly or wrongly, that he had been murdered by the agents of the earl and countess of Somerset, the coup de grâce having been administered with a poisoned enema.[5]

Overbury never, therefore, saw any of his works printed. Three months after his death, on December 13, 1613, the rights of the bookseller and publisher Lawrence Lisle in "a poeme called *a wife* written by Sir THOMAS OVERBURYE" were recorded in an entry in the *Stationers' Register*. Lisle's career and connections will be important to the ensuing argument. He was not, when he entered *A Wife* in 1613, an important publisher. He had married the widow of another publisher and bookseller, Matthew Cooke, and had succeeded to Cooke's shop and to Cooke's rights in certain works by Joseph Hall. Besides these works, he had entered Jeremy Corderoy's *Warning for Worldlings* in the *Stationers' Register* in late 1607, and a Paul's Cross sermon, a prospective translation of a French anti-Catholic tract, a book called *An Inventarye of Churche Goodes*, and Dekker's *Ravens Almanacke* in 1608. Then, after an interval of five years, Lisle entered Daniel Tuvill's *Dove and the Serpent*, a book of sententious advice on godly discourse, two months before Overbury's poem. Tuvill's last book had been published by Samuel Macham, who was Lisle's partner in rights to works by Hall. These entries are the only evidence of Lisle's publishing activity before *A Wife*: it was mainly of godly texts, and was evidently a sideline to bookselling. Between 1608 and 1610, a few books were identified as sold at Lisle's address:

4. BL MS Cotton Titus B VII, fol. 483v; HMC *Mar and Kellie*, Supplementary Report 51.

5. For Overbury's death and the ensuing trials, see Samuel R. Gardiner, *History of England from the Accession of James I to the Outbreak of the Civil War, 1603–1642*, 10 vols. (London: Longman, 1883–1884), 2:175–87; pp. 331–63 are still useful. Subsequent work is cited and improved upon by Chester Dunning, "The Fall of Sir Thomas Overbury and the Embassy to Russia in 1613," *Sixteenth Century Journal* 22 (1991): 695–704; David Lindley, *The Trials of Frances Howard: Fact and Fiction at the Court of King James* (London: Routledge, 1993), 145–92; and Alistair Bellany, "The Poisoning of Legitimacy? Court Scandal, News Culture, and Politics in England, 1603–1660" (Ph.D. diss., Princeton University, 1995).

Chapman's *Conspiracie and Tragedie of Charles Duke of Byron*, Jonson's *Masque of Blackness* and *Masque of Beauty*, a volume of epigrams by an Oxford man called Richard West (these three were all published by Thomas Thorpe), and an anonymous account of the funeral of Henri IV.[6]

After the first edition of Overbury's *Wife*, though, Lisle's output changed markedly. In 1614, he published Christopher Brooke's *Ghost of Richard III*, Thomas Campion's *Somerset Masque*, George Chapman's *Andromeda Liberata* and his *Free and Offenceless Justification*, four enlarged editions of *A Wife*, a companion poem called *The Husband*, and a volume of epigrams. Another edition of *A Wife* followed in 1615, and three more in 1616 together with the lost "Sir Thomas Overburyes Ghost" of John Ford, engraved portraits of Overbury and George Villiers (then earl of Buckingham), another work by Tuvill, a poem on the decay of St. Paul's, and a translation of Aelian. In 1616, he also entered Overbury's *Observations*, but did not proceed with their publication; they were finally published by John Parker in 1626. After 1616, Lisle published two more editions of *A Wife*, an account of a murder, a manual for surgeons' mates, and a mock almanac.[7] By 1619, his former apprentice Henry Seile had taken over his affairs. A man called Lawrence Lisle married a kinswoman of the duke of Buckingham around 1617, he or a namesake was granted a share in the exclusive right to varnish and repair armor in 1620, and he was granted an impost on tobacco and pipes imported into Ireland in early 1622. His positive identification with the publisher is elusive, but their careers and, as far as can be told, their private lives dovetail; the publisher's first wife was dead by March 1616.[8]

The collection centered on *A Wife*, then, was first advertised as being the work of Overbury and his friends in May 1614, eight months after Overbury's

6. *A Wife* is entered in *Stationers' Register*, ed. E. Arber (London: for the author, 1877), 3:538. For Lisle and Joseph Hall, see *Stationers' Register*, 3:585, and *STC* 12644, 12644.5, 12670, 12682 (all 1609), 12706 (1614); for his early activity as publisher, see *Stationers' Register*, 3:366 (published as *STC* 5757), 3:373, 3:376, 3:384, 3:385 (published by Thomas Archer as *STC* 6519); books to be sold by Lisle are *STC* 4968, 14761, 25262 (all 1608), 13136 (1610).

7. To the list in *STC*, 3:108, add entries in *Stationers' Register*, 3:578 (Ford) and 3:590 (portrait of Villiers); for the latter, see A. M. Hind, *Engraving in England in the Sixteenth and Seventeenth Centuries*, vol. 2, *The Reign of James I* (Cambridge: Cambridge University Press, 1955), 253 and plate 148.

8. For the marriage, see Sheffield City Libraries, Wentworth Woodhouse Muniments Str P 7, item 32 (April 19, 1637): "The humble peticō of Lawrence L'isle Humbly shewing That hee aboue 20 yeares since marryed wth a neere kinswomā of ye late D: of Buckingham . . ."; for the right to repair armor, see the printed proclamation of July 11, 1620; for the impost on tobacco pipes, granted February 8, 1622, see the petition to Strafford and *CSPDom*, 1660–1661, 396; for the death of the bookseller's wife, see *Stationers' Register*, 3:585.

death. The publisher who made this claim appears to have had no connection with Overbury or with the court before 1614. The extraordinary success of the collection almost certainly owed something to the publisher's ascription of authorship. Early modern publishers were certainly capable of issuing books with false ascriptions of authorship in order to make them more salable, and there is a prima facie case for asking whether this could have happened here. John Owen and Ben Jonson testify to the authorship of the title poem, *A Wife*, but is it possible to confirm that the numerous texts that accompany it were all "written by himselfe and other learned Gentlemen his friends"?

Because the collection was progressively enlarged, what is true of the authenticity of one text may not be true of the authenticity of others. This discussion will work backward chronologically, beginning with the late miscellaneous additions to the collection. They fall into two categories: liminary elegies on Overbury, and texts connected with the Inns of Court or with titled people. The elegies were added after Overbury's death had become a matter of scandal. Seven appeared in the seventh edition, and nine more in the ninth. Their effect was to make the collection's opening pages look more and more like a humanistic tumulus, a published record of shared distress. James Binns has discussed liminary verses as records of "a complex of literary, political and social webs linking writer to writer and book to book," but this discussion rests on the argument that "the normal practice was for an author to ask his friends for verses."[9] This author was dead, though—so who was soliciting these poems? Lawrence Lisle, presumably, and it is by no means clear that he was turning to Overbury's friends.

In at least one case, he was clearly printing the work of a hack. Despite the grand title of the elegy from the seventh edition, *In obitum intempestiuum & lachrimabilem Illustrissimi Equitis Aurati* TH: OVERBURI *magnæ spei & expectationis Viri*, its signature is that of Thomas Gainsford, "a poore Captaine about London," whose windy Latinity here is part of the same struggle for acceptance as a gentleman and scholar, a courtly humanist, as his history of Trebizond, or his facetious verses about women. In other cases, something more interesting appears to be going on. Another elegy from the seventh edition is signed "W. B. Int. Temp." This is certainly William Browne of Tavistock; there is a manuscript copy of the poem in a collection of Browne's verse. Browne had already, in 1614, contributed a liminary verse to another book published by Lisle, Christopher

9. Binns, *Intellectual Culture in Elizabethan and Jacobean England: The Latin Writings of the Age* (Leeds: Francis Cairns, 1990), 169, 166.

Brooke's *Ghost of Richard III* (the C. B. who contributed an elegy to the seventh edition of *A Wife* may indeed be Brooke). Other contributors of verses to Brooke's volume were Chapman, two of whose poems Lisle published in 1614, and Jonson, who also contributed a verse to *The Husband*, which Lisle also published in 1614. The D. T. who contributed an elegy to the seventh edition has been identified as Daniel Tuvill, two of whose books Lisle published. John Ford, who contributed an elegy to the ninth edition, was at the time doing other hackwork for Lisle, writing an ephemeral book for him called *Sir Thomas Overburyes Ghost contayneinge the history of his life and vntimely death*. It is clear that Lisle was obtaining work not from Overbury's associates, but from his own.[10]

Other additional verses that appeared in Sir Thomas Overbury's *Wife* commemorated Lord Howard of Effingham and the countess of Rutland. The first of them was by Richard Corbett, and entered the collection at the same time as his elegy on Overbury himself. The second is associated with it in a number of manuscripts.[11] They both had a wide manuscript circulation; likewise, Francis Beaumont's elegy, "Ad Comitissam Rutlandiae," which appeared in the eleventh edition, is still extant in at least twenty-six manuscripts.[12] The "Essay of Valour" printed in the same edition was so much a piece of literary common property as to be attributed both to Donne and to Sidney by midcentury.[13] The extracts from the Grays Inn *Masque of Mountebanks*, which also appeared in the eleventh edition, are still extant in five manuscripts.[14] Sir Henry Wotton's poem "How happie is he borne or taught," printed in the fourth edition onward as

10. For Gainsford, see S. L. Adams, "Captain Thomas Gainsford, the 'Vox Spiritus' and the *Vox Populi*," *Bulletin of the Institute for Historical Research* 49 (1976): 141–44. The verses are ascribed to "Sr Tho: Gainsford" in BL Add. MS 15527, fol. 17^r, and to "Sr Thom Gansforde" in Bodleian MS Ashmole 38, p. 146 (this would have pleased Gainsford); further locations and references in M. Crum, ed., *First-Line Index of English Poetry, 1500–1800, in Manuscripts of the Bodleian Library, Oxford* (Oxford: Clarendon Press, 1969), A 1076. For Browne, see BL MS Lansdowne 777, fol. 56 (Beal, *Index*, BrW 35); for Tuvill, see Douglas Bush, *The Earlier Seventeenth Century*, rev. ed. (Oxford: Clarendon Press, 1962), 654; for Ford, see *Stationers' Register*, 3:578.

11. For the poem on Howard, see Richard Corbett, *The Poems*, ed. J. A. W. Bennett and H. R. Trevor-Roper (Oxford: Clarendon Press, 1955), xix, 114–15. The manuscripts recorded by Beal in which it is associated with the poem on Lady Rutland are BL MS Egerton 2230 (CoR 119, BmF 35); Bodl. MS Rawl. poet. 117 (CoR 116, BmF 30); Bradford, Hopkinson MSS 34 (CoR 117, BmF 32); Folger MSS V. a. 319 (CoR 123, BmF 42) and V. a. 322 (CoR 124, BmF 43); Harvard MS Eng 966.7 (CoR 125, BmF 45); and Rosenbach Foundation MS 239/22 (CoR 126, BmF 51).

12. Beal, *Index*, BmF 1–26.

13. It is rightly rejected from the canon in John Donne, *Paradoxes and Problems*, ed. H. Peters (Oxford: Clarendon Press, 1980), xlviii.

14. See Beal, *Index*, 2:330, and Albert H. Tricomi, "John Marston's Manuscripts," *Huntington Library Quarterly* 43 (1980): 87–102 (esp. 102 for the suggestion that the masque, presented in 1618, had been written some years earlier).

"The Character of a happie life," is extant in fifty-two. Ted-Larry Pebworth has described the text printed by Lisle as "undoubtedly pirated and derivative." The only surprising addition to the late editions of *A Wife* is "Certaine Edicts from a Parliament in *Eutopia;* Written by the Lady *Southwell*," which was added in the sixth edition.[15] The others include some of the commonest texts of Jacobean scribal culture, and give the entirely false impression that Lawrence Lisle had privileged access to the manuscripts exchanged between eminent persons. This was no doubt what Lisle intended.[16]

These late additions, then, were by no means the products of a courtly literary circle. What, in that case, about the "witty Characters, and conceited Newes" of the second edition's title page? They can be considered in the order in which the title page advertises them. "Characters" were essays of a specialized kind: each was a collection of about twenty epigrammatic sentences describing a given kind of person. Although the title pages of the enlarged editions of *A Wife* subsequent to the second claim that all the "Characters" printed in them are the works of Overbury or his learned friends, this claim need not be taken seriously. The convenient regularity of their appearance—no fewer than seven editions have new installments of what one calls "diuers more Characters (neuer before annexed) written by himselfe and other learned Gentlemen"—makes their origins quite clear. Rather than making seven separate manuscript discoveries, Lisle was evidently commissioning "Characters" to complement those that he had printed with the second edition of Overbury's poem. These commissioned pieces are anonymous. Six have been attributed to Dekker, on stylistic grounds, and the attribution is made more likely by the fact that Lisle had planned to publish Dekker's *Ravens Almanacke* early in his career. Thirty-two others have been attributed convincingly to Webster, on the basis of a series of verbal parallels. A comprehensive discussion of the authorship of these additional "Characters" is not important for the purposes of this argument.[17] The point is that if Lisle did, as he claimed, print "Characters" written

15. Beal, *Index*, WoH 1–48, and addenda; Ted-Larry Pebworth, "New Light on Sir Henry Wotton's 'The Character of a Happy Life,'" *Library*, 5th ser., 33 (1978): 223–26. Three possible Southwells, for none of whom there is a compelling case, are mentioned by Sr. Jean Klene, *The Southwell-Sibthorpe Commonplace Book: Folger MS. V. b. 198* (Tempe, Ariz.: Medieval and Renaissance Texts and Studies, 1997), xxviii–xxix n. 39.

16. For an eccentric recent proposal that since Robert Sidney had been created Viscount Lisle, Lawrence Lisle "had, if in name only, a connection" with him and therefore "may well have received the manuscript of *A Wife*" from a member of the Sidney family, see Bruce McIver, "'A Wife now the Widdow': Lawrence Lisle and the Popularity of the Overburian Characters," *South Atlantic Review* 59 (1994): 27–44, esp. 35.

17. The fullest treatment of the subject at present is in J. P. Considine, "The Humanistic Antecedents of the First English Character-Books" (Ph.D. diss., University of Oxford, 1995), 72–79.

by the members of a courtly literary circle, those texts must be the ones that appeared with the second edition of *A Wife,* and should be distinguished from those that appeared with later editions.

Were, then, the "Characters" that were printed with the second edition by Overbury and his friends? Their manuscript circulation suggests that they were not. If the "Characters" had been written as a form of courtly recreation within a literary circle, then the consistency of their style would need to be explained by common or mutual influence: in other words, by the coterie circulation of texts. The printed texts should therefore be supplemented by manuscripts that antedate them or offer variant textual traditions. This is not the case. Apart from obvious apographs of the printed editions, such as those that supply missing pages in defective printed copies, and a few extracts from the eleventh edition (or a later one) in a binding fragment, there are only three manuscripts in which the texts of any of the "Characters" appear.[18]

These are Trinity College Dublin, MS 877; Texas Tech University, MS Dalhousie I; and British Library, MS Lansdowne 740. They all contain poems by John Donne; readers of the Variorum Edition of Donne will know them as DT1, TT1, and B40, respectively, and I shall refer to them by those sigla. Beal dates all three to the 1620s.[19] They are mutually independent, but closely related.[20] They each contain texts of the first three "Characters," which are of good and bad women, and of a short poem, supposedly Overbury's epitaph on himself, which begins, "The Spann of my daies measur'd, hear I rest." DT1 and B40 also have the text of Overbury's *Wife,* omitted in TT1. They both provide it with the

18. Defective printed copies supplied in manuscript include Bodleian Bliss B. 330 (1), a copy of the sixth edition with three leaves supplied, and Huntington RB 62806, a copy of the ninth edition in which a "Character" printed in only the sixth and eighth is copied onto the blank S3v (facsimile in James E. Savage, "An Unpublished Epigram, Possibly by John Webster," *University of Mississippi Studies in English* 8 [1967]: 15); for the binding fragment, see Murphy, *Bibliography,* 22.

19. Ernest W. Sullivan II has argued that TT1 was largely transcribed before 1617, and therefore antedates the others (*The First and Second Dalhousie Manuscripts: Poems and Prose by John Donne and Others, a Facsimile Edition* [Columbia: University of Missouri Press, 1988], 4–12). A terminus a quo can be established for it—the first items copied are letters between Archbishop Abbot and James I on the Essex divorce, written in August 1613—but Sullivan's efforts to establish a terminus ante quem are not convincing. The only real evidence is that the manuscript was still being added to in 1624, but that poems were copied from it into another manuscript that may well have been completed not long after August 1628.

20. Sullivan, *Dalhousie Manuscripts,* 8–10; this is confirmed by the textual work on individual poems in the ongoing *Variorum Edition of the Poetry of John Donne;* see, for example, Gary A. Stringer et al., eds., *The Anniversaries and the Epicedes and Obsequies* (Bloomington: Indiana University Press, 1995), 131–32.

same set of explanatory glosses, which do not appear in any of the printed editions.[21] B40 also introduces *A Wife* and the "Characters" with the following epistle (fol. 74v), which explains their relationship. It appears in no other manuscript, and in none of the printed editions.

> *The occation of the wrightinge viz*
>
> Pietie and Truth in whom soeuer makes vnitie, and vnitie | is the substance of ffrendship: Beeleeuing of both of them, or the | loue of both in >each of< vs, I take it for acquaintance enoughe to send | yo^w my slender Labour following. If yor vnder standing p^rvent | the purpose of it in yor self, yett through yor handes maye | the benefitt passe to others. If not (as I allow a sufficient | woman to be some degrees beneath the sufficiencye of man) | I am glad to make the waie cleare betweene sight, and Truth. | High Truth hath almost invisible beginnings, and hides her self | in her owne puritie, scarclie yelding to be represented in | wordes, But when Truth looseth knowledg it seemes to loose | it self, since it is vnprofittable. Therfore haue I assaied | to bring it downe to my self, and my wordes, that in them, | the inquiering mynde maye meet it, and that a highe meaninge | made more bodelie by outward wordes, may be rede easier, | as written in a greater letter. Toward the doing of this, I | haue the libertie of words, wch verse denied the autho^r, | both by measure and Comelines; both wch in verse stopp from | fair runing in on breath of Sence: And yett I thinke | some Truthes in me as in him, will hould stiffe to their nature, | and not looke through wordes verie clearlie. /
>
> Yett neither this, nor any othe^r seruice would I doe to | ~~Pietie~~ knowledge only, but that knowledge maye doe the like | to Pietie. ffor Knowledg is not her owne End, but she is | the seruant of Goodnesse. And this I heare yo^w put in | action: so that I rather assent to yo^w then tell yo^w any | new matter. Therfore I maie leaue, but first add arequest | there being in vs that vnitie, the soule of ffrendship, | only by reson to be discerned; That it maie hereafter | walke abroad more visiblie, in writing wordes or Actions. /

This epistle is evidently by a man, sending a composition, "my slender labour following," to a woman he hopes will be his patron. It is not by Overbury, to whom it refers in the third person. The writer of the epistle has returned to the topic of *A Wife*, hoping that since he is writing prose, "the liberty of words, which verse denied the author," will allow him to make Overbury's topic clearer. His prose composition is evidently the three descriptions (he does not call

21. I am grateful to Dr. Robin Robbins of Wadham College, Oxford, for lending me photographs of DT1.

them "Characters") that follow. Their verbal echoes of Overbury's poem are therefore a consequence of their having been written by another author as a sort of key to the poem, not, as has often been supposed, a consequence of their having been written by Overbury.[22]

The relationship between *A Wife* and the prose "Characters" should now be clear. The writer of the epistle in B40 knew the poem in manuscript. He embellished it with glosses and appended three prose descriptions to it, and sent it to a potential patron, who must, since he supposed that her understanding might have anticipated the purpose of his paraphrase, previously have had an opportunity to read the poem by itself. His work was then copied into the common ancestor of the miscellanies DT1, TT1, and B40, the copyist of TT1 omitting the text of *A Wife* and the epistle, and the copyist of DT1 omitting the epistle.

This is the only evidence for the transmission of the first three "Characters" in manuscript; they were clearly part of a bid for patronage, and not of a process of friendly textual exchange. If their author's request for a response "in writing, words, or actions" had been answered by the composition of prose descriptions imitating his, those responses would naturally have been copied with his. The absence from the manuscript tradition of the other nineteen "Characters" that were printed with the second edition of *A Wife* is striking. It points rather strongly to the likelihood that the manuscript of *A Wife* that was obtained by Lawrence Lisle in 1613 included the three descriptions, and that when he decided to produce a second edition, it occurred to him that it could be enlarged by printing them and commissioning more to go with them.

None of the "Characters," then, were written by Overbury, nor is there any evidence to suggest that any of them were written by anyone associated with him. If any item in the second edition of his poem was by him or his circle, it must have been part of the "conceited Newes," or as their heading in the second edition of *A Wife* calls them, "Newes from Any Whence, or Old Truthes vnder a supposall of Nouekie, Occasioned by divers Essaies, and private passages of Wit, betweene sundrie Gentlemen upon that subject." Each item of "Newes" was, like each "Character," a collection of twenty or so aphoristic sentences. The items of "Newes" had initials appended to them, as follows: "Newes from

---

22. W. J. Paylor, ed., *The Overburian Characters: To Which Is Added "A Wife," by Sir Thomas Overbury* (Oxford: Basil Blackwell, 1936), 109, with the fanciful embellishment that two of them "may be an attack upon Frances Howard," cited, for example, by Sullivan, *Dalhousie Manuscripts*, 4; and McIver, "'A Wife,'" 31.

Court," T. O.; "Answer to the Court newes," A. S.; "Country Newes," S^r. T. R.; "Newes from the very Country," I. D.; "Answer to the very Country Newes," A. S.; "Newes to the Vniuersitie," anonymous; "Newes from Sea," W. S.; "Forrein Newes of the yeere 1604," anonymous; "Newes from my Lodging," B. R.; "Newes of my morning worke," M^{ris}. B.; "Newes from the lower end of the table," J. C.; and "Newes from the Bed," R. S.

There are arguments for and against the authenticity of the "Newes" as a document from a real literary circle. The clearest argument against is that since Lisle's statement that the "Characters" originate in exchanges within an Overbury circle was false, his similar statement about the "Newes" cannot be trusted. Moreover, one more item of "Newes" was added to the sixth edition, and one more to the seventh; it is certainly easier to imagine that they were being written for publication than that an initial authentic document was being supplemented by the convenient discoveries of two more much shorter documents, both also authentic.

A second argument against Lisle's statement that the "Newes" was a coterie document is that attempts to assign the items to real people have not been supported by manuscript evidence. So, for instance, Sr. Jean Klene regards it as certain, on the evidence of two verbal parallels, that Anne Southwell wrote one piece; but why, in that case, did Southwell not include it in her manuscript "Workes"?[23] Helen Peters places "Newes from the very Country," initialed "I. D.," among the *dubia* in her edition of the minor prose of Donne (to whom it has been ascribed), on the grounds that it shows "few of the flashes of wit that are associated with Donne"; she might have added that his other short prose works, with the exception of one of dubious authenticity, are all associated with other works of his in at least one manuscript, whereas this one is not.[24]

A third argument against is that there are no independent manuscripts of the "Newes." There are two collections of excerpts from certain items, but they cannot be shown to be independent of the printed editions. One is the "Burley manuscript," collected by Henry Wotton's secretary, William Parkhurst, which contains a number of sentences from three items. The other is a commonplace

---

23. Klene, *Southwell-Sibthorpe Commonplace Book,* xxviii–xxxi. The strongest verbal parallel that Klene adduces is from a letter from Southwell written in 1628 that suggests at most that she had by that date read one of the many editions of *A Wife* (possibly the Dublin edition of 1626, since she lived in Ireland). The appearance in this item of "Newes" of the aphorism "That Man, Woman, and the Diuell, are the three degrees of comparison" does make male authorship of the piece likelier than female authorship.

24. Donne, *Paradoxes and Problems,* xlix.

book of Sir Constantijn Huygens, of 1621.[25] Besides these two, there is evidence that a few items of "Newes" were written in response to the printed texts of 1614 onward. One such piece, "newse ffrom the grave," alludes darkly to the trials of Overbury's alleged murderers in 1615, remarking "That most are to begin there lives, when the end thereof drawes them hether, so that a man may begin where overburie endes, whoe ended for all that, sooner then was look't for."[26] As with the "Characters" printed by Lisle, the consistency of the "Newes" argues either for their commissioned production or for their ready circulation in manuscript. There is a significant lack of evidence for the latter. This is not an *argumentum ex silentio:* there are manuscripts of the "Newes," but they are all posterior to printed texts.

The weakest argument for the coterie production of the "Newes" is that of James Savage, founded on Jonson's lines about Cecilia Bulstrode in *Vnder-Wood* XLIX:

> What though her Chamber be the very pit
> >Where fight the prime Cocks of the Game, for wit?
> And that as any are strooke, her breath creates
> >New in their stead, out of the Candidates?
> What though with Tribade lust she force a Muse,
> >And in an Epicoene fury can write newes
> Equall with that, which for the best newes goes,
> >As aërie light, and as like wit as those?
> What though she talke, and cannot once with them,
> >Make State, Religion, Bawdrie, all a theame?
>
> >>>>(ll. 3–12)

25. For the "Burley manuscript," now Leicestershire Record Office, DG.7/Lit.2, see Beal, *Index,* 2:561–62. The excerpts from the "Newes" are at fols. 255v–56. Beal's account modifies Evelyn Simpson, "John Donne and Sir Thomas Overbury's 'Characters,'" *Modern Language Review* 18 (1923): 410–15; see also John Sparrow, "Donne's Table-Talk," *London Mercury* 18 (1928): 45. The Huygens manuscript is in The Hague: Koninklijke Bibliotheek, MS Akad. XLVIII, with excerpts from the news at fol. 311ff. See A. G. H. Bachrach, "Constantijn Huygens's Acquaintance with Donne: A Note on Evidence and Conjecture," in *Litterae textuales: Essays Presented to G. I. Lieftinck,* ed. J. P. Gombert and M. J. M. de Haan (Amsterdam: A. L. van Gendt, 1976), 3:111–17; and Paul R. Sellin, *So Doth, So Is Religion: John Donne and Diplomatic Contexts in the Reformed Netherlands, 1619–1620* (Columbia: University of Missouri Press, 1988), 23–30. Sellin argues that Huygens copied a manuscript independent from the printed "Newes"; all the evidence he presents suggests otherwise. In particular, the fact that Huygens's sentences are in precisely the reverse order to that of their appearance in print implies a close relationship between his manuscript and the printed text.

26. Bodl. MS Rawlinson D. 692, fol. 66.

This, Savage has suggested, makes it clear that the "Newes" were produced by a circle of friends who met in Bulstrode's bedchamber to make up witty essays.[27] It is hard to imagine how this could actually have worked. Did a group gather in Bulstrode's bedchamber with paper and ink, have the rules explained to them, and sit down to write? Did they assemble to hear the rules, go away to their own lodgings to write their essays, and gather again a week later to read their results to each other? Neither supposition commands ready assent: why should Jonson write with such anger about what sounds like a solemn Victorian parlor game? The silly games of the courtiers in *Cynthias Reuells* (IV.iii.81ff) are the closest analogy, but they are played by word of mouth, and their products are far slighter than the "Newes."

Another passage in Jonson, in fact, makes it quite clear what the making of "newes" means in the attack on Bulstrode: the bad wife in *Epicoene* will "be a states-woman, know all the newes, what was done at *Salisbury,* what at the *Bath,* what at court, what in progresse . . . and then skip to the *Mathematiques,* and demonstration and answere, in religion to one; in state, to an other, in baud'ry to a third" (II.ii.114–23). The two passages, which are chronologically close to each other, are reworkings of the same material. The "newes" that is part of the furious and inept verbal activity described in *Epicoene*, like that attributed to Bulstrode, is gossip, rumormongering, not the writing of essays. As Jongsook Lee puts it in a discussion of the poem, "The product of her 'Tribade lust' is 'newes,' which belongs to the order of rumor Captayne Hungry spreads in a tavern." Lee concludes, rightly, that "As historical documents about Jonson and Cecilia Bulstrode, these poems do not say much."[28] There is no need to labor the point further, and there would have been little cause to mention it were it not that the "news-game" that Savage has proposed has been accepted uncritically by other scholars.[29]

An argument stronger than Savage's is that if the "Newes from Any Whence" is the work of a single author, the initials appended to certain items of news must be explained. They were presumably not randomly assigned; if they had been, then the "Characters" could as readily have been initialed to strengthen

---

27. James E. Savage, ed., *The "Conceited Newes" of Sir Thomas Overbury and His Friends* (Gainesville, Fla.: Scholars' Facsimiles and Reprints, 1968), xxiv ff.

28. Jongsook Lee, "Who Is Cecilia, What Was She? Cecilia Bulstrode and Jonson's Epideictics," *Journal of English and Germanic Philology* 85 (1986): 20–34, quotations from pp. 30, 34.

29. See Arthur Marotti, *John Donne: Coterie Poet* (Madison: University of Wisconsin Press, 1986), 184, 205–6; Barbara K. Lewalski, *Writing Women in Jacobean England* (Cambridge: Harvard University Press, 1993), 109, 364 n. 68, 365 n. 69.

Lisle's claim about their coterie origins. They are enigmatic, though, and cannot have meant much to most buyers of printed copies. They must therefore have been an in-joke of some kind, originating either in the Inns of Court or in a similar London milieu. It might be thought appropriate that "Newes from Court" should bear the initials of a thrusting courtier, or that "Newes of my morning worke" should be identified as by "M^ris. B.," presumably Cecilia Bulstrode, the object of a number of male witticisms.[30] In that case, the best explanation for the presence of the "Newes" in *Sir Thomas Overbury's Wife* is that when Lisle was commissioning "Characters" to bulk out the first edition of the poem, one of the people to whom he made his requirements known was able to offer him a preexisting manuscript that included a text with Overbury's initials appended to it. In that case, he may have advertised the "Newes" as a coterie text in good faith, knowing that he had not commissioned it, and not knowing that it was a single-authored satire.

The liminary verses printed in the first two editions of *A Wife*, and the poem itself, are the only other elements of the collection published by Lisle. There is no reason to doubt that the poem that Lisle published was Overbury's. The question of how it reached him, though, is worth asking. I have suggested that the manuscript he was given was related to the archetype of the copies of *A Wife* and the three characters in B40, TT1, and DT1. Who was the owner of that manuscript, and why did he suggest its publication to Lisle, who did not specialize in the publication of poetry? Lisle's business dealings in 1614 do not suggest a ready answer. Chapman may plausibly have chosen him as the publisher for *Andromeda Liberata* and Campion for the *Somerset Masque* because they supposed the publisher of a poem by Somerset's client and friend to be a suitable publisher for work in praise of Somerset himself (it will be remembered that Somerset was not accused of complicity in Overbury's murder until 1615); Brooke may have chosen him for *The Ghost of Richard III* at Chapman's suggestion. Publishing Overbury's *Wife* was the beginning of Lisle's career as a publisher of important literary and political works. The questions remain: Why did he publish it, and how did he obtain it? Could the person who communicated the manuscript to Lisle have written liminary verses for it? There are thirteen of

---

30. For Bulstrode's reputation, see Jonson's epigram and his epitaph on her (*Works* 8:222–23 and 371–72, commentary 11:87–88 and 130–31) and his conversations with Drummond (1:135, 150); the two epicedes by Donne (Stringer et al., *Anniversaries,* 129–59); the erotic poem "Shall I goe force an Elegie?" in John Donne, *Poems,* ed. H. J. C. Grierson, 2 vols. (London: Oxford University Press, 1912), 1:410, which purports to be addressed to her; and Lewalski, *Writing Women,* 120–22.

them, one of which purports to be Overbury's epitaph on himself. Three are signed D. T., and may be by Tuvill. Two appear to be by John Ford. One, signed "W: Stra:," has been ascribed to William Strachey, who had contributed a commendatory verse to Jonson's *Sejanus*, or to Ford's cousin William Stradling.[31] If these suggest an origin for Lisle's publication, it is one among educated but not particularly successful minor writers, people on the edges of literary distinction, a far cry from the courtier Overbury.

Sir Thomas Overbury's Wife does not record the literary exchanges of Overbury and his friends. It is the document not of a literary circle but of an invented literary circle. Inventing a literary circle was Lisle's business throughout the early publication history of *A Wife*. It gave him the opportunity to bring out one enlarged edition after another of his book without appearing to intrude extraneous material. It gave his readers a sense that the printed book they bought encapsulated a world of courtly textual exchange. The scandal of Overbury's death was one window by which middle-class Londoners could look into the private transactions of the court. The publication of what appeared to be the passages of wit that he had shared with his friends was another.

In the previous decade and earlier, verse miscellanies in the tradition that ends with *The Phoenix Nest* (1593) and Francis Davison's *Poetical Rhapsody* (1602) had given their middle-class readers a similar impression of access to the products of coterie textual culture. Their invocation of Sir Philip Sidney can be compared to Lisle's of Sir Thomas Overbury. In all three cases, the use of the dead knight's name, and the presence of at least one text by or legitimately associated with him, in Arthur Marotti's words, gave "a certain legitimacy to the published writings of lower-born poets"—or, in the case of *A Wife*, prose writers. Davison even protested, perhaps disingenuously, against this as an unworthy trick of the book trade in his introduction to *A Poetical Rhapsody*: "If any except against the mixing (both at the beginning and ende of this booke) of diverse thinges written by great and learned Personages, with our meane and worthles Scriblings, I utterly disclaime it, as being done by the Printer, either to grace the forefront with Sir *Ph. Sidneys*, and others names, or to make the booke grow to a competent volume."[32] Lisle was to grace his title page, and enlarge his book, by closely analogous means. He was, however, to go further, presenting the whole book as the work of a single literary circle, appealing, perhaps, to

31. Lisa Hopkins, "'Elegy by W. S.': Another Possible Candidate?" *Philological Quarterly* 76 (1997): 159–68.

32. Arthur Marotti, *Manuscript, Print, and the Renaissance Lyric* (Ithaca: Cornell University Press, 1995), 234; Davison quoted on pp. 235–36

middle-class book buyers' increasing awareness of a system of coterie trans-mission of texts from which they were substantially excluded.

His strategy worked beautifully, but it is time to understand it now, and to understand that the literary circle of Sir Thomas Overbury "and other learned Gentlemen his friends" was made up by Lawrence Lisle. It was, as Francis Ba-con wrote of the world in the last item to be added to an early modern edition of *A Wife*, not so much a circle as a bubble.

Robert C. Evans

"This Art Will Live"
Social and Literary Responses to Ben Jonson's *New Inn*

One of the most intriguing but also one of the least-studied aspects of Ben Jonson's long career is the controversy that followed the famous failure of his 1629 play *The New Inn*. Until recently, the play itself was rarely read, rarely respected, and almost never staged: even for many admirers of Jonson, it seemed to epitomize Dryden's view of the late dramas as "dotages." More recently, all the late plays, and especially *The New Inn*, have benefited from far more detailed (and in some cases enthusiastic) attention. But even if we continued to see this work as a "dotage" and its opening-night failure as a fitting example of poetic justice, we would still be wrong to ignore its first performance, which offers compelling evidence of the social forces and literary milieu that helped shape Jonson's life and writings. His extant responses to the play's failure—and the surviving replies of numerous other authors, including persons both within and outside his immediate circle of literary and social allies—are in some ways at least as interesting as the play itself.[1]

The entire *New Inn* episode, in fact, raises a number of intriguing questions about (and offers much suggestive evidence concerning) the role of literary circles in Jonson's era. To what degree, for instance, could members of Jonson's circle exercise independent judgment on controversial issues? How, if at all, were the responses of one circle determined by the responses of other, perhaps

1. For a wealth of information about the play and its reception, three modern editions are especially helpful. These include the early Yale text, prepared by George Bremner Tennant (New York: Henry Holt, 1908); the recent Revels Plays edition, prepared by Michael Hattaway (Manchester: Manchester University Press, 1984); and the text, notes, and other materials printed in C. H. Herford, Percy Simpson, and Evelyn Simpson, eds., *Ben Jonson*, 11 vols. (Oxford: Clarendon Press, 1925–1952). In citing these editions, I shall abbreviate them respectively as "Tennant," "Hattaway," and "H&S"—in the last case also giving appropriate volume and page numbers.

more powerful, factions? In what ways could membership in (or leadership of) a circle help a writer deal with feelings of larger social or political isolation? How might the failures or misfortunes of one member of a circle affect the reputation and social standing of the circle as a whole? To what degree were circles stable entities, and to what degree were they necessarily unstable, contingent, and constantly in flux? What evidence is there for conflict *between* and also conflict *within* circles? To what extent were members of any given circle jockeying for power or influence *inside* the group? How could the "leader" of a circle maintain his leadership, especially as he aged and his mortality (and even his fallibility) became more and more apparent? These are just a few of the many questions the *New Inn* affair raises concerning the importance and impact of literary and social factions in Jonson's life and larger culture.

The sinking of *The New Inn* generated plenty of flotsam and jetsam as well as a whole navy of emergency craft, including lifeboats, rescue ships, and even a few destroyers bent on menacing any survivors and preventing much from being salvaged. Jonson himself produced two poems defending the play, especially the notorious "Ode to Himselfe." That poem, in particular, generated great interest and many replies, from both within and outside his literary circle. The poem was, apparently, his *only* work ever translated three times, by three different authors, into Latin (H&S, 10:333–38). The translators—John Earle, William Strode, and Thomas Randolph—were all themselves significant writers, and Randolph was one of a number of noted authors (such as Thomas Carew, George Chapman, and Owen Felltham), obscure writers (such as James Clayton, John Polwhele, and Richard Goodwin), and anonymous writers (such as "C. G." and the author of a poem titled "The Countrys Censure") to participate in the extended controversy. Also sucked into the whirlpool were such minor lights or major luminaries as Richard Brome, Inigo Jones, King Charles, Queen Henrietta Maria, and the earl of Newcastle. The *New Inn* fiasco therefore offers important evidence of how interlocking literary circles, personal friendships and rivalries, and patronage relations could all interact in Jonson's era.

The *New Inn* affair is thus worth examining for many reasons. First, it involves poems by Jonson not usually accorded much close attention. Second, it provoked responses from numerous other writers, from both within and without his own literary circle, as well as from Jonson's most significant patrons. Third, it helped shape (for better or worse, but mainly for the worse) his whole subsequent reputation, from 1629 down to the present day, thus affecting his standing in literary circles from his time to ours. Fourth, it helps illuminate the complex position in which Jonson's admirers—the most immediate members of his own literary circle—often found (and still do find) themselves. Fifth, it helps illustrate his *personal* complexity—his complicated combination of lofty ideals and practical concerns and fears. Sixth, it helps suggest that such complexity was not simply unique to him but was instead typical of his whole literary and social milieu, with its many interlocking and conflicting factions. And, finally, the *New Inn* controversy helps shed new light on some of our own current critical, theoretical, and factional disputes—especially the question of how far literature, in Jonson's time, was judged in "macropolitical" terms and how far it was judged instead as written *art*. The latter question seems particularly important, since recent interpretations of *The New Inn* itself (and of much other early modern literature) have often emphasized ideological rather than more narrowly aesthetic issues. In the case of *The New Inn*, however (and, I would argue, in the case of Jonson's contemporary reception in general), Politics with a capital *P* clearly took a backseat to debates about *literary* merit. To say this is not to argue that politics were unimportant. Rather, it is simply meant to suggest that in some cases the most useful kind of historicist criticism might be called "historical formalism"—that is, an approach that seeks to understand how contemporary audiences judged artists precisely *as* artists and literary works precisely *as* works of literature. These were the terms in which persons both within and outside Jonson's circle seem to have responded to *The New Inn*, and perhaps this fact will interest readers in some circles today who are also inclined to view literature, first and foremost, as art.

Among the most interesting of the original responses to Jonson's play were those penned by Jonson himself, including the epilogue apparently prepared for the first night's performance. This is one of Jonson's most unusual poems, partly because it is both so humble and so intensely personal. In addition, the fact that it was not written for manuscript circulation among a few close friends or patrons (the members of his immediate circle) but composed to be spoken from a public stage makes it all the more remarkable. In the epilogue, Jonson (who was now paralyzed and bedridden by a stroke in 1628) almost seems to have anticipated his play's failure:

> If you expect more then you had to night,
> > The maker is sick, and sad. But doe him right,
> He meant to please you: for he sent things fit,
> > In all the numbers, both of sense, and wit,
> If they ha' not miscarried! if they haue,
> > All that his faint, and faltring tongue doth craue,
> Is, that you not impute it to his braine.

> That's yet vnhurt, although set round with paine,
> It cannot long hold out. All strength must yeeld.
>   (H&S, 6:490, ll. 3–11)²

   This passage is full of surprises. Thus, just when we might expect Jonson (after the first quoted line) to launch into one of his famously explosive preemptive strikes on an ignorant audience, he abruptly confesses not only his physical debility but also his mental depression. From a poet normally so proud and publicly self-reliant, both confessions seem startling—especially the second. No sooner does he appeal to our sympathies, however, than he offers what can be read either as a self-respectful demand or as another pleading appeal (*or* as both at once): "But doe him right, / He meant to please you" (ll. 4–5). His latent self-respect more obviously dominates the ensuing reference to having sent "things fit," but such confidence is soon undercut by his concern that these fit things have nonetheless "miscarried" (l. 7). Once again we might expect him typically (at this point) to blame any such miscarriage on ignorant auditors or incompetent actors, but once more he surprises by making his "faint, and faltring tongue . . . craue" (a startling verb) that his audience not blame the play's weaknesses on any weakness of his "braine," which (he insists) is "yet vnhurt" (ll. 8–10). This insistence, though, is immediately followed by the literally pathetic admission that his mind, besieged by pain, "cannot long hold out" (l. 11). Yet, just when he might seem more frankly personal and confessional than almost anywhere else in his writings, he immediately reminds us that *his* current suffering is merely the human condition: "All strength must yeeld" (l. 11). Thus, just when he seems to admit his personal vulnerability (thereby displaying, paradoxically, a kind of strength), he pulls back and alerts us that *his* weakness will someday be our own. In the lines just quoted, then, Jonson seems implicitly to acknowledge that his social and literary status cannot rest securely merely on the approval of his own limited circle of friends and imitators. He both concedes and bristles against the need to appeal to a broader public.

   Such complexity continues throughout the epilogue. Immediately after confessing the ultimate weakness of all strength, for instance, Jonson nevertheless asserts that in the case of a true poet, "iudgement would the last be, i' the field" (l. 12). Here again the phrasing mixes confidence and uncertainty (especially since "would . . . be" can seem conditional, implying a mere hope or intent): the poet prides himself on his judgment but can never really assure himself (or

---

   2. In the original printed source, this passage is in italic type. I have silently changed it to roman and will do so with other such passages throughout the rest of this chapter.

us) that it will indeed be his last quality to concede defeat. All he can do is explain his desires and then hope for the best—from himself, the actors, and their mutual audience. Thus, after further outlining his plans, he concludes as follows:

> This he did thinke; and this doe you forgiue:
>   When e're the carcasse dies, this Art will liue.
> And had he liu'd the care of King, and Queene,
>   His Art in somthing more yet had beene seene;
> But Maiors, and Shriffes may yearely fill the stage:
>   A Kings, or Poets birth doe aske an age.
>
> (ll. 19–24)

The second half of line 19 can be read as either a plea or an implied command (or both), and the whole line's balanced syntax implies the ideal reciprocity between a well-intentioned poet and an understanding audience. Similarly, the word *carcasse* can suggest not only the poet's body but also the physical staging of the play—the first possibility implying Jonson's human vulnerability, the second signaling sturdy confidence in the endurance of his writings. Meanwhile, the ironic echo of "carcasse" in "care" typifies a vital, playful, perhaps sarcastic wit we might not expect from a poet so pained, while the juxtaposition of "Art will liue" with "had he liu'd" (ll. 20–21) emphasizes "he," contrasting art's immortality with the precarious condition of the artist, who must fear not only the weakness of his own mind and body but also the fickle judgments of audiences who, unlike the members of his literary circle, may lack either sympathy with or understanding of his artistic aims.

Here and throughout the epilogue, Jonson somehow manages to avoid sounding baldly self-pitying. Perhaps his complicated blend of tones prevents it: modesty balanced by pride, weariness set against pugnacious grit, contemptuous disdain offset by an obvious devotion to Art, defiance counteracted by a plea for forgiveness (a plea that itself seems difficult to take entirely at face value). Even his irritation with King Charles (another expression of strength or desperation or both at once) hardly seems simple. The word *more*, for instance, suggests not only Jonson's frustration with the king but also his disappointment with himself and his play, as well as his fear that sickness might render any hope of "more" plays pointless. "[S]omthing more" (l. 22), in this context, seems to mean both "something better" and simply "something else." Here again the poem touches on death—a theme it constantly emphasizes, but one that is balanced, as one might expect, by countervailing references to creation and life.

Thus, even as Jonson confronts the inevitable death of his own "carcasse" and the possible miscarriage of his "sense, and wit" (l. 5), he ends with a favorite thought: the double rarity of kings and poets. The final line compliments Charles, but the compliment follows the rebuke of the king's neglect (l. 21). Rhetorically complex, Jonson's poem is at once highly personal and highly public, yet also aimed (indirectly) at two special persons in particular: the "King, and Queene" (l. 21). In the Britain of Jonson's day, they were the exclusive members of the social circle whose approval carried the most weight.

Jonson in fact composed a second epilogue for *The New Inn* intended for a planned (but cancelled) performance at court. The play's disastrous failure instead prompted a fiery, indignant "Ode to Himselfe," which circulated in manuscript well before it first appeared in print (along with the play) in the 1631 first edition (Tennant, xxi). It clearly aroused great interest, not only generating the Latin translations already mentioned but also prompting many replies. If documented reader response indicates a work's impact, then this poem might seem one of the most significant Jonson ever wrote. Its complexities begin at once:

> Come leaue the lothed stage,
> And the more lothsome age:
> Where pride, and impudence (in faction knit)
> Vsurpe the chaire of wit!
> Indicting, and arraigning euery day
> Something they call a Play.
> Let their fastidious, vaine
> Commission of the braine
> Run on, and rage, sweat, censure, and condemn:
> They were not made for thee, lesse, thou for them.
> (H&S, 6:492–94, ll. 1–10)

The first line already contains an implicit contradiction: the very call to leave the loathed stage enacts Jonson's inability to abandon it entirely, to give it up altogether. His leave-taking signifies his reluctance or incapacity to take leave; he must—he *will*—have the final word. The poem is built on the necessary pretense that if Jonson does leave the stage, he will leave it by his own choice; yet, the "Ode" itself shows that this choice is partly forced. Even as he rejects both the "stage" and the "age," he implicitly acknowledges how much both still mean to him. The word *vaine* embodies this tension: on the one hand it puns, implying that the malice of Jonson's antagonists (who constitute, in his eyes, a

vicious "faction" and ignorant "Commission"—a perverse circle) is both egotistical and futile; on the other hand the mere existence of the poem shows the
effectiveness of their attacks. Meanwhile, the "Ode" itself (as the replies it provoked will show) paradoxically made *Jonson* seem (in many eyes) the person
most motivated by ego.

Jonson, though, was not the only authority figure being publicly challenged
early in 1629. At just this time, the power of King Charles was being put to quite
dramatic tests. The last Parliament before the long years of his personal rule
would either shortly be or had already been dissolved in disarray.[3] On March
2, when the Speaker of the House of Commons rose to announce the king's desire that Parliament adjourn for a week, a near riot erupted. Doors were bolted
shut, and the Speaker was pushed back down—twice—into his seat to prevent
his leaving. With royal troops dispatched to force the doors and compel ad-
journment, the House hastily adopted three resolutions and then adjourned itself. Immediately afterward Charles dissolved Parliament, and for the next
eleven years he ruled without their advice or consent.[4]

Jonson's implied comparison in his "Ode" between the larger problem
of political insubordination (particularly in the tantalizing reference to
"Vsurp[ing] the chaire of wit" [l. 4]) and the ignorant unruliness displayed by
the first audience of *The New Inn* is thus variously intriguing. The self-pitying,
self-righteous tone of the "Ode" (embarrassing even to some of Jonson's allies)
is at least partially mitigated by this attempt to set his complaints in a larger
context. By presenting himself as simply another figure whose rightful authority was being undermined by "pride, and impudence (in faction knit)" (l. 3),
he makes his difficulties seem to reflect a more general problem: both he and
the king were victims of malicious circles of impudent malcontents. This interpretation of events must have been consoling: his failure thus resulted less from
any defect in his creativity than from the same kind of perverse insubordination he laments in various poems he wrote supporting Charles at around this
time. It hardly seems surprising, then, that the "Ode" ends by proclaiming Jonson's plan to abandon the stage and instead "sing / The glories of thy *King,* /

3. Most scholars have assumed that *The New Inn*'s first (and only) contemporary performance occurred on January 19, 1629. Hattaway, however, offers reasons for thinking
that it may have occurred shortly after March 25. Either date is consistent with my ensuing comments.

4. For a superbly detailed account of this entire episode, it is still difficult to surpass
Samuel R. Gardiner, *History of England from the Accession of James I to the Outbreak of the
Civil War, 1603–1642,* 10 vols. (London: Longmans, 1883–1884), 7:67–69.

His zeale to *God,* and his iust awe o're men," thereby "tuning forth the acts of his sweet raigne" (ll. 51–53, 59).[5] He thereby seeks to establish himself as the lead chorister in Charles's circle of literary supporters.

One great irony of the "Ode" is that it provoked perhaps even more discomfort (and often derision) than the play itself. Especially fascinating, for instance, were the reactions of some of Jonson's poetic "sons"—self-professed members of his own literary circle, such as Carew and Randolph. Carew's poem cleverly strikes a note of intelligent balance: its first words—"'Tis true (deere Ben:)"—lead us to expect a ringing endorsement of Jonson's stance, and in fact the opening lines seem to offer just that. By the end of line 4, however, Carew repeats the "'tis true" clause, but this time it introduces a concession that Jonson's talents have indeed declined. This concession is then itself balanced, though, by an optimistic prediction about his later reputation:

> 'Tis true (deere Ben:) thy iust chastizing hand
> Hath fix'd vppon the sotted age, a brand
> To they'r swolne Pride, & empty scribling due,
> It can nor iudge, nor write: & yet 'tis true
> Thy comique Muse from the exalted line
> Toucht by thy Alchymist, doth since decline
> From that her Zenith, & foretells a redd
> And blushing Euening, when she goes to bedd.
> Yet such, as shall outshine the glimmering light
> With which all starrs shall guilde the following night.
>   (H&S, 11:335–36, ll. 1–10)

Carew thus pays Jonson the subtle compliment of exercising the discriminating judgment Jonson himself always extolled. Imitation, he thereby tries to show, need not imply flattery.[6] Membership in a common literary circle, he attempts to demonstrate, need not imply servility. His independent judgment, in this view, affirms one of the deepest values to which Jonson and his "sons" had

5. Jonson fulfilled this promise in a number of poems that are often overlooked by critics who wish to stress the "subversive" possibilities of his writings. These include especially *Vnder-Wood* LXII, in which he thanks Charles for a gift of one hundred pounds and wonders whether the king can "cure the Peoples Evill" (H&S, 8:235), and also *Vnder-Wood* LXIV, a ringing endorsement of Charles's rule written in the immediate aftermath of the debacle in Parliament. For possible explanations of why and how Jonson could, in good conscience, have supported Charles this early in his reign, see Robert C. Evans, *Jonson, Lipsius, and the Politics of Renaissance Stoicism* (Wakefield, N.H.: Longwood Academic, 1992), 114–30.

6. On this point, see Earl Miner, *The Cavalier Mode from Jonson to Cotton* (Princeton: Princeton University Press, 1971), 268–70.

committed themselves. At the same time, Carew's implicit criticism of Jonson serves to distance him from his faltering mentor.

The rhetorical balance of Carew's poem continues throughout, especially when he asks Jonson, why should "the follies . . . of this dull Age" draw from the old poet's "penn such an immodest rage, / As seemes to blast thy else immortal bayes, / When thyne owne tongue proclaymes thy itch of prayse?" (ll. 23–26). "Itch" suggests an almost physical compulsion, thus challenging Jonson to exercise greater mental self-control. All in all, Carew's poem adroitly defends what is best in Jonson without defending him blindly. It displays the very modesty and judgment it celebrates, presenting an attractive image of Carew even while showing how Jonson's effort to enhance his own image had proved largely self-defeating. The poem shows how the failure of one member (especially the leading member) of a literary circle might embarrass its other participants and how the more intelligent of them might seek to respond both with loyalty and with judgment—judgment that might seem autonomous but was itself influenced by various social pressures.

Similarly interesting is the response of Randolph (H&S, 11:333–35), another of Jonson's professed admirers. Unlike Carew, he never concedes any disappointment with *The New Inn*. Instead, he more nearly follows Jonson's own cues: significantly, his poem (unlike Carew's) closely imitates the phrasing, imagery, argument, and even the shape of Jonson's "Ode," and (in an interesting bit of sibling rivalry) it also echoes Jonson in taking a swipe at Richard Brome, another of the old poet's "sons."[7] Randolph thereby illustrates the tensions that might exist not only between but also *within* literary and social circles:

> And let those things in plush,
>   Till they be taught to blush,
> Like what they will, and more contented bee
>   With what *Broome* swept from thee.
> I know thy worth, and that thy lofty straines
>   Write not to clothes but Braines:
>   But thy great spleene doth rise
>   Cause moles will have no eyes;
> This only in my *Ben*, I faulty find

7. Brome's play *The Love-sick Maid* was produced with great success at around the same time that *The New Inn* failed. In an early manuscript version of the "Ode to Himselfe," Jonson mocked Brome (who had once been his personal servant), but he later cut the allusion from the printed text of the poem (see Tennant, xxi–xxix). Randolph, then, was apparently responding to one of the early manuscript copies of the "Ode."

He's angry, they'le not see him that are blind.
(H&S, 11:333–35, ll. 31–40)

Randolph's only explicit criticism of Jonson is for showing such "great spleene" at moles for lacking eyes—that is, for being "angry" because "they'le not see him that are blind" (ll. 37–40). Yet, Randolph, like Carew, achieves the double purpose of defending Jonson while distinguishing himself from the old man's excesses. Both his and Carew's poems are socially and psychologically complex, demonstrating both loyalty and independence. Both sons defend the father while also distancing themselves from his failings. And, in doing so, they paradoxically exhibit the very sort of autonomous judgment the old man always prized and preached. They thereby discharge their obligations as members of his circle while also showing their capacity to create and lead circles of their own. Their status as "sons of Ben" does not prevent them from also operating as fundamentally independent agents who present their interests as reflecting allegiance to higher values that are even more important than personal loyalty.

Such complexity also characterizes Richard Goodwin's lengthy *Vindiciae Jonsonianae*, perhaps the best poem prompted by the "Ode" (H&S, 11:340–44). Jonson himself apparently liked the work well enough to pass it along to the earl of Newcastle, an important patron and therefore the center of still another literary and social circle. Although Goodwin counsels Jonson fairly bluntly not to "Staine . . . [his] Well-gaind Honour, with the Crude, / or the rash Censure, of a Multitude / of Silken fooles" (ll. 5–7), these lines typify his complex wit: they can be read both as a criticism of Jonson's "Crude" and "rash Censure" of his attackers and as an attack on the idiotic opinions of his critics. The shift from line 6 to line 7 is equally clever, since "Multitude" at first seems to imply a plebian crowd, while "Silken fooles" makes clear the social prominence of the critics. It was their status, in fact, that made their attacks bite, for although Goodwin, Jonson, and others ridicule these landowning *"Gallants"* (l. 35) as being beneath contempt, it was precisely their wealth and social power that made their literary judgments at all threatening. Goodwin's poem, in fact, twice suggests Jonson's "fear" of them. He advises his friend to

feare not to fall, by Votes
of such imbroyered-glittering-Siluer Coates!

.   .   .   .

Thy dareing Pen,

> that may contend with Fate, can that feare men?
>   (ll. 79 – 80, 85 – 86)[8]

In any case, Goodwin advises Jonson to avoid giving the *appearance* of being afraid, since any public sign of fear would only further erode his power. It would erode the confidence of Jonson's own circle while encouraging the aggressiveness of the anti-Jonsonian faction.

Ironically, for Goodwin and others Jonson's efforts at self-defense often seemed self-defeating. His best response to the attacks (they repeatedly suggest) would have been no response. By responding themselves, however, they show how difficult it was to practice such stoic wisdom. Thus, Goodwin counsels Jonson to ignore his critics and rely instead on his self-conviction of virtue, merit, and innocence: "Their dislike," he insists, "is thine Honour; Hee that's moued, / With such mens censures; graunteth it half prou'd / that he is guiltie" (ll. 611 – 63). Yet, Goodwin himself feels compelled to reply, not only to defend Jonson but also implicitly to defend the good judgment of Jonson's supporters, such as himself. Indeed, the whole controversy was shot through with such paradoxes. Calm, stoic prudence was easily undercut by real social pressures: an attack on Jonson was not merely an attack on Jonson but also an implied attack on the other members of his circle. By replying to his critics, Jonson might seem weak while trying to seem strong; yet, by failing to reply (and thus attempting in another way to seem strong), he might still seem weak. His weakness, moreover, might reflect on his friends. No wonder he and his supporters sometimes sound exasperated.

To make matters worse, of course, it was not only Jonson's original critics— the original spectators—with whom he and his circle now had to contend. Ironically, his attacks (in his epilogues and "Ode") on the ignorance of his original audience now began to generate a new series of counterattacks. In fact, it seems to have been his defense of his play, far more than the play itself, that provoked irate response. One such reply apparently came, ironically, from a one-time member of Jonson's own literary circle, George Chapman—although Chapman's probable allusion to this specific controversy seems to have gone unnoticed.[9] Far

8. The same motive is also twice implied by John Polwhele, who wrote a brief poem encouraging Jonson (see Hattaway, 227 – 28). Hattaway notes that when Herford and the Simpsons reprinted Polwhele's poem in their edition, they inadvertently omitted the crucial third line. That line suggests that as long as Jonson enjoys the king's support, he has nothing to fear from his critics.

9. For the text of Chapman's "Inuectiue" against Jonson, see H&S where it is dated as having been written in 1633 or 1634 (11:406 – 12). Establishing the relevance of this poem to the *New Inn* controversy would take far more space than I have available here, but I do discuss this matter in a piece forthcoming in *Notes and Queries.* Suffice it to say that lines 12 – 14, 31 – 32, and 35 – 37 seem especially pertinent.

more effective, though, was an indictment penned by Owen Felltham. Although Felltham (like Chapman) probably in some respects admired Jonson, his poetic riposte mockingly urges the old poet to "Come leave this saucy way / Of baiting those that pay / Dear for the sight of your declining wit" (H&S, 11:339–40, ll. 1–3). Even his praise is backhanded: he commends Jonson as a "Translator" but claims that the old man lacks true "*genius* and fire," and he asserts that when Jonson's works are rejected, "You bellow, rave and spatter round your gall" (ll. 13–14, 20). Ironically turning Jonson's own standards against him, he implies that *The New Inn* is even worse than Shakespeare's *Pericles*—a play Jonson had attacked when defending his own (ll. 21–30). Felltham accuses Jonson of prostituting his art merely to make money; of trying to "rail men into approbation," thereby raping Fame; and of indulging in "self-conceit and choler of the bloud" (ll. 40, 45–50, 53). He urges the old man to "Leave then this humour vain, / And this more humorous strain" (ll. 51–52). These adjectives and nouns are cleverly selected: Felltham essentially mocks Jonson for behaving like a fool from one of his own "humour" plays, and he not only makes the standard pun on "vain" (implying that Jonson's conduct is both egotistical and futile) but also puns on "straine"— suggesting that Jonson's self-defense is at once labored, excessive, ungracious, and embarrassing (at least to his erstwhile admirers). All in all, Felltham's poem (which seems to have circulated widely) is devastating satire, especially since it so skillfully parodies both the structure and the diction of Jonson's "Ode." The fact that it was penned by a man who elsewhere expressed admiration for Jonson must have sharpened its sting.[10] From one perspective this poem illustrates Felltham's lack of servility; from another perspective it exemplifies his inevitable self-interest. All the writers who participated in the *New Inn* controversy must have realized that in commenting on Jonson they were also presenting themselves for judgment by competing social and literary circles.

This kind of complexity can be seen, for instance, in the work of the anonymous author who composed "The Countrys Censure of Ben Johnsons New Inn," which opens by offering "Counsell" to "decaying Ben," asserting that "Age, steept In sacke, hath quencht thy Enthean fire" (H&S, 11:344–46, ll. 1–3). The author claims to "pittye now, whom once, wee did Admire," and (like Felltham) he turns many of the old playwright's own standards (and standard arguments) against him. *The New Inn*, he claims, makes Jonson seem a mere

10. On Felltham's poem, see Ted-Larry Pebworth, *Owen Felltham* (Boston: Twayne, 1976), 90–93. Felltham contributed an elegy to *Jonsonus Virbius* (1638), published not long after the old poet died in 1637. His attack on Jonson was not printed until 1661 (H&S, 11:340, 460–62).

poetaster—a member of "the *Vnbrowed* Thronge" (l. 14). Actors, he notes, cannot breathe life into dead lines, and he argues that Jonson's original audience was angered less by *The New Inn* than by the self-betrayal it represented. The anonymous author of this poem shows little patience even for Jonson's somewhat pathetic references to his physical illness:

> But lett me tell thee this, Ben, by the way,
> Thy Argument's as tedious as thy play;
> Thou saist noe Palsye doth thy Brayne pan vex,
> I praye the<e> tell me what? an Apoplex?
>
> (ll. 25–28)

The unknown prosecutor attacks the indecorous, excessive language of *The New Inn*'s subplot, he indicts the work for being boring, and he subtly alludes to *Cynthias Revels*, one of Jonson's earliest plays, suggesting that the old poet has now shown himself guilty of the very self-love (or *"Philautie"*) he often openly mocked.[11] In short, he subjects Jonson to precisely the kind of literary and personal satire Jonson himself had mastered. He turns the teachings against the fallen teacher, showing (in the process) how well he has learned the master's lessons. His poem is, ironically, a thoroughly Jonsonian indictment of Jonson himself.

Indeed, what seems at once most interesting and most impressive about all the attacks on *The New Inn* is the generally *literary* focus of the charges. (This fact seems especially relevant to debates among present-day critical factions.) Jonson's contemporary critics berated him less for bad politics than for failed art. The lofty literary standards he had done so much to inculcate were now being turned against him, but at least those standards *were* mostly literary.[12] And when they were not literary, they were mainly moral or ethical. Admittedly, his attackers sometimes mock his great girth and his taste for sack, but mainly they indict his alleged pride or arrogance—the very faults he himself had so often assaulted and always considered so threatening to a healthy commonwealth. Once again, in other words, Jonson essentially wins while losing: the mainly ethical and literary values he and his circle had long championed are the very

---

11. This allusion seems not to have been previously noticed.
12. Jonson's champions also defend him mainly on literary grounds. See, for instance, the poem by "I. C." (probably James Clayton [Hattaway, 213 n]), which praises the skilled combinations of "Art, and Nature" in Jonson's works (H&S, 11:336–38, l. 26). See also the poem by "C. G.," published in 1640 (Tennant, 136), that explicitly alludes to *The New Inn* and claims that in this work "comely action graced each learned line."

values his critics (who were sometimes also his "sons") invoke when they assail him. Ethics and art: these are the criteria by which he both judged and was eventually judged himself.

Interestingly, the controversy surrounding *The New Inn* only confirms what a larger study of Jonson's seventeenth-century reputation would also seem to indicate: that Politics—macropolitics, Politics with a capital *P*—seem to have played a far less important role in contemporary judgments of the poet than our own recent preoccupations with ideology might lead us to expect.[13] In the "Ode to Himselfe," for instance, Jonson emphatically embraced King Charles at exactly the time when embracing the king might have seemed impolitic. Yet, almost no response to the "Ode" attacks Jonson on ideological grounds. No respondent indicts him as a supporter of monarchy, or even of this monarch; no one suggests that he betrays republican ideals; no one either praises, condemns, or even mentions his opinions on the large ideological matters that have seemed so important to so many modern scholars.[14] Instead, in the immediate aftermath of *The New Inn* (and indeed for most of the rest of the century, including during the Commonwealth and after the Restoration), Jonson was evaluated mostly as a worthy or unworthy man and as a skilled or unskillful artist—but *especially* as an artist. If the responses of contemporary individuals and circles are any indication, then, there may be some real historical sanction for confidently reading the works of Jonson and his fellow writers chiefly in formalistic terms—as works of successful or unsuccessful *art*. Both the attackers and the defenders of Jonson are, in this sense, members of his own *literary* circle in the simplest sense of that term: for them, it is Jonson's *literary* failure or success that seems most important, not his macropolitical ideology or opinions

13. I am currently completing a book on this matter, tentatively titled "Ben Jonson: Reception and Reputation." Study of seventeenth-century allusions to the poet suggests that ideological matters rarely figure in contemporary assessments of him or his work.

14. "I. C." (James Clayton?) does emphasize the poet's proclamation (in the "Ode") of his plans to praise Charles, and Felltham alludes to Jonson's "braver Theme," but they endorse such praise. Similarly, John Polwhele implies that Jonson enjoys Charles's support (Hattaway, 227–28). These comments, however, are about as close as any of the respondents ever get to offering macropolitical judgments. To the extent that politics are mentioned, then, the references hardly imply a "subversive" or "republican" tinge to Jonson's views. Such evidence is relevant to recent debates about the political resonance of *The New Inn* itself. See, for instance, Martin Butler, "Late Jonson," in *The Politics of Tragicomedy: Shakespeare and After*, ed. Gordon McMullan and Jonathan Hope (London: Routledge, 1992), 166–88; and Julie Sanders, "'The Day's Sports Devised in the Inn': Jonson's *The New Inn* and Theatrical Politics," *Modern Language Review* 91 (1996): 545–60. Sanders takes a somewhat "progressive" or "subversive" view of Jonson's politics in this play, opposing Butler, who sees him as more "conservative." Butler, I think, stands on firmer ground.

on topical issues. Both his friends and his foes respond to him mainly as a *writer*, not an ideologue, and perhaps in this sense they offer a useful model for the literary-critical factions who, even today, vie over the proper response to the works of Jonson and other writers of his age.

In any case, the evidence provided by the *New Inn* controversy does suggest a few tentative answers to the questions with which this essay began. Thus, members of Jonson's circle could indeed exercise some independent judgment on controversial issues, although their judgments would inevitably also be affected by social pressures from within and outside their circle. Individual writers were probably conscious, when they wrote, of the effects their words might have (and the responses they might elicit) both within their own circle and in circles outside their own. Membership in a circle could help an individual cope with the frustrations of larger social isolation, but embarrassing behavior might also cause greater isolation—not only for himself within his circle but also for his circle in society at large. Almost inevitably, circles were constantly in flux—gaining members, losing members, and perhaps even losing leaders as social and personal circumstances changed. Membership in a circle meant acquiring both a group of (temporary) allies and a collection of (potential) rivals, and rivalry might especially become an issue when the leader of a circle seemed to be losing influence both within and outside his own group.

Inevitably, politics seem to have had a major impact on Jonson's standing inside and outside his circle, but we should probably be careful not to restrict our definition of "politics" (as we have so often seemed to do in recent theory and criticism) to "large" ideological issues. The evidence provided by the *New Inn* controversy suggests that such issues were usually by no means the most immediately pressing or dominant ones in the day-to-day lives of Jonson and many of his contemporaries, just as they rarely are in the day-to-day lives of many people today. Instead, the issues probably of most immediate concern to Jonson, his circle, and those outside it seem to have been perennial "micropolitical" problems—the kind that are probably rooted as much in biology, sociology, and ethics as in ideology per se. The most immediate concerns faced by Jonson, other writers, and other people in general at his time were the ones that have always faced human beings in all societies. They involve such questions as: What is my status? Is that status secure? Do I have enemies? Do I have friends? Which of the two groups is more influential? Do I have a comfortable degree of economic security and (especially) of psychological autonomy and peace of mind? Does my social position allow me to feel respected and (perhaps more important) to feel *self*-respect?

Jonson's ideological attitudes and positions, of course, inevitably affected such practical questions, especially if we construe the word *ideology* in a broader sense than is typically used today. Thus, if Jonson had not been a Christian— if he had been a Jew or Moslem or atheist—his social position would have been highly insecure. If he had not been a heterosexual—if he had been an open "sodomite" or sexual transgressor in some other flagrant way—his life might literally have been at risk.[15] If he had advocated regicide (at least before the late 1640s!) or if he had attacked all notions of private property, he undoubtedly would have been in danger. But Jonson was not an atheist, openly homosexual, a proponent of king killing, or a protocommunist. He did not openly attack the established church (although for a decade he refused to join it), and he did not openly advocate wholesale political revolution. If he had been or done any of these things, "politics" in the "larger" sense—in the sense of ideology— would surely have had a highly dramatic impact on his life.

Instead, Jonson—like most of his contemporaries—had to be most concerned with politics in a less dramatic but perhaps more intimate and pervasive sense: the kind of politics that seem nearly inescapable, no matter what particular ideological system happens to prevail. And in politics on this scale (if the *New Inn* controversy is any guide), what seem to have mattered most were not so much Jonson's opinions on the "large" issues of the day as his *artistic* ability and *literary* skill. In the matter of the *New Inn* as in so many other matters and moments in his life, Jonson was judged by his contemporaries first and foremost as he wanted to be judged: as a *writer*, as a craftsman skilled (or unskilled) at using words. His talent as an artist, more than almost anything else, primarily determined his social standing and social security.

If Jonson had not been able to write well, he would become the butt of painful jokes (as indeed happened with *The New Inn*), and even his friends and other supporters (such as patrons) might have deserted him. His ideological opinions—whether he was a royalist or "republican," a Laudian or a Puritan— would be matters of concern mainly to his limited circle of friends and family. The real social power he enjoyed, as well as the real influence he exercised over his literary circle, depended at least as much on his talent as an author as on his more narrowly "political" opinions. It was primarily his skill at writing well,

---

15. I use the word *sodomite* as a way of acknowledging the arguments of many modern scholars who contend that certainly the word, and perhaps also the concept, of "homosexuality" did not even exist in Jonson's day. Behavior and feelings that *we* would call "homosexual" obviously did, however, and often provoked intense criticism and violent punishment.

not his personal ideological attitudes, that would determine his social status, literary influence, economic security, and (most significant) his peace of mind, sense of worth, and self-respect.

Of course, to say that Jonson needed to write "well" might seem to beg many complex questions, including the following: What did it mean, in Jonson's time, to write "well"? By what artistic standards were literary works judged? How much agreement was there about such standards? To what degree were such standards in flux? To what extent were such "literary" standards themselves influenced by social factors, such as class or education or even "ideology"? Although there is no space to address such questions here, these problems (and others like them) are precisely the kinds that might be addressed by a "historical formalist," if such a term did not strike so many contemporary theorists as obviously oxymoronic, and if our preoccupations today were not so exclusively (and narrowly) "Political." Perhaps one fruitful way, therefore, to understand Jonson and his literary circle would be to study the ways in which—and the reasons—they seem to have taken artistic talent as seriously as they seem to have done. This, at least, seems one matter obviously raised by the whole *New Inn* affair.

Timothy Raylor

Newcastle's Ghosts
Robert Payne, Ben Jonson, and the "Cavendish Circle"

When we talk about literary circles in Renaissance England, we use an elegant, geometric figure to explain a wide range of complex, often messy, social interactions. It is a useful shorthand that none of us, I suppose, takes too literally. We work the term hard, distributing it broadly over a spectrum that ranges from tightly knit communities with dense social, geographical, and intellectual bonds to loose networks of correspondents linked by only, perhaps, one or two shared interests. At the dark end of the spectrum, thick with threads, we find the intimate family groups that flourished in the provinces: one thinks, for example, of the Cottons and the Cokaynes of the Derbyshire Peak, linked in manifold ways by marriage and by locale, sharing political and literary attitudes that meshed in the vigorously royalist verse of Sir Aston Cokayne and Charles Cotton. Somewhere near the middle we find the drinking clubs of early-seventeenth-century London: the self-styled Orders—of the Bugle, the Blue, and the Fancy—involving young men on the make, bound together by secret passwords, ritualized debauches, and a fascination with impromptu literary composition, both competitive and collaborative.[1] At the lighter end of this spectrum, geographically and socially disparate, we find the Hartlib circle: an international group of learned men and women connected largely—in some cases, solely—through Samuel Hartlib's London office, and joined not by bonds of lineage or camaraderie but by a shared commitment to the Comenian project of pansophia, or universal reformation.

Yet, so handy a term is always in danger of suggesting a false uniformity among different kinds of groups. There is a world of difference between, on the

1. Timothy Raylor, *Cavaliers, Clubs, and Literary Culture: Sir John Mennes, James Smith, and the Order of the Fancy* (Newark: University of Delaware Press; London and Toronto: Associated University Presses, 1994), 69–110.

one hand, the Cokayne and Cotton families, bound tightly together by geography and blood, and, on the other, Hartlib's correspondents, scattered across the Atlantic seaboard, many of whom were unknown to one another. We would gain much precision by following the example of historians of science who, taking the lead from modern social network theorists, have begun to insist on a distinction between the closed circle (tightly knit, with "strong ties") and the open network (large, disparate, and held together by "weak ties").[2] In the case of Hartlib, for example, we would still find ourselves dealing with a circle, but it would be an inner core of trusted advisers, each known to the other (including Comenius, John Dury, and Sir Cheney Culpeper); it would be found nestling within a larger and more disparate network, a vast web of correspondents covering most of the known world and drawing together such unlikely associates as Balthazar Gerbier and John Winthrop.[3]

But there are other problems with the image of the circle, the most serious of which is that it describes only two dimensions. As such, it has a leveling effect, reducing all participants in an activity to the same size or, in social terms, to the same rank and status. There can be few less appropriate ways of describing the social formations of Renaissance England than a model that fails to incorporate the most important determinants of a person's social existence. A thorough three-dimensional analysis would be likely to reveal that many of the literary circles of Renaissance England might more aptly be imagined by the use of alternative conceptual models.

Modern scholars have displayed considerable curiosity about the group that revolved around the figures of William Cavendish, successively first earl, marquess, and duke of Newcastle (1593–1674), and his brother, Charles (1595?–1654), a group known variously as the Newcastle, Cavendish, or Welbeck circle (after the family estate of Welbeck Abbey, Nottinghamshire). Newcastle was probably the most powerful nobleman in northern England; he was certainly the most munificent. He staged for King Charles I two entertainments of unparalleled extravagance, and he was lavish in his patronage of the arts and sciences: Jonson and Dryden, van Dyck and Fanelli, Hobbes and Descartes were

2. For a helpful analysis making use of this distinction, see David S. Lux and Harold J. Cook, "Closed Circles or Open Networks? Communicating at a Distance during the Scientific Revolution," *History of Science* 36 (1998): 179–211.

3. For an example of this double-level of operation, see Timothy Raylor, "Samuel Hartlib and the Commonwealth of Bees," in *Culture and Cultivation in Early Modern England: Writing and the Land*, ed. Michael Leslie and Timothy Raylor (Leicester and London: Leicester University Press, 1992), 95–96.

among those who enjoyed his support. But Newcastle was no mere Maecenas; he was avid in the pursuit of his own literary, political, and scientific projects. He composed plays and masques and penned vast numbers of poems, wrote a manual on government for Charles II, printed two huge and supposedly definitive works on horsemanship, and prepared for the press but never printed an equally hefty tract on swordsmanship. By the early 1630s, he and his scholarly brother, Charles, were at the forefront of the new philosophy in England, promoting theoretical research and practical experiment on optics, mathematics, and mechanics. They established correspondence with such European scholars as Claude Mydorge and Marin Mersenne the Minim friar, who acted as a conduit for Continental ideas.[4]

To aid them in their investigations, the Cavendish brothers drew upon the help of several expert assistants. One of them was Robert Payne (circa 1595–1651), an Oxford scholar and cleric who entered into a mathematical correspondence with Sir Charles Cavendish in 1631 and joined the household at Welbeck as chaplain by April 1632, a position he retained until his departure for Christ Church, Oxford, in 1638. Another was Walter Warner (circa 1557–1643), the aged associate of Thomas Harriot and Henry Percy, ninth earl of Northumberland. Warner had no official connection with Welbeck, and was never resident there; during the 1630s he divided his time between his lodgings in Charing Cross, London, and the house of his patron, Sir Thomas Aylesbury, in Windsor Park. But during this period he corresponded with Payne and with Sir Charles Cavendish on optical and psychological questions. Yet another figure associated with the brothers and their researches into optics, mechanics, and psychology in the 1630s was Thomas Hobbes, who had been in the service of the senior Chatsworth branch of the family on and off since the 1610s, acting variously as tutor and secretary. In the autumn of 1636 Hobbes contemplated a move to Welbeck in order to pursue his studies in peace but was ultimately unable or perhaps unwilling to disentangle himself from his domestic responsibilities to the Chatsworth Cavendishes.[5]

4. The best modern account of Newcastle remains Geoffrey Trease's romantic *Portrait of a Cavalier: William Cavendish, First Duke of Newcastle* (London: Macmillan, 1979). Among more specialist studies of the circle, see, for example: Jean Jacquot, "Sir Charles Cavendish and His Learned Friends," *Annals of Science* 3 (1952): 13–27, 175–91; Robert Hugh Kargon, *Atomism in England from Hariot to Newton* (Oxford: Clarendon Press, 1966), 40–42, 54–58, 63–76; Harold W. Jones, "Der Kreis von Welbeck," *Grundriss der Geschichte der Philosophie: Die Philosophie des 17. Jahrhunderts*, vol. 3, *England*, ed. Jean-Pierre Schobinger (Basel: Schwabe, 1988), 186–209; and *The Cavendish Circle*, special issue of *Seventeenth Century* 9 (1994): 141–287.

5. On Payne, see Noel Malcolm, ed., *The Correspondence of Thomas Hobbes*, 2 vols. (Ox-

Although some commentators have extended the boundary of the circle by including additional figures, such as John Pell and Sir Kenelm Digby, its generally accepted nucleus in the 1630s remains William and Charles Cavendish, Robert Payne, Walter Warner, and Thomas Hobbes.[6] What may be said of such a group? At one extreme it has been suggested that the Newcastle circle was a tight-knit intellectual community that engaged in the collaborative composition of works in which it laid out collectively held views on natural philosophy. At the other extreme, the idea that these men formed a distinct circle has been called into question, and the notion that they engaged in any kind of collective authorship has been dismissed as an absurd anachronism.[7] In this paper I propose to examine in general terms two areas of dispute: the nature of the group and the question of collaborative authorship within it. Let us begin by examining the connections among these figures, to determine how aptly we think of them as forming a circle.

That they were closely connected is clear. All of them knew one another, and all were engaged in investigations in a small number of related fields about which they exchanged information and criticism. Payne corresponded with both Warner and Hobbes on optics, passing on to the latter his criticisms of Warner's work. Warner corresponded on the same subject with Sir Charles and with Payne. And Hobbes corresponded with the brothers and with Payne about optics and psychology, slyly undermining Warner's claims to distinction in these areas. The only weak link here is that between Hobbes and Warner, whose knowledge of one another's work appears to have been transmitted primarily via Welbeck (even when the two were residing a mere few miles apart in Sur-

---

ford: Clarendon Press, 1994), 2:872–77; and Mordechai Feingold, "A Friend of Hobbes and an Early Translator of Galileo: Robert Payne of Oxford," in *The Light of Nature*, ed. J. D. North and J. J. Roche (Dordrecht: Nijhoff, 1985), 265–80. On Warner, see Jan Prins, *Walter Warner (ca. 1557–1643) and His Notes on Animal Organisms* (Utrecht: privately published, 1992); John W. Shirley, *Thomas Harriot: A Biography* (Oxford: Clarendon Press, 1983), 362–71; and John Aubrey, *"Brief Lives," Chiefly of Contemporaries, Set Down by John Aubrey, between the Years 1669 and 1696*, ed. Andrew Clark, 2 vols. (Oxford: Clarendon Press, 1898), 2:16. For their correspondence, see British Library, MSS Additional 4395, fols. 102, 116–18; and Additional 4279, fol. 307. On Hobbes, see Malcolm, *Correspondence of Hobbes*, 1:xxxvii, 37.

6. Pell is included by Jones, "Der Kreis von Welbeck," and Digby by Arrigo Pacchi, *Introduzione a Hobbes* (Bari: Laterza, 1971), 16.

7. Pacchi, *Introduzione a Hobbes*, 16; Thomas Hobbes, *Court Traité des Premiers Principes: "Le Short Tract on First Principles" de 1630–1631*, ed. and trans. Jean Bernhardt (Paris: Presses Universitaires de France, 1988), 89; Noel Malcolm, "A Summary Biography of Hobbes," in *The Cambridge Companion to Hobbes*, ed. Tom Sorrell (Cambridge: Cambridge University Press, 1996), 22–23; Karl Schuhmann, "Le *Short Tract*, première oeuvre philosophique de Hobbes," *Hobbes Studies* 8 (1995): 6.

rey) and whose relations were evidently a little cool. Although Warner esteemed Hobbes, Hobbes was hostile and competitive in respect to Warner, never hesitating to promote his own work at the expense of the older man's, and even urging Newcastle to withhold his support of Warner.[8] What we have here is less a single unitary circle than a complex solar system: Welbeck and the Cavendish brothers its center, Payne a dependent satellite in close orbit around it, and Warner and Hobbes moving in wider, separate, but overlapping orbits around it and other centers of power. Hobbes's orbit was determined by the influence of several Cavendish houses: Welbeck, Chatsworth, and Byfleet. Warner, meanwhile, moved primarily around the axes of Northumberland House and Windsor Park, but he was influenced nonetheless by the more distant gravitational pull of Welbeck.

Perhaps we would be better advised to think in terms not of a Welbeck or Newcastle circle, but of an extended Newcastle entourage. As domestic chaplain, Payne was simply a paid member of the household. Although Warner was not officially connected with Welbeck (a pension from the earl of Northumberland gave him a degree of financial independence, as did the support of Aylesbury), he did receive financial support from the brothers: Sir Charles, for instance, sent him twenty pounds "as our acknowledgement of your favour" on May 2, 1636. Hobbes's relation to Newcastle was similar to that of Warner, but a little closer: he hovered on the fringes of Welbeck. Although for many years a servant of the Cavendish family, he held no post at Welbeck; however, he received financial support from Newcastle in the form of gifts, and he came close to taking up residence in the household in 1636. Payne, Hobbes, and Warner were therefore linked to Sir William and Sir Charles Cavendish not by fellowship but by the obligations of clientage.[9]

When we reconceive the relationships among the Cavendish brothers and their associates in terms of patronage, rather than in terms of a circle drawing together men with a shared interest in science, our picture of the group becomes a little more supple and inclusive. We are able, for example, to incorporate another satellite in orbit around Welbeck—although this may not be the most appropriate way of describing the aging Ben Jonson. Jonson is not usually included in accounts of the Welbeck circle because he did not participate in the

8. British Library, MSS Harleian 4458, fols. 26–27, Harleian 6083, fol. 104 (quoted in Prins, *Warner and His Notes,* 15); Malcolm, *Correspondence of Hobbes,* 1:28–29, 32, 33–34, 40; Malcolm, "Summary Biography," 22.

9. Prins, *Warner and His Notes,* 12; British Library, MS Additional 4405, fol. 307; Malcolm, *Correspondence of Hobbes,* 1:28.

scientific activities that supposedly formed its binding agent. Yet, he was linked to the Cavendish brothers in the same way as Hobbes or Payne, and was intimate with both of them. Although he had been writing addresses to the family since the 1620s, in the early 1630s Jonson came to rely heavily upon the financial support of Newcastle, who employed him to write texts for the royal entertainments at Welbeck in May 1633 and Bolsover in July 1634. Jonson was intimate with at least two of our satellites. Writing to thank Newcastle for a gratuity sent to acknowledge one of the texts just mentioned (probably the latter), Jonson speaks warmly of the bearer, "my beloued friend Mr Payne": "I am in the number of your humblest seru^{ts}: my Lo: and the most willing; doe ioy in the good friendship and fellowship of my right learned friend Mr Payne, then whom your Lo^P: could not haue imployed a more diligent & iudicious Man, or that hath treated mee wth more humanitie, wch makes mee cheerfully to insert my selfe into yor lo:^{ps} commands, and so sure a Clientele."[10] Jonson was also a close friend of Hobbes, close enough to be given access to the latter's translations of the newsletters of Fulgenzio Micanzio in the 1620s, and to be called upon to criticize his translation of Thucydides at the end of that decade.[11] There is no likelihood that Jonson took any part in the optical or mechanical researches of the brothers, but he was no less a part of their milieu in the mid-1630s than Hobbes or Warner.

To emphasize the overriding importance that must be assigned to matters of rank in any assessment of the nature of the Welbeck group is not to suggest that relations among the brothers and their assistants were stiff or lacking in warmth: indeed, the relaxed tone of such relations is indicated by the remarkable informality displayed in Hobbes's letters to the earl, or by the affection clearly discernible in the letters of Ben Jonson; it is merely to insist that we give adequate attention to the grounds that made such exchanges possible.[12] However direct and friendly their tone, Jonson's are still fundamentally begging letters. We might illustrate this point by turning briefly to the image Newcastle himself provided of the chemical experiments he undertook with Payne:

> Dr. *Payn*, a Divine, and my Chaplain, who hath a very Witty Searching Brain
> of his own, being at my House at *Bolsover*, lock'd up with me in a Chamber,

10. C. H. Herford, Percy Simpson, and Evelyn Simpson, eds., *Ben Jonson*, 11 vols. (Oxford: Clarendon Press, 1925–1952), 1:212; see the editors' note for the reasoning behind the suggestion that the letter pertains to the second entertainment (212–13).

11. Ibid., 11:244; Aubrey, *"Brief Lives,"* 1:365.

12. Cedric Brown offers a perceptive reading of the letters in such terms in "Courtesies of Place and Arts of Diplomacy in Ben Jonson's Last Two Entertainments for Royalty," *Seventeenth Century* 9 (1994): 166–67.

to make *Lapis Prunellæ*, which is salt-petre and Brimstone inflamed, look-ing at it a while, I said, Mark it Mr. *Payn*, the Flame is pale, like the Sun, and hath a Violent Motion in it like the Sun; saith he, It hath so, and more to Confirm you, says he, look what abundance of Little Suns, Round like a Globe, appear to us every where, just the same Motion as the Sun makes in every one's Eyes; So we concluded, the Sun could be nothing else but a very Solid Body of Salt and Sulphur, Inflamed by his own Violent motion upon his own Axis.[13]

This is a charming vignette, generous to a fault, yet even here one cannot avoid noticing the hierarchical structure within which such apparently infor-mal collaboration and exchange takes place. Payne's is a limited, supporting role: he does not contradict, preempt, or seek to outstrip his patron; rather, he makes himself useful by confirming the truth of the earl's remark, and by teas-ing out of it an explanatory analogy that converts a random and platitudinous observation into a dazzling philosophical insight.

It is in the context of the noble household that we can best make sense of the scientific work of Payne, Warner, and, to an extent, Hobbes during their as-sociation with Welbeck. Although Payne's official position was that of do-mestic chaplain, he played several additional roles in the household. We have just seen him acting both in the guise of private secretary, ferrying money to Jonson, and in the guise of chemical operator, undertaking experiments with the earl. His surviving writings from the period also show him acting as re-search assistant to the brothers, translating Italian works of mechanics for their benefit, including Benedetto Castelli's *Della misura dell'acque correnti* and Galileo's *Della scienza mecanica*.[14] Such assistance did not stop at the transla-tion of texts on mechanics into English; it also extended to the application of mechanical principles to areas of interest to the Cavendish brothers. Indeed, it is only in terms of Sir William's interest in both mechanics and horseman-ship that we can make sense of Payne's provision for him of an extraordinary essay titled "Considerations touching the facility or Difficulty of the Motions of a Horse," in which equine motion is subjected to a mechanical analysis. And it is in terms of the collaborative work of the household that we can best un-derstand the nature, purpose, and authorship of the most important document to have been produced at Welbeck, *A Short Tract on First Principles*: a work at-tributed variously to Hobbes, Payne, and the Cavendish circle itself, which at-

13. William Cavendish, "Opinions Concerning the Ground of Natural Philosophy," in *Philosophical and Physical Opinions*, by Margaret Cavendish (London, 1663), 463.
14. British Library, MS Harleian 6796, fols. 309 – 16, 317 – 39.

tempts to use the mechanical method to provide an account of human psychology.[15]

Although Warner's research on optics predated his encounter with the Cavendish brothers, he was financially rewarded for his *favoring* of them: a term that refers, one assumes, to his concentration on matters of particular concern to them. In 1640 Hobbes presented *The Elements of Law* to Newcastle as a work of political psychology undertaken at his request: "Now (my Lord) the principles fit for such a foundation, are those which I have heretofore acquainted your Lordship withal in private discourse, and which by your command I have here put into method."[16] That so major a text was developed and written under Newcastle's auspices underlines the importance of the Cavendish family in the history of English intellectual life. And the doubts that prevent us from speaking with confidence about the character and authorship of the *Short Tract* underscore how far we are from understanding the precise nature of its contribution. This brings us to the second of our issues for investigation: the question of collaborative authorship at Welbeck.

The objection that to speak of collective authorship in this period is anachronistic may be swiftly dismissed. It has recently been argued that "collaboration was a prevalent mode of textual production" at this time, and collective writing was a vital aspect of social and literary life in the Cavendish household. We find evidence for this claim in the joint authorship of poems and plays by Newcastle's daughters, Elizabeth (Brackley) and Jane, some parts of which are, in surviving manuscript collections, initialed by their respective authors, but are not attributed in any thorough or systematic manner. We find it also in the reappearance of characters and plot elements from plays by William in the dramatic works of his second wife, Margaret, as well as in the appearance of William's verses in works printed as hers. The haphazard manner in which such attributions are registered—some announced in the printed titles of individual works, others inserted in ink, in certain copies and apparently at random, by Margaret

15. For the text of "Considerations touching the facility," a facsimile, and its attribution to Hobbes, see S. Arthur Strong, *A Catalogue of Letters and Other Historical Documents Exhibited in the Library at Welbeck* (London: Murray, 1903), 54–55, 237–40; for the attribution to Payne, see Malcolm, *Correspondence of Hobbes*, 2:875. For a full examination of the hand and authorship of this and other disputed documents, see Timothy Raylor, "Hobbes, Payne, and *A Short Tract on First Principles*," forthcoming in *Historical Journal* (2001). The authorship and context of *A Short Tract* have been hotly disputed in recent years. These matters are discussed at length in Raylor, "Hobbes, Payne, and *A Short Tract*."

16. Quoted from the edition of Ferdinand Tönnies, *The Elements of Law*, introduced by M. M. Goldsmith, 2d ed. (London: Cass, 1969), xv–xvi.

herself—is suggestive of the promiscuous collaboration and relaxed attitude toward literary ownership characteristic of the Cavendish family.[17]

But it is one thing to show that collaboration and collective authorship was standard practice among members of the Cavendish family, quite another to claim that domestics such as Payne or clients such as Hobbes participated in these practices. What we can show, however, is that within the patronage-client dynamic we have so far traced, various people in diverse fashions did so. The surviving literary manuscripts of William Cavendish, distributed between the British Library in London and the Hallward Library of the University of Nottingham, allow us to study his habits of composition: they attest to Newcastle's habitual reliance upon various kinds of secretarial assistance. Since there is so little evidence about the processes of composition in the early modern period, such evidence warrants our attention, regardless of the literary value of Newcastle's works themselves.

Newcastle's manuscripts comprise a series of separates (single sheets or bifolia) bound up in several volumes in the early part of this century under the auspices of his descendant, the sixth duke of Portland. These sheets contain rough and fair drafts of plays, masques, and poems in Newcastle's hand, and fair copies (sometimes multiple copies) in the hand of his secretary, John Rolleston. Many of these drafts and copies are endorsed by Rolleston "Intr[ata]," indicating entry into a lost master volume. In each stage of drafting or copying, a work might display orthographic corrections in the hand of Rolleston, and substantive revisions in the hand of Newcastle, as well as those of several unnamed assistants.[18]

If we restrict our attention for the moment to works of the mid-1630s, we

17. The quotation is from Jeffrey Masten, *Textual Intercourse: Collaboration, Authorship, and Sexualities in Renaissance Drama* (Cambridge: Cambridge University Press, 1997), 4. On the writings of Newcastle's daughters, see Margaret J. M. Ezell, "'To Be Your Daughter in Your Pen': The Social Functions of Literature in the Writings of Lady Elizabeth Brackley and Lady Jane Cavendish," *Huntington Library Quarterly* 51 (1988): 282, 284–85. For Margaret Cavendish's registration of debts to her husband, see, for example, *Natures pictures drawn by Fancies Pencil to the Life* (London, 1656), British Library, shelf mark G. 11599, 20, 25, 64, 65, 79, 94, 97. Her use of slip cancels to indicate William's authorship in *Plays* (London, 1662) is noticed by James Fitzmaurice, "Margaret Cavendish on Her Own Writing: Evidence from Revision and Handmade Correction," *Papers of the Bibliographical Society of America* 85 (1991): 305.

18. For analyses of the provenance, composition, and scripts of these volumes, see Lynn Hulse, ed., *Dramatic Works by William Cavendish*, Malone Society Reprints, 158 (Oxford: Malone Society, 1996), xvii–xx; and Hilton Kelliher, "Donne, Jonson, Richard Andrews, and the Newcastle Manuscript," *English Manuscript Studies, 1100–1700* 4 (1993): 134–73. Explicit endorsements regarding entry into a master volume appear on several poems in the hands of Cavendish and Rolleston: see, for instance, Hallward Library, University of Nottingham, PwV 25, fols. 5r, 7r, 19r, 54r, and 57r.

find one hand in particular making substantive revisions to Newcastle's writings. Rolleston's copy of the play *Wit's Triumvirate, or the Philosopher* (written 1634–1636)—a play recently attributed to Newcastle by Hilton Kelliher—displays, in addition to numerous revisions by Newcastle himself, a number of "cuts and additions, mainly to the final Act . . . in a small rounded hand that is also occasionally seen in the autograph drafts of verse preserved among the Portland manuscripts in Nottingham." As the play's editor observes, this is a "mixed" hand (combining italic and secretary forms), and it introduces several additions and rewrites. They are directed toward the enlivening of dull passages and the clearing up of dramaturgical problems (the latter not always successfully). The same hand is found performing similar work on Newcastle's Christmas masque of the mid- to late-1630s. And we find it undertaking major revisions to Newcastle's poem on the death of Jonson, "To Ben Jonson's Ghost" (after August 1637). Kelliher concludes his brief comments on the hand by noting that "so far it has eluded identification" and by proposing various professional playwrights of Newcastle's acquaintance as possible candidates. I believe, however, that the identity of the hand is to be found within the Welbeck household: I suggest that this small, rounded, mixed hand is that of Robert Payne.[19] Not only is it extremely similar to those undisputed examples of Payne's writing (it exhibits the same mixed cursive appearance; the right-handed slant; the long descenders; the open-shouldered *r;* the full-bodied letters; the open-bowled *a, o,* and *p;* and the mixture of Greek, reversed, two-stroke, and italic *e*), but its appearance in works of the mid-1630s also coincides exactly with Payne's sojourn at Welbeck (1632–1638). Our tendency to pigeonhole such figures by dint of modern disciplinary categories may make this chemical operator and translator appear an unlikely assistant on literary matters, but he was in fact the author of at least one surviving poem—a short epitaph for Queen Anne, published in 1619.[20]

The nature of Payne's work is nicely illustrated in the evolution of Newcastle's poem on his deceased client, Ben Jonson. The poem was first printed by

---

19. British Library, MS Additional 45865; Kelliher, "Donne, Jonson," 152; Cathryn Ann Nelson, ed., *A Critical Edition of "Wit's Triumvirate, or The Philosopher,"* 2 vols., *Salzburg Studies in English Literature: Jacobean Drama Studies,* 58, (Salzburg: Institut für Englische Sprache und Literatur, Universität Salzburg, 1975), 1:67–69; the hand is visible in the right margin of the facsimile reproduced on p. 79. Nelson labels it Hand 3. Regarding the Christmas masque, see Hulse, *Dramatic Works by Cavendish,* xxii, xxvi (pl. 4). Hulse labels it Hand C to distinguish it from the two other correcting hands she detects in these manuscripts. For a full discussion of Payne's hand, see Raylor, "Hobbes, Payne, and *A Short Tract.*"

20. Malcolm, *Correspondence of Hobbes,* 2:872.

Francis Needham in the *Welbeck Miscellany* of 1934, whence it was reprinted by Herford and the Simpsons in the Oxford *Ben Jonson* in 1952. Kelliher describes it as a private lamentation, but it might just have been intended for *Jonsonus Virbius*. Be that as it may, Needham prefaced his edition by noticing that "An autograph draft, with corrections partly in the author's and partly in an unrecognized hand, suggests that this poem was not Newcastle's unaided work," but discussion of the composition of the poem has not been taken further.[21] Let us look, then, at "To Ben Jonson's Ghost."

The poem exists in two versions: the first is a once neat working draft written by Newcastle on the recto of a single sheet (pl. 1). It is overscored by corrections, deletions, and insertions in his hand, and also in that of Payne, the latter being distinguishable with some ease because it uses a darker ink and a blunter nib. The second is Rolleston's clean and elegant transcript of the corrected text (pl. 2), written on the first recto of a bifolium containing two additional poems on Jonson's death by Newcastle and by William Alabaster—poems that have not, to my knowledge, ever been printed.[22]

If we peer beneath the surface of Payne's revisions, as I have tried to do in the first of my figures (fig. 1), the earliest version of the poem emerges as a fairly typical Newcastle production, replete with idiosyncratic orthography, redundant or vaporous phrasing, and lifeless syntax. Its governing conceit is that Jonson's death has robbed poetry of the only voice worthy enough to compose a funerary poem on his death: Poetry herself is dead. Newcastle makes one or two desultory attempts to bring this tedious poem to life: he tinkers with the opening in an effort to create some syntactic and semantic interest. The earliest version of the opening reads: "Ben I woulde write off thee, nott to Aproue / My witt, my Lerninge, Iudge-mente, butt my Loue." In his revision, Newcastle attempts to dispose of the plodding list of the second line by shifting the relationship of the intellectual qualities, creating the slightly more pointed and balanced "My Lerninge, witt, butt Iudge-mente & my Loue." And he fiddles with the final line in search of a conclusion that closes resoundingly without recourse to loud assertion or swearing: "Is any Infidell Lett him butt Looke / Ande he's conuerted by thy Glorius Booke" (ll. 19–20); "Is any Infidell Lett him butt Looke . . . / And I dare sweare thourte saued by thy booke" (ll. 19, 21). Not until the third try does he hit on the idea that the would-be convert might actually

---

21. Francis Needham, ed., *A Collection of Poems by Several Hands*, vol. 2 of *Welbeck Miscellany* (privately printed, 1934), 43; Herford, Simpson, and Simpson, *Ben Jonson*, 11:489; Kelliher, "Donne, Jonson," 158; Needham, *Welbeck Miscellany*, 42.

22. Hallward Library, University of Nottingham, PwV 25, fols. 23r, 25r.

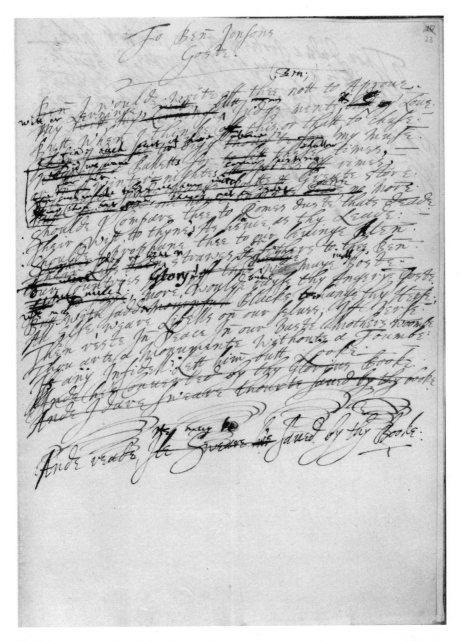

Plate 1
University of Nottingham MS PwV25, fol. 23r. Reproduced by permission
of the University of Nottingham, Department of Manuscripts

To Ben Jonson's Ghost.

I would write of Thee, Ben; not to approue
My witt or Learneing; but my Iudgment, Loue.
But when I thinke, or this, or that, to chuse;
Each part of Thee, is too big for my Muse.
Should I compare Thee to Romes dust, that's dead?
Their witt, to Trines as heauy as thy Lead:
Should I prophane Thee to our liueing Men?
Th'are light as strawes, and feathers to Thee, Ben.
Did wee want Ballads, for these shallow tymes,
Or, for our winter Nights, some sporting rhymes;
For such weake trifles, wee haue witts great store:
Now thou art gone, there's not a Pott more.
Our Countrey's Glory! Wee may iustly boast
Thus much; more would but raise thy angry Ghost.
Wee may with sadder blackes bthange thy hearse:
All els, were Libells on our selues, if verse.
Rest then, in Peace, in our vast Mothers wombe:
Thou art a Monument, wythout a Tombe:
Is any Infidell? Let nim but Looke,
And read, Hee may be saued by thy Booke.

Plate 2
University of Nottingham MS PwV25, fol. 25r. Reproduced by permission
of the University of Nottingham, Department of Manuscripts.

To Ben Ionsons
Goste:

_____

Ben I woulde write off thee, nott to Aproue._
My [witt,] ,Lerninge,. [my Lerninge], <witt,>, <butt>
    Iudge-mente, [butt] <&> my Loue._
Butt When I thinke off this, or thatt, to chuse._
Then I doe see to bigg though'te for my muse._
Weare Itt a Ballett for to fitt these times_   5
or In a winter's nighte att sportes off rimes
Wee coulde finde manye Poetts & Greate store._
Butt for a good one nowe thou arte [heare] <gone> no more._
Shoulde I compare thee to Romes duste thats deade._
Their Witt, to thyne As heuie, as thy Leade:_   10
Shoulde I prophane thee to our liuinge Men._
[Their Less] <Lighter> then strawes [&] <or> fethers to thee
    Ben._
Our Country'es ???? [off thee] <Iustlye>wee maye Boste..._
For to saye more, woulde rayse thy Angerye Goste._
Butt with sadd mournfull Blacks behange thy Herse;_   15
All else, weare Libells on our selues, Iff verse._
Then reste In Peace In our vaste mothers woombe
Thou arte a Monumente withoute a Toumbe:_
Is any Infidell Lett him butt Looke._
[Ande he's conuerted by thy Glorius Booke.]   20
[Ande I dare sweare thourte saued by thy booke.]

<Ande reade, Ile sweare he's saued by thy Booke:_>

Figure 1
William Cavendish, "To Ben Jonson's Ghost": authorial draft (with author's corrections)

Source: Hallward Library, University of Nottingham, PwV 25, fol. 23r
Notes: Square brackets enclose deletions; pointed brackets, insertions. Italicized queries represent unreadable letters. Otiose strokes over nasal consonants are not transcribed.

have to *read* Jonson's book in order to be saved by it: "Is any Infidell Lett him butt Looke . . . / And reade, Ile sweare he's saued by thy Booke" (ll. 19, 22).

Let us now turn to Payne's treatment of his patron's draft. His revisions are displayed in boldface in figure 2. He ranges widely over the text, making substantive alterations to its diction, syntax, and organization. In doing so, he repeatedly discovers the precise idea underlying Newcastle's fuzzy phrasing. Thus, for example, the vague claim that living poets are "Less then straws & fethers to thee Ben" becomes, in Payne's hands, the more precise assertion that "Theyre light as straws & feathers to thee Ben" (l. 12). He cuts needless huffing, such as Newcastle's "sadd mournfull Blacks," which he deftly reduces to "sadder Blacks" (l. 15). And he makes some effort to impose decorum on the earl's wayward language, bringing the inept and indecorous "Then I doe see too bigg though'te for my muse" within the bounds of propriety in "I finde each part of thee aboue my muse" (l. 4).

Less immediately obvious, but no less significant, are Payne's attempts to breathe life into the poem by giving balance, point, and edge to its variously clumsy and pedestrian syntax. By simply moving the name "Ben" from the start to the middle of the opening line, where it acts as a fulcrum between two unequal halves, Payne animates a plodding phrase by balancing its parts. That tension is heightened by a slight rearrangement of the relations between Newcastle's dull list of qualities in the next line. By simply removing an ampersand, Payne fundamentally alters the sense of the line, refiguring the relationship between judgment and love: the two are no longer opposed (as in Newcastle's first version) or aggregated (as in Newcastle's second); in Payne's revision, the latter becomes the product of the former.

One is repeatedly struck by how nimbly the secretary has managed to work within the framework imposed by his patron. In Payne's revisions of lines 5–8, the subjects, objects, and rhyme words are almost all that remain of the original. Newcastle's phrasing here is vague, windy, and redundant:

> Weare Itt a Ballett for to fitt these times.
> or In a winter's nighte att sportes off rimes
> Wee coulde finde manye Poetts & Greate store.
> Butt for a good one nowe thou arte heare no more.
>
>   (ll. 5–8)

Such loosely woven phrases are merely a gesture in the direction of poetry, sketched out with the clear expectation that someone would tidy them up: it is impossible to imagine that they were ever intended to stand thus. Payne

To Ben Ionsons
Goste:

I woulde write off thee **(Ben;)**, nott to Aproue._

My **witt or** Lerninge, butt [my] **my** Iudge-mente, [&] Loue._

Butt When I thinke or this, or thatt, to chuse._

I finde each part of thee aboue my muse._

{**Did we want** Balletts for **these shallow** times,_   5

{or **for our** winter=nightes, **some sporting** rimes,_

{**For such weake trifles wee haue wits** Greate store._

{**Now thou art gone there's not a Poet** more._

·Shoulde I compare thee to Romes duste thats deade._

·Their Witt, to thyne**'s** As heauie, as thy Leade:_   10

·Shoulde I prophane thee to our liuinge Men._

·**Theyre light as** straws & feathers to thee Ben._

Our Country'es **Glory! wee maye iustly** Boste.._

Thus much, more, woulde **but** rayse thy Angerye Goste._

We may with sadd**er Blacks** behange thy Herse;_   15

All else, weare Libells on our selues, Iff verse._

Then reste In Peace In our vaste mothers woombe

Thou arte a Monumente withoute a Toumbe:_

Is any Infidell? Lett him butt Looke._

Ande reade **He may be** saued by thy Booke:_   20

Figure 2
William Cavendish, "To Ben Jonson's Ghost": corrected authorial draft (with corrections by Robert Payne)

Source: Hallward Library, University of Nottingham, PwV 25, fol. 23r
Notes: Square brackets enclose deletions. Payne's corrections are registered in bold. Otiose strokes over nasal consonants are not transcribed.

manages this tidying with great efficiency and some flair. In the first couplet he provides a context for the ballads, clarifies the nature of the times and rhymes through the judicious insertion of adjectives, and establishes clear relationships among the various components of the verse by the addition of pronouns. He thoroughly rewrites the second couplet, removing the redundancy of "manye Poetts & Greate store" and adding point to the bland claim that as Jonson is gone there are no more good poets by establishing an antithesis between wits, who are plentiful, and poets, who are not. Payne's version of the lines runs:

> Did we wante Balletts for these shallow times,_
> or for our winter=nights, some sporting rimes,_
> For such weake trifles wee haue witts Greate store._
> Now thou art gone there's not a Poet more._
>
> (ll. 5–8)

Although not fine poetry, this is a remarkable improvement on Newcastle's draft. And one's admiration for the secretary's deftness and tact increases when one takes note of the constraint within which he clearly felt obliged to work. Payne's refusal to touch the rhyme words of his text reveals a reluctance to meddle too obviously, too noticeably, with the framework laid down by his patron. He is happy to make substantial alterations within a line, willing even to move couplets around freely (in the final version, the couplets here quoted are exchanged with the two that, in this version, follow), but he does not feel free to discard entirely a line of Newcastle's devising. One feels in consequence that there were clearly understood limits to the kinds of improvement Payne was expected to undertake.

Consistent with this attempt to work within the framework laid down by Newcastle is the fact that Payne undertakes only one major act of reorganization: the switching off of lines 5–8 and lines 9–12, as indicated on the corrected draft and carried out in the fair copy. The move connects two sets of couplets that operate in the first-person singular, thus allowing the opening section of the poem to take the form of a personal meditation prior to moving into the second-person plural that becomes its middle section. The change coincides with the reworking of lines 7–8 to give an illusion of logical and rhetorical development to an otherwise random series of apostrophes.

Neither this change nor the others discussed can ultimately save Newcastle's poem from failure, but they reveal much about the process of collaborative composition underlying it. Evidence for the dynamic character of this collabo-

To Ben: Ionson's Ghost.

I would write of Thee, Ben; not to approue
My witt or Learneing; but my Iudgment, Loue.
But when I thinke or this, or that, to chuse;
Each part of Thee, is too big for my Muse.
Should I compare Thee to Romes dust, that's dead?   5
Their witt, to Thine's as heauy as thy lead:
Should I prophane thee to our liueing Men?
Th'are light as strawes, and feathers to Thee, Ben.
Did wee want Ballads for these shallow tymes,
Or for our winter Nights, some sporting rhymes;   10
For such weake trifles, wee haue witts great store;
Now thou are gone, there's not a Poett more./
Our Country's Glory! Wee may iustly boast
Thus much; more would but raise thy angry Ghost.
Wee may with sadder blackes behange thy hearse;   15
All els, were Libells on our selues, if Verse.
Rest then, in Peace, in our vast Mothers wombe,
Thou art a Monument, without a Tombe.
      Is any Infidel? Let him but looke
And read, Hee may be saued by thy Booke.   20

Figure 3
William Cavendish, "To Ben Jonson's Ghost": scribal copy by John Rolleston

Source: Hallward Library, University of Nottingham, PwV 25, fol. 25r
Note: Substantive changes to corrected authorial draft are registered in bold.

ration appears in the final version of the poem (fig. 3). The most obvious changes in this version are to the accidentals, which Newcastle's secretary, Rolleston, has carefully regularized. There is, however, one substantive alteration, to the fourth line. It was originally the tasteless, "Then I doe see too bigg though'te for my muse," which Payne had recast as, "I finde each part of thee aboue my muse." In the final version, Payne's syntax is retained, but his delicate "aboue" is rejected in favor of "too big for"—a return to the coarser but more Jonsonian and therefore ultimately more decorous image of physical bulk.[23] But whether this represents a second thought by Payne or a reinsertion by Newcastle we do not know.

The division of labor between Newcastle's assistants in the Jonson poem points to a separation of secretarial responsibilities. Rolleston was responsible for ensuring the accuracy of his transcriptions and for regularizing Newcastle's highly eccentric orthography; he made no substantive alterations to the text he copied. Such improvements were the province of Payne, who was entrusted with a wide range of responsibilities, stretching from the regularization of spelling through the settling of rough-hewn lines, to the thorough reworking of sizable passages of awkward verse.

The general pattern of revision in the surviving literary manuscripts suggests that revisers such as Payne were called in to assist primarily with works intended for some kind of public appearance, whether dramatic performance or circulation beyond the household itself. A degree of caution is necessary in advancing such a claim: it may be that "To Ben Jonson's Ghost" was not intended for wide circulation. And the very concept of a public appearance may need to be interpreted rather broadly: it has been proposed that Newcastle's "Phanseys"—the love lyrics he sent to Margaret Lucas on something like a daily basis during his courtship of her in the 1640s—were similarly worked over by an assistant.[24]

This general pattern of revision is confirmed when we broaden our focus to include the dramatic works of Newcastle, most of which rely upon the paid assistance of professional dramatists. He regularly brought in professionals to give structure (particularly in respect to plots) to what were rough sketches or mere conceits for plays. We do not know how much Newcastle was responsible for the themes and formats of the Welbeck and Bolsover entertainments, but it is reasonable to posit some input on his behalf, particularly in respect to the underlying conceit of each. In fact, Jonson's slightly puzzling praise of Payne's friendship, fellowship, diligence, and judiciousness—praise that seems to gesture at something more substantial than the mere conveyance of a cash payment—may perhaps be explained in the context of our new understanding of the latter's involvement in Newcastle's literary projects. Is it not possible that

23. Compare *Vnder-Wood*, ix. 17, lii. 1–6, lvi. 9; Herford, Simpson, and Simpson, *Ben Jonson*, 8:150, 226–27, 230.

24. Doubts about their status were raised by Francis Needham, librarian of Welbeck Abbey and editor of several of Newcastle's works, in response to Norman Ault's printing of five poems from the sequence in his anthology, *Seventeenth-Century Lyrics* (London: Longman, 1928), 175–78: see William Cavendish, *A Pleasante & Merrye Humor off A Roge*, vol. 1 of *Welbeck Miscellany*, ed. Francis Needham (privately printed, 1933), vii.

Payne provided input on Newcastle's behalf as the housebound Jonson worked up the texts?[25] Few of us, however, would be willing to go as far down this road as James Fitzmaurice, who treats these entertainments as full-blown collaborations between poet and patron, with Newcastle providing the lion's share of their content and Jonson taking care of such technical matters as the fine-tuning of verse.[26]

About other dramatic collaborations we can generally speak with more confidence. Comparison of Newcastle's manuscript version of *The Country Captain* with the anonymously printed version of 1649 shows that James Shirley was brought in to take a rambling and weakly plotted draft, trim it, and then re-frame it as a subplot in an altogether new work. In the case of *The Triumphant Widow*, as Francis Needham and Lynn Hulse have shown, Shadwell fused to-gether two earlier works by Newcastle—the brief comedy "A Pleasante & mer-rye Humor off a roge" and "The King's Entertainment"—and on their basis cre-ated an entirely new play.[27] The nature of Shadwell's work on *The Humorous Lovers* has not been so certainly determined (a few of Newcastle's manuscript songs are pressed into service, but no draft for the play survives); we are prob-ably safe to assume that it was similar in kind to his efforts on *The Triumphant Widow*. Certainly, in 1677 the playwright received twenty-two pounds from the Newcastle family steward for seeing the two plays through the press.[28] Finally, the extent of Newcastle's contribution to *Sir Martin Mar-All* is a matter of de-bate. Geoffrey Trease, the duke's most recent biographer, follows Gerard Lang-baine in crediting him with only the idea of the play, assigning the writing of it wholly to Dryden. However, in the most substantial and authoritative exami-nation of the authorship of the play to date, the editors of the "California Dry-den" incline to the contemporary view, crisply recorded by Pepys, that the play was "made by my Lord Duke of Newcastle, but, as everyone says, corrected by Dryden." Be that as it may, Dryden clearly felt confident enough of his own con-tribution to claim the play as his own—though he did not do so until several years after Newcastle's death.[29]

25. Brown has already speculated along these lines ("Courtesies of Place," 166).

26. James Fitzmaurice, "William Cavendish and Two Entertainments by Ben Jonson," *Ben Jonson Journal* 5 (1998): 67–68.

27. Sandra A. Burner, *James Shirley: A Study of Literary Coteries and Patronage in Seven-teenth-Century England* (Lanham, Md.: University Press of America, 1988), 146–47, 167 n. 32; Cavendish, *A Pleasante*, v–vii; Hulse, "'The King's Entertainment' by the Duke of Newcastle," *Viator* 26 (1995): 375–83.

28. Hulse, *Dramatic Works by Cavendish*, vii–viii, xvi; Cavendish, *A Pleasante*, v.

29. Trease, *Portrait of a Cavalier*, 191; John Loftis and Vinton Dearing, eds., *The Works of John Dryden* (Berkeley: University of California Press, 1966), 9:353–64.

The kind of collaborative authorship we have witnessed at Welbeck does not fit snugly within the postromantic taxonomy of agents, editors, friends, publishers, readers, sources, and spouses laid out by Jack Stillinger in the major study of this subject. We need to search for Renaissance terms in order to account for such practices. The contributions of Newcastle's assistants amount to more than merely scribal regularization of spelling and grammar, and to less than the kind of joint authorship we find in the collaborations among social equals. They involve the fleshing out and tidying up of drafts, through the settling of problems of diction, syntax, and organization that Newcastle, with aristocratic indifference, felt it beneath his dignity to resolve.[30] We are dealing with a division of labor that can partly be understood in rhetorical terms by distinguishing invention from elocution and disposition: by separating the idea or governing conceit of a work from its style, its diction, and, to some extent, its organization. This division is a natural one for the early modern period: we find it invoked, for instance, in regard to the distribution of responsibility for masques and pageants, the published texts of which are not infrequently advertised as "invented by X; written by Y."[31] But these distinctions are encountered in collaborations where the question of priority was a sensitive one; in cases of collaboration among Newcastle and members of his household and his clients such questions did not arise. It will be more helpful for our purposes to turn from literature to science, setting this rhetorical distinction in the context of the contemporary organization of scientific research.

Contemporary scientific practice relied heavily, as Steven Shapin has shown us, upon the labor of "invisible assistants": they bought supplies, organized laboratories, conducted experiments in them, and wrote up experimental narratives that were then circulated under the names of gentlemanly patrons. In this system, a gentleman was not required to master the actual technologies required to perform his experiments, nor was his direct involvement in any stage of the experimental process required. As Thomas Sprat explained in his *History of the Royal Society,* there was a clear distinction between dignified gentlemanly invention and merely mechanical skill; indeed, an advantage lay in not being too weighed down with the latter. "There is some privilege," wrote Sprat, "to be allow'd to the *generosity* of their *spirits,* which have not bin subdu'd, and

30. Stillinger, *Multiple Authorship and the Myth of Solitary Genius* (Oxford: Oxford University Press, 1991); Douglas Grant, ed., *The Phanseys of William Cavendish, Marquis of Newcastle* (London: Nonesuch, 1956), xxi–xxii.

31. D. J. Gordon, *The Renaissance Imagination,* ed. Stephen Orgel (Berkeley: University of California Press, 1975), 80–85, 269–71.

clogg'd by any constant *toyl*, as the others. *Invention* is an *Heroic* thing, and plac'd above the reach of a low, and vulgar *Genius*."[32] It is this distinction between noble invention and mechanical execution that best accounts for the roles played by invisible assistants in the composition of Newcastle's works. In the language of modern publishing, Robert Payne is Newcastle's "ghost."

It would be nice to leave the matter here, with this tidy distinction between invention and execution in place. But there is still another species of collaboration discernible in the poetic and dramatic works of Newcastle that demands our attention both because it undermines this distinction and because, in doing so, it offers further evidence for my contention that relations among the Cavendish brothers and their associates are best understood in terms of patronage. The alert reader will have noticed that, in addition to Payne and Rolleston, a third assistant is at work on "To Ben Jonson's Ghost": Ben Jonson's ghost itself. Not only does Newcastle lift an entire line from Jonson's poem to the memory of Shakespeare—Jonson's "Thou art a Moniment, without a tombe" (l. 22) appears verbatim as Newcastle's line 18—but he also borrows from it his founding conceit: the notion that Jonson is beyond the praise of living poets. Newcastle's lines "Butt When I thinke off this, or thatt, to chuse / Then I doe see too bigg though'te for my muse" (fig. 1, ll. 3–4) rely upon Jonson's "I confesse thy writings to be such, / As neither *Man*, nor *Muse*, can praise too much" (ll. 3–4).[33] From the perspective of elegiac decorum, such borrowings may be defended as an apt compliment to the dead poet. But there is another angle for evaluating them.

Struggling through the vast stretches of Newcastle's literary oeuvre one is struck, time and again, by his habitual, promiscuous reliance upon Jonsonian themes, phrases, and plots. A charitable reader might argue that Newcastle is here practicing the time-honored technique of imitation, but there is a difference between imitation and copying, between adopting the spirit or form of a work for present purposes and merely plundering it for details. It is the latter we frequently find in Newcastle. There are many local borrowings, such as the use of "To Penshurst"'s "The purpled pheasant, with the speckled side: / The painted partrich" (ll. 28–29) in this line from an incomplete pastoral entertainment: "The Paynted Phesante, with the spekelde side" (l. 185). One could

---

32. Sprat, *History of the Royal Society,* ed. Jackson I. Cope and Harold Whitmore Jones (St. Louis: Washington University Press; London: Routledge, 1958), 392; quoted in Steven Shapin, *A Social History of Truth: Civility and Science in Seventeenth-Century England* (Chicago: University of Chicago Press, 1994), 397.

33. Herford, Simpson, and Simpson, *Ben Jonson,* 8:390–92.

try to defend this as an allusion, but nothing in the context suggests that anything so explicit is intended. More telling in this respect is Newcastle's reliance
on the crutches provided by Jonsonian conceits and Jonsonian plots. For his
Christmas masque of the mid-1630s, for example, Newcastle models his anti-
masque tradesmen on the builders of Jonson's Bolsover entertainment; in writing "The King's Entertainment" he copies the comic Welshmen of Jonson's *For
the Honour of Wales* (1618); and in writing *Wit's Triumvirate* he relies almost exclusively upon the conceit and plot structure of *The Alchemist*, diverging from it
only when he is able to turn to other plays for structural support—as in his use
of the old trick of changing the clothes of a drunken man while he sleeps, employed in *The Taming of the Shrew* and more recently in Henry Glapthorne's *Lady
Mother* (licensed in 1635).[34] Jonsonian conceits and plots repeatedly provide
the structural foundations and scaffolding for Newcastle's own inventions,
which are frequently excursions on Jonsonian ideas. This is not imitation; it is
appropriation. Indeed, the brazen manner in which Newcastle takes over Jonson's texts forces one to wonder whether his support of the poet during the late
lean years did not, in his view, give him some kind of proprietary rights over
the whole of Jonson's canon.

Appropriations of this kind, whether of dead poets or live assistants, provide
further evidence that the so-called Cavendish, Newcastle, or Welbeck circle is
really best understood as an extension of the aristocratic household. This is not
to suggest that all literary circles in Renaissance England must be similarly dissolved; it is merely to argue for the value of attending to the three-dimensional aspect of a particular group before reaching for that handy catchall, the idea
of the circle.

---

34. On imitation, see Fitzmaurice, "William Cavendish," 64; see M. H. Abrams, *A
Glossary of Literary Terms*, 6th ed. (New York: Harcourt Brace Jovanovich, 1993), 89.
Quotes are in Herford, Simpson, and Simpson, *Ben Jonson*, 8:94; and Hulse, *Dramatic
Works by Cavendish*, 53. On the Christmas masque, see Hulse, *Dramatic Works by
Cavendish*, xi; Hulse, "'The King's Entertainment,'" 372; Nelson, *Critical Edition of "Wit's
Triumvirate*," 1:1–25

Paul A. Parrish

Reading Poets Reading Poets

Herbert and Crashaw's Literary Ellipse

"Poetry was very much in the air," observes Graham Chainey of Cambridge in the 1630s and 1640s. And indeed it was. Poetry was the usual, sometimes the official, mode of expression and response—to a royal visit, to an important birth, death, wedding, or other important occasion—or, in another vein, an opportunity for an individual writer to make his mark, announce his arrival among the literarily accomplished. Although the wisdom of appearing in print was not without its naysayers and skeptics, the early publications of Abraham Cowley and Richard Crashaw—their *Poetical Blossomes* (1633 and 1636) and *Epigrammatum Sacrorum Liber* (1634), respectively—were designed in part to identify each as a poet worthy of having his writings made more widely available to others. Broader evidence of the extent of poetic expression at Cambridge in the years leading up to the intrusion by parliamentary forces is found in the numerous poetic collections emanating from the university and in the number of students and fellows who contributed to those volumes. At Peterhouse alone, nearly twenty different students, fellows, or masters contributed to as many as seven different university collections, including the commemorative volume on Edward King to which Milton contributed his "Lycidas."[1]

To write verse is not, of course, necessarily to be a poet, but it is useful to recall that the Cambridge community can claim Herbert, Crashaw, Cowley, Joseph Beaumont, John Cleveland, Francis Quarles, Henry More, and others—

---

1. Chainey, *A Literary History of Cambridge*, rev. ed. (Cambridge: Cambridge University Press, 1995), 49. See Thomas A. Walker, *A Peterhouse Bibliography* (Cambridge: Cambridge University Press, 1936), for a listing of Peterhouse students and fellows, including a brief record of their writings. A number of the Peterhouse men who contributed to university collections were ejected from their fellowships in 1643–1645. See John Twigg, *The University of Cambridge and the English Revolution, 1625–1688* (Woodbridge: Boydell Press, Cambridge University Library, 1990), 294–95.

not to mention Milton—as students, fellows, or university officials from, say, 1625 to 1645, and each might appropriately be designated a "poet."[2] In the broadest sense, therefore, there existed at Cambridge an environment conducive to poetry, an environment in which poetry was not only "in the air" but also manifested in some significant and enduring examples.

My interests here are at once grounded in a view of a vital literary community in and around Cambridge and more narrowly focused. I believe there existed in the Cambridge environs—and I use this term in part to acknowledge the continuing influence of Herbert, if not his actual residency, in the Cambridge community, and in part to encompass the involvement of Nicholas Ferrar and the community of Little Gidding near Cambridge—not so much a literary circle as a literary ellipse, with the two foci being Herbert and Crashaw. Against these central figures—especially Herbert—a number of poets measure their art, and to them several of their contemporaries, notably Ferrar, Beaumont, and Cowley, respond in specific and revealing ways.

Having advanced the figure of the ellipse I am prepared, at the outset, to acknowledge its limitations. Of the two writers I nominate as the foci, Herbert is the more important and lasting influence on a greater number of writers. There may even be, as Stanley Stewart has argued, a "School of Herbert" in which Crashaw is one of the more important students.[3] Nonetheless, I will argue that, if only briefly, the positions of Herbert and Crashaw were regarded with equal attention by a few. Nicholas Ferrar and Joseph Beaumont reinforce the implications of the image most readily, as each responds to Herbert and Crashaw with what appear to be equal measures of recognition and appreciation. With Cowley the relationships are more complex. A friend and admirer of Crashaw and the author of the most important elegiac tribute to him, Cowley also acknowledges the superiority of devotional poetry, the prime original of which at this time was Herbert. Cowley, however, very much goes his own way, honoring the two "poets and saints" who preceded him but demonstrating in his own writings a breadth of interest in both secular and religious affairs that is not evident in either Herbert or Crashaw.

---

2. To cite one indicator only, in the *Concise Dictionary of National Biography* each of them is so identified, either by being nominated a "poet" or by having his verse noted for specific comment.

3. Stewart discusses in *George Herbert* (Boston: G. K. Hall, 1986, esp. 118–56) a "School of Herbert" that included somewhat slavish imitators such as Christopher Harvey (*The Synagogue; or, The Shadow of the Temple: Sacred Poets and Private Ejaculations: In Imitation of Mr. George Herbert* [1640]) and Ralph Knevet (*A Gallery to the Temple*), as well as more independent figures such as Crashaw, Vaughan, and Traherne.

The personal associations among Herbert, Ferrar, Crashaw, Beaumont, and Cowley are suggestive and intriguing, and since they figure importantly in the discussion that follows, I will outline them here. The friendship of Herbert and Ferrar probably began during their Cambridge years and had certainly become important for each by the late 1620s. When he realized that his own death was imminent, Herbert saw to it that his papers, including the manuscript of what would become *The Temple*, were left in the hands of Ferrar and Arthur Woodnoth, Ferrar's cousin, and Ferrar was soon busily involved in shepherding the poems through publication and contributing the preface to the reader in the 1633 edition. Although it is unlikely that Crashaw and Herbert were personally acquainted, Crashaw's poetic interest in Herbert has long been established, as seen in the title of his first published volume of poems (apart from the epigrams), *Steps to the Temple*, and in his poem "On Mr. G. Herberts booke intituled the Temple of Sacred Poems, sent to a Gentlewoman." Equally certain is Crashaw's attachment to Ferrar and the Little Gidding community. It is possible that Crashaw and Ferrar first became acquainted in London, before each settled in and around Cambridge; it is more likely that Crashaw established a relationship with Ferrar and Little Gidding after he matriculated at Cambridge in 1631, by which time the community had been functioning for some five years. Contemporary accounts cite Crashaw's visits to Little Gidding, his poem "Description of a Religious House" is likely written with Little Gidding in mind, and we have certain evidence that, after Nicholas's death, Crashaw maintained and perhaps strengthened his associations with the Ferrar and Collet families.[4] Joseph Beaumont was a friend of Crashaw at Peterhouse and a fellow of the college; they are identified together by Puritan authorities, both because of the "popish" theology and ceremonies they are accused of endorsing and because they are among five fellows cited for ejection on April 8, 1644.[5] Moreover, Beaumont is the likely author of the preface to the 1646 *Steps to the Temple* (he eas-

---

4. I am thinking in particular of Crashaw's letter from Leyden in which he wrote, possibly to a member of the Little Gidding community, possibly to Joseph Beaumont, of the "mother" of Little Gidding, Mary Collet, whose intimacy and influence he obviously felt very deeply. See L. C. Martin, ed., *The Poems English, Latin, and Greek of Richard Crashaw*, 2d ed. (Oxford: Clarendon Press, 1957), xxvii–xxxi; and Paul A. Parrish, "Richard Crashaw, Mary Collet, and the Arminian Nunnery of Little Gidding," in *Representing Women in Renaissance England*, ed. Claude J. Summers and Ted-Larry Pebworth (Columbia: University of Missouri Press, 1997), 187–200. I use Martin's edition in my citations from Crashaw's poetry and from the "Preface to the Reader."

5. For further discussion of the issues and incidents surrounding the ejections, see Allan Pritchard, "Puritan Charges against Crashaw and Beaumont," *TLS* (July 2, 1964): 578.

ily qualifies as "The Authors friend"), and he is the certain author of verses explicitly paying tribute to both Herbert and Crashaw. The friendship and the artistic relationship of Crashaw and Cowley are confirmed by their acquaintance both at Cambridge and, later, in Paris, by their jointly written poem "On Hope," by Crashaw's tribute to Cowley in "Upon two greene Apricockes sent to Cowley by Sir Crashaw," and, especially, by Cowley's impressive elegy on his friend, "On the Death of Mr. Crashaw." That poem also indicates, if it does not make explicit, Cowley's familiarity with and attention to Herbert's poetic legacy.

I want to move from these biographical connections to look more closely at the occasions when these five—Herbert, Ferrar, Crashaw, Beaumont, and Cowley—wrote to or about each other, in letters, prefaces, and poems. There emerges, I believe, a revealing set of literary relationships and interactions, one in which Herbert and Crashaw are dominant and inescapable forces, engaging others in sometimes similar, sometimes different ways.

During his first year at Cambridge, in 1609–1610, Herbert wrote to his mother, commenting on the effects of a recent illness on his poetic efforts but also confirming that he seeks not the inspiration of the Muses, but the divine inspiration of God:

> I fear the heat of my late *Ague* hath dryed up those springs, by which Scholars say, the Muses use to take up their habitations. However, I need not their help, to reprove the vanity of those many Love-poems, that are daily writ and consecrated to *Venus;* nor to bewail that so few are writ, that look towards *God* and *Heaven.* For my own part, my meaning . . . is in these Sonnets, to declare my resolution to be, that my poor Abilities in *Poetry*, shall be all, and ever consecrated to Gods glory.[6]

The record of Herbert's poetry testifies to his having maintained this commitment to shun the temptations of secular poetry in favor of making his poems "ever consecrated to Gods glory." When, more than twenty years later, Ferrar saw *The Temple* through to publication, he commented with equal precision about what Herbert's verse is and is not. Ferrar stresses the singularly sacred quality of the poems assembled and explicitly separates Herbert's sacred muse from the more worldly inspiration that marks efforts of his predecessors and contemporaries. Herbert, we are told, has dedicated his poetry "to the *Divine Majestie*," and beyond that, little need be said or added to what the life and the poetry themselves reveal. "How should we now presume to interest any mor-

6. F. E. Hutchinson, ed., *The Works of George Herbert* (Oxford: Clarendon Press, 1941), 363.

tall man in the patronage of it?" Ferrar asks. "Much lesse think we it meet to seek the recommendation of the Muses, for that which himself was confident to have been inspired by a diviner breath then flows from *Helicon*. The world therefore shall receive it in that naked simplicitie, with which he left it, without any addition either of support or ornament, more then is included in it self." Ferrar's comments on Herbert's life complement his view of his art, as he observes that having quitted "both his deserts and all the opportunities that he had for worldly preferment, he betook himself to the Sanctuarie and Temple of God, choosing rather to serve at God's Altar, then to seek the honour of State-employments."[7]

The statement of purpose Herbert announces to his mother, which Ferrar in turn confirms through Herbert's poetry and his life, becomes a kind of touch-stone for later writers, pointing to their kinship with, and occasional departure from, the compelling example of poetry written with a "diviner breath."

Whether Crashaw's *Steps to the Temple* is an authorial title we cannot be sure, but it substantiates that either Crashaw or the friend—I believe it is Beau-mont—who helped arrange for the publication during Crashaw's absence in Paris saw Crashaw as a fitting follower of Herbert.[8] Crashaw's poem about *The Temple* makes even more explicit this identification of the two. To the "Gentle-woman" to whom the poems are sent, he says,

> And though *Herberts* name doe owe
> These devotions, fairest; know
> That while I lay them on the shrine
> Of your white hand, they are mine.
>   (ll. 15–18)

When we read Beaumont's "Preface to the Reader," however, a more subtle portrait of Herbert and Crashaw emerges, one that I want to relate to two important facets of the Little Gidding community to which each was committed. On the one hand, the religious community of Little Gidding emphasized the necessity of private devotions. Contemporary accounts and the numerous biographies of Nicholas confirm the importance of regular and frequent devotions, of nightly vigils, of the practice of private readings and meditations. In these practices one easily imagines Herbert and Ferrar finding meaningful ac-

7. Ibid., 3.
8. See the discussion of Elsie Duncan-Jones, "Who Was the Recipient of Crashaw's Leyden Letter?" in *New Perspectives on the Life and Art of Richard Crashaw*, ed. John R. Roberts (Columbia: University of Missouri Press, 1990), 174–79.

cord and responding with mutual admiration and influence. But Little Gidding was also a community that valued a more public expression of worship, and the family invested both time and resources into transforming the church, which had fallen into disrepair prior to the family's purchase of the property, into a modest but elegant site for worship in a Laudian mode. Peter Peckard, Nicholas Ferrar's early biographer, describes the "new font" that was brought in, "the leg, laver, and cover all of brass, handsomely and expensively wrought and carved," and he further describes the "blue taffety, and cushions of the finest tapestry and blue silk," and other costly items that were placed on the Communion table.[9] There is at Little Gidding, in short, both the simplicity of personal and private devotions and the beauty of worship with appropriate and expensive accoutrements. The one, I would argue, had greatest appeal to and influence on Herbert, the other the greatest attraction to and effect on Crashaw.

Beaumont's "Preface to the Reader" calls immediate attention to the different quality of Crashaw's verse while also stressing that it is rooted in the devotional aim that also characterizes Herbert's work. *"Here's Herbert's second, but equall,"* he affirms, *"who hath retriv'd Poetry of late, and return'd it up to its Primitive use."* The ambiguous antecedent of *"who"*—is it Herbert or Crashaw who has restored poetry "to its Primitive use"?—may not be intentional, but it is fitting, for indeed both are committed to a sacred, not secular, art. But it is also a commitment with a difference. One cannot imagine Beaumont saying of Herbert, as he does of Crashaw, that his poems *"shal lift thee Reader, some yards above the ground. . . . So maist thou take a Poem hence, and tune thy soule by it, into a heavenly pitch; and thus refined and borne up upon the wings of meditation, in these Poems thou maist talke freely of God, and of that other state."* Beaumont does, nonetheless, reinforce the theme suggested in the prefatory material to *The Temple* and confirmed throughout Herbert's verse (one thinks of the Jordan poems, for example): the superiority of divine poetry over its secular counterparts. *"Think yee,"* Beaumont asks, *"St. Augustine would have steyned his graver Learning with a booke of Poetry, had he fancied their dearest end to be the vanity of Love-Sonnets, and Epithalamiums? No, no, he thought with this, our Poet, that every foot in a high-borne verse, might helpe to measure the soule into that better world: Divine Poetry."* Beaumont proceeds to contrast this *"Language of the Angels,"* this *"Quintessence of Phantasie and discourse center'd in Heaven,"* with *"those under-headed*

9. Peckard, *A Life of Nicholas Ferrar* (London: Joseph Masters, 1852), 108–9.

Poets, Retainers to seven shares and a halfe; Madrigall fellowes, whose onely businesse in verse, is to rime a poore six-penny soule, a Subburb sinner into hell." "*[O]ur Poet,"* Beaumont confidently asserts, will in the "*general arraignment of Poets*" be able to "*looke downe upon poore*" Homer, Virgil, Horace, and others.[10]

A final point to be made about the preface is that it at least hints at Beaumont's association of Crashaw with Herbert and his distinctive claims for the younger poet. When he specifically mentions the "*aptly*" styled title of the collection, Beaumont in fact says nothing about Herbert but rather focuses on Crashaw's service at Little St. Mary's Church near Peterhouse. "*There,*" he says, "*he penned these Poems,* Stepps *for happy soules to climbe heaven by.*"

Beaumont's poetic tributes to Herbert and Crashaw can be found in his *Psyche,* and both they and Beaumont's verse taken as a whole reveal his recognition of and indebtedness to each. If on a personal level Ferrar may be arguably equally close to Herbert and Crashaw (though, as I have suggested, for somewhat different reasons), on an artistic level Beaumont is a descendant of each. He is, to cite the ellipse again, on the circumference of the figure, sometimes writing in the mode of Herbert, sometimes clearly emulating Crashaw, but often seemingly equidistant between the two, producing verse that bears the marks of the influence of each.[11]

Beaumont's preface to the first edition of *Psyche* (1648) recalls his preface, written only two years earlier, to Crashaw's *Steps.* After explaining briefly what *Psyche* is about and why he chose to write the poem, he addresses the matter of

10. Having decried secular verse, it would appear that Beaumont, unlike Ferrar in *The Temple,* does have to account for the fact that there is in the volume he is introducing both sacred and secular verse, the latter headed *The Delights of the Muses.* Beaumont does so briefly, almost offhandedly, saying simply: "And those other of his pieces intitaled, The Delights of the Muses, (though of a more humane mixture) are as sweet as they are innocent." In the first edition of *Steps* (1646), a printing error requires one other acknowledgment of the secular poems. Before the first poem in the volume ("The Weeper") there is this apology and explanation: "Reader, there was a sudden mistake ('tis too late to recover it) thou wilt quickly find it out, and I hope as soone passe it over, some of the humane Poems [that is, secular verse such as "Loves Horoscope," "To the Morning. Satisfaction for sleepe," and others] are misplaced amongst the Divine." In the second (1648) and subsequent editions, the "offending" poems are placed where they belong, and the apology is omitted.

11. A full reading of Beaumont's shorter lyric poems confirms, I believe, the presence of poems clearly reminiscent, both in content and in title, of Herbert, along with others that bear equal evidence of the influence of Crashaw. I have explored these issues in "Ravishing Embraces and Sober Minds: The Poetry of Joseph Beaumont," in *Discovering and (Re)Covering the Seventeenth-Century Religious Lyric,* ed. Eugene Cunnar and Jeffrey Johnson (Pittsburgh: Duquesne University Press, forthcoming). See also Eloise Robinson, ed., *The Minor Poems of Joseph Beaumont, D.D.* (London: Constable, 1914), xxviii–xliii.

divine verse.[12] Revealingly, he does so with an apparent lack of confidence in readers, especially readers who are capable of being attentive to a persistently sacred intent:

> I am not ignorant, that very few Men are competent Readers of *Poems,* the true *Genius* of *Poetrie* being little regarded, or rather not subject at all to common Capacities: so that a discourse upon this Theam would bee to smal purpose. I know also, how little Prefacing Apologies use to be credited: Wherefore, though I had much (very much) to say, and justly, in this kinde, I will venture to cast my self upon thy Ingenuitie, with this onely Protestation, that *If any thing throughout this whol* Poem, *happen [against my intention] to prove Discord to the Concent of Christs Catholicke Church, I here Recant it aforehand.*

In spite of these stated reservations, Beaumont announces his hope that his book may "prompt *better Wits* to believe, that a *Divine Theam* is as capable and happy a Subject of *Poetical Ornament,* as any *Pagan* or *Humane Device* whatsoever." With this "Divine Theam" comes, as it does with Herbert and Crashaw, a devotional intent. If his readers come to appreciate verse with a divine theme and, moreover, are led "into any *true degree* of *Devotion,* I shall," concludes Beaumont, "be bold to hope that I have partly reached my *proposed Mark,* and not continued *meerly Idle.*"[13]

Within his long poem—perhaps the longest poem in the English language—Beaumont cites the accomplishments of Herbert and Crashaw, among others. His several stanzas about Crashaw appear in 1648, but the stanza about Herbert does not appear until 1702 in a posthumous edition. Although we need not conclude that the added verse about Herbert amounts to a poetic afterthought, the occasions of the two tributes suggest a greater degree of immediacy and intimacy with Crashaw's life and art.

In canto 4, which includes his observations on both ancient and contemporary poets, Beaumont calls attention to the writings of Pindar and Horace,

---

12. In fact, Beaumont wrote *Psyche* and most of his other poems after he, like Crashaw and many others, had been ejected from his fellowship at Peterhouse. He alludes to this context in the opening of "The Author to the Reader": "The Turbulence of these Times having deprived mee of my wonted Accommodations of Study; I deliberated, *For the avoyding of meer Idlenesse,* what Task I might safelyest presume upon, without the Society of Books: And concluded upon Composing this *Poem.* In which I endeavor to represent a *Soule* led by divine *Grace,* and her *Guardian Angel,* (in fervent *Devotion*)" (*Psyche: or Loves Mysterie in XX Canto's: Displaying the Intercourse Betwixt Christ, and the Soule* [London: printed by John Dawson for George Boddington, 1648], sig. A4r).

13. Ibid.

and then opens the way for Herbert (st. 102). As we would expect, Beaumont announces Herbert's aims as different, for he works in "holier moulds":

> Yet neither of their Empires was so vast
> But they left *Herbert* too full room to reign,
> Who Lyric's pure and precious Metal cast
> In holier moulds, and nobly durst maintain
> > *Devotion in Verse,* whilst by the spheres
> > He tunes his Lute, and plays to heav'nly ears.[14]
> > > > (st. 102)

Beaumont's verses about Crashaw (sts. 94–95 [1648 ed.]) suggest that he also plays to "heav'nly ears," and the lines have a more deeply felt and more personal quality than those on Herbert. Beaumont sees Crashaw as one who follows the pattern of Gregory of Nazianzum. What Beaumont sees in Gregory's verse is perfectly in tune with how Crashaw's poetry is characterized in the preface to *Steps to the Temple.* Other literary ancestors, among them Homer and Tasso, are first mentioned, but superior to each of these is Gregory, "whose Heav'n-tuned soul did sweetly soar / Unto the top of every stage and story / Of Poetry; through which, as hee did pass, / He all the *Muses* made *Urania's*" (st. 93). The two stanzas on Crashaw follow, and reveal the close personal relationship of author and subject as much as the important artistic connection:

> And by this soul-attracting Pattern, *Thou,*
> *My onely worthy self,* thy Songs didst frame:
> Witnesse those polish'd *Temple-Steps,* which now
> Whether thou wilt or no, this Truth proclaim,
> > And, spight of all thy Travels, make't appear
> > Th'art more in *England,* than when thou wert here.
>
> More unto Others; but not so to Me
> Of old acquainted with thy secret worth:
> What half-lost I endure for want of Thee
> The World will read in this mis-shapen *Birth:*
> > Fair had my *Psyche* been, had she at first
> > By thy kinde-censuring hand been dress'd and nurst.
> > > > (sts. 94–95)

All evidence suggests that, among poets at Cambridge, Crashaw's two closest friends were Beaumont and Cowley. In Beaumont, as I have indicated, he

14. *Psyche,* 2d ed. with "Corrections throughout, and Four new Cantos, never before Printed" (Cambridge: printed at the University Press, for Tho. Bennet, 1702).

found someone of similar temperament and religious sensibilities, albeit one whose poetic talents were clearly less impressive. With Cowley, the artistic relationship is similarly avowed but is also more problematic. Crashaw's tribute to Cowley's precocious talent in his "Upon two greene Apricockes sent to Cowley by Sir Crashaw" and their joint effort in the poem "On Hope" confirm their close relationship, as does evidence that when Crashaw was down and out in Paris, Cowley came to his assistance. But the poem on hope suggests divergence more than convergence, as the two poets take a topic and address it in two different ways, not so much answering each other as speaking on two different planes. This suggestion of difference within a context of interaction and appreciation is further implied in Cowley's preface to his 1656 poems and made explicit in his elegy "On the Death of Mr. Crashaw." In each of these instances—the poem on hope, his prefatory comments to his own poems, his poetic tribute to Crashaw—Cowley breaks the mold of sacred verse, acknowledging it, appreciating it, even elevating it, but not being limited by it.

In some respects the poet of the 1656 poems is not so different from the young author of *Poeticall Blossomes*, first published some twenty-three years earlier when Cowley was only fifteen. In the preface to the second edition of *Poeticall Blossomes* (1636), Cowley admits that some objected to the first edition either because of his age or because they thought he should have written anonymously. Not to be deterred, the young Cowley says that "the itch of Poesie by being angered encreaseth, by rubbing, spreads farther; which appeares in that I have ventured upon this second Edition." If you want to use it to light tobacco or as wrapping paper for cooks and grocers, he says to a skeptical reader, go ahead; it will not be the first time the pages of a book were used in that way: nonetheless, "it shall something content mee, that it hath pleased My selfe and the Bookseller."[15] The more mature Cowley is no less forthright about his intentions. Acknowledging that works are more typically published posthumously, he says he has determined "to produce these *Poems* to the light and view of the World; not as a thing that I approved of in it self, but as a lesser evil, which I chose rather then to stay till it were done for me by some body else, either surreptitiously before, or avowedly after my death."[16]

The conclusion of this lengthy preface—more than thirteen pages—finds Cowley addressing the central theme that takes us back to *The Temple:* the worth

15. Cowley, *Poeticall Blossomes by A. C.*, 2d ed. (London: printed by E. P. for Henry Seile, 1636), sigs. A3v–A4r.
16. *Poems . . . written by A. Cowley* (London: printed for Humphrey Moseley, 1656), sig. (a)2r.

of sacred verse relative to secular poetry. Beaumont had acknowledged Crashaw's secular poetry in *Steps to the Temple*, but did so briefly, almost so a reader might not notice. Cowley's secular poetry is much more prominent, and he does not shrink from commenting on it and its value. His approach grows out of the arrangement of the contents of the collection, as the four parts are, successively, "Miscellanies" (including the elegy on Crashaw), "The Mistress, or, Love Verses" (including the poem[s] on hope), "Pindarique Odes," and "Davideis, or, a Sacred Poem of the Troubles of David." Cowley's aim in his preface is in part to repeat what we have read in other comments, that sacred verse is inherently superior to all other forms, and indeed this final section begins much as we might expect: "What can we imagine more proper for the ornaments of *Wit* or *Learning* in the story of *Deucalion*, then in that of *Noah*? why will not the actions of *Sampson* afford as plentiful matter as the *Labors of Hercules*? . . . what do I instance in these few particulars? All the *Books* of the *Bible* are either already most admirable, and exalted pieces of *Poesie*, or are the best *Materials* in the world for it."[17]

Cowley, however, follows this by-now conventional claim with an important "Yet," and in that "Yet" he argues the value of secular ("prophane") verse:

> Yet, though they be in themselves so proper to be made use of for this purpose; None but a good *Artist* will know how to do it: neither must we think to cut and polish *Diamonds* with so little pains and skill as we do *Marble*. For if any man design to compose a *Sacred Poem*, by onely turning a story of the *Scripture*, like Mr. *Quarles*'s, or some other godly matter, like Mr. *Heywood of Angels*, into *Rhyme*; He is so far from elevating of *Poesie*, that he onely *abases Divinity*. In brief, he who can write a *prophane Poem well*, may write a *Divine one better*; but he who can do that but ill, will do this much worse. The same fertility of *Invention*, the same wisdom of *Disposition*; the same *Judgement* in observance of *Decencies*, the same lustre and vigor of *Elocution*; the same modesty and majestie of *Number*; briefly the same kinde of *Habit*, is required to both; only this latter allows better *stuff* and therefore would look more deformedly, if *ill drest* in it.[18]

Within the contexts I have tried to establish in this essay, Cowley's elegy on his friend, the "poet and saint" Richard Crashaw, seems to me very much a piece with his preface to his own poems. In terms of its representations of the deceased poet and those left alive, the elegy can, certainly, be regarded as largely

17. Ibid., sig. (b)3r.
18. Ibid., sig. (b)3r–v.

conventional: the dead poet is elevated above those left to celebrate him; his verse soars with a "spotless *Muse*," while mere mortals, the "wretched *We, Poets of Earth*" (ll. 29, 9), are left to deal with worldly challenges posed by *"Chance," "Envy," "Ignorance," "Beauty,"* and *"Desires"* (ll. 61–63). Beyond the convention, however, is a more telling recognition of two poetic worlds, the sacred and the secular: to the one, Cowley says, Crashaw was fully devoted; to the other, Cowley acknowledges, he is at least partly bound. Crashaw's otherworldly spirit is identified and reiterated throughout the poem: he was on earth "the same *Poet* which thou'rt *Now*" (l. 10), in both roles providing music fit for angels:

> Whilst *Angels* sing to thee their ayres divine,
> And joy in an applause so great as *thine.*
> Equal society with them to hold,
> Thou need'st not make *new Songs,* but say the *Old.*
> (ll. 11–14)

The ending lines of the poem bring us back to the duality announced at the beginning: the sacred muse of the *"Bard Triumphant"* found superior to concerns and subjects of "the *Poets Militant* below" (ll. 59–60). The lines end, as well, with a more personal note that aligns them with Beaumont's tribute in *Psyche;* Crashaw is cast as a superior and transcendent Elijah, Cowley as a humble Elisha still confronting the vagaries of life on earth:

> Thou from low earth in nobler *Flames* didst rise,
> And like *Elijah,* mount *Alive* the skies.
> *Elisha*-like (but with a wish much less,
> More fit thy *Greatness,* and my *Littleness*)
> Lo here I beg (I whom thou once didst prove
> So humble to *Esteem,* so Good to *Love*)
> Not that thy *Spirit* might on me *Doubled* be,
> I ask but *Half* thy mighty *Spirit* for Me.
> And when my *Muse* soars with so strong a Wing,
> 'Twill learn of things *Divine,* and first of *Thee* to sing.
> (ll. 65–74)

Cowley's elegy closes the literary ellipse I have drawn here, and he no doubt aims as well to push beyond its circumference. The foci of Herbert and Crashaw are compelling to Ferrar and—at times at least—defining for Beaumont, but as we progress beyond the immediacy of the lives and art of Herbert and Crashaw, their influence is less controlling, particularly on a poet such as Cowley who es-

tablishes a more independent voice shaped by diverse antecedents and contemporary associations. Cowley is not resistant to Herbert's influence, but it is
present more tenuously and implicitly. The personal and artistic interaction of
Cowley and Crashaw is more evident and more important, but the encounter
is also, as David Trotter has observed, one "between radically different person-
alities and cultural assumptions."[19] In short, while conceiving of these various
poetic relationships as an ellipse — rather than a circle or line or other more de-
limiting figure — is more accurate and more revealing, the ellipse, like any other imposed construct, is itself eventually subject to interrogation. We reach that
point when we consider Cowley, who, at moments, might be described variously as Spenserian, Jonsonian, or Donnean.[20] Nonetheless, understanding the
continuing — if more subtle or complicated — presence of two focal points for
devotional poetry among his influences provides further insights into a poet
such as Cowley, who, merging his own distinctive poetic with other voices, is
also capable of singing with "diviner breath" and, in so doing, allows his muse
to soar in the company of Herbert and Crashaw.

19. Arthur Nethercot notes occasions where Cowley "seems to refer to . . . [The Tem-
ple] indirectly" or where there is a "possible glancing allusion" to Herbert's volume
(Abraham Cowley: The Muses' Hannibal [London: Oxford University Press, Humphrey
Milford, 1931], 48, 166); Trotter, The Poetry of Abraham Cowley (London: Macmillan,
1979), 79.
20. See, for example, Trotter, Poetry of Cowley, 27–35, 110–12; and Earl Miner, The
Metaphysical Mode from Donne to Cowley (Princeton: Princeton University Press, 1969),
110–17. Miner says that "in some ways Cowley is more like Donne than is Marvell" but
goes on to observe that he is "sometimes more Cavalier or even more proto-Restoration
than he is Metaphysical" (111).

Anna K. Nardo

A Space for Academic Recreation
Milton's Proposal in *The Reason of Church-government*

The preface to book 2 of *The Reason of Church-government* is perhaps the most well-known passage in Milton's prose. This autobiographical digression, which justifies his entry into the episcopal controversy that would within the year escalate into civil war, displays Milton's remarkable self-consciousness about his poetic career: his long preparation, his ambition to "leave something so written to aftertimes, as they should not willingly let it die," and his survey of potential subjects for epic, tragedy, odes, and hymns.[1] In the midst, however, of this ethical appeal for his audience's indulgence, Milton interposes a specific recommendation that the magistrates create literary academies, associations more formally structured than the "circles" surrounding Sir Philip Sidney or Ben Jonson.

Interrupting his portrait of the poet as a young man—a digression that is itself interposed within an argument against prelatical government—Milton pauses to imagine a space that did not exist in England, but flourished throughout Italy.[2] Whereas in England literary circles were fluid—forming, dissipating, then reforming around a charismatic figure or a generous patron—in Italy literary academies were civic institutions. In *The Reason of Church-government*, Milton imagines transplanting across the Alps the ideal of recreative discourse

1. Milton, *The Reason of Church-government Urg'd against Prelaty*, ed. Ralph A. Haug, in *Complete Prose Works of John Milton*, ed. Don M. Wolfe et al., 8 vols. (New Haven: Yale University Press, 1953–1982), 1:810. All subsequent quotations from Milton's prose are from this edition and are cited parenthetically in the text.
2. Timothy Raylor has surveyed the kinds of loose literary clubs (such as those centering on Ben Jonson) and rowdy fraternities (such as those often formed by professional soldiers) that were active in early-seventeenth-century England (*Cavaliers, Clubs, and Literary Culture: Sir John Mennes, James Smith, and the Order of the Fancy* [Newark: University of Delaware Press; London and Toronto: Associated University Presses, 1994], 69–110).

among learned men that he so admired in the Italian academies he had visited only two and one-half years earlier. Briefly, I want to elucidate this recommendation for a space of academic dialogue, first by mapping Milton's representation of space in the autobiographical digression, second by surveying the social functions of academies in early-seventeenth-century Florence, third by locating academic space within the context of Milton's reconfiguration of space in his argument against the bishops, and finally, in a postscript, by comparing this early hopeful recommendation to Milton's later celebrations of the civilized pleasures of academic recreation despite the failure of his hopes to reform church and state.

In the preface to book 2 of *The Reason of Church-government*, Milton portrays himself as having been thrust out of "a calme and pleasing solitarynes fed with cherful and confident thoughts" by a divine call "to imbark in a troubl'd sea of noises and hoars disputes" (1:821). He imagines this raucous space of controversial prose as a marketplace in which merchants trade their wares. Like the servant in the parable of the talents, he believes that he bears "summes of knowledge and illumination, which God hath sent him into this world to trade with" (1:801). His merchandise is "pretious truths of such an orient lustre as no diamond can equall" and "treasure inestimable without price" (1:801–2). His opponents, however, merely trade with "trash," with "the fals glitter of their deceitfull wares wherewith they abuse the people, like poor Indians with beads and glasses" and with "antiquities sold by the seeming bulk" and carted by "good sumpters [who lay] ye down their hors load of citations and fathers at your dore" (1:802, 822).[3] Milton pointedly contrasts the uproar in this marketplace of controversy to the quiet of leisured study—a retired space where Milton, the poet, has been pursuing "the full circle of [his] private studies," where "in the spacious circuits of her musing [the poet's mind] hath liberty to propose to her self" lofty subjects for future poetry (1:807, 812–13).

Although these two spaces—the retired leisure of study and the marketplace of trade—may seem antithetical, Milton asserts that the former has been purchased in the latter. The son of an indulgent father who took great pains for his education at home, at Cambridge, and during a grand tour of Italy, Milton reminds himself that "ease and leasure was given thee for thy retired thoughts out of the sweat of other men" (1:804). Now he believes himself called to enter if

---

3. Thomas N. Corns reads these references to the marketplace of controversy as indicating Milton's growing reservations about his role as just another Presbyterian controversialist (*Uncloistered Virtue: English Political Literature, 1640–1660* [Oxford: Clarendon Press, 1992], 33).

not the financial marketplace where his scrivener father amassed the sufficient wealth to educate his son, then certainly the marketplace of spiritual controversy where he must invest what he calls "those few talents which God at that present had lent me" (1:804).

Despite his present embroilment in tumult, Milton imagines a future entrance into a public sphere more congenial to the use of these talents—a space comparable to that of the pulpit, where the poet will teach "over the whole book of sanctity and vertu" through a subject carefully chosen to be "doctrinal and exemplary to a Nation" (1:817, 815). This rostrum for the public poet is the space he claims for his future, but it is, as yet, only a vision. The present state of poetry is far different, and he laments "the corruption and bane which [our youth and gentry] suck in dayly from the writings and interludes of libidinous and ignorant Poetasters" (1:818).

At this point, frustrated by what he sees as the decadence of contemporary poetry and drama, Milton proposes the creation of a new kind of space—neither the retired study of leisured contemplation, nor the marketplace of ideas, nor the rostrum from which the future poet will both teach and delight. This space will be, first and foremost, ludic, because, he admits, "the spirit of man cannot demean it selfe lively in this body without some recreating intermission of labour, and serious things" (1:818). In contemporary society, he argues, the space of recreation has been usurped by corrupting plays and public sports that have become mere "provocations of drunkennesse and lust" (1:819). Here Milton calls attention to Charles I's reissue in 1633 of his father's 1618 *Book of Sports*—the declaration authorizing the enjoyment of dancing, archery, May games, Whitsun ales, morris dances, and other forms of innocent mirth after Sunday services. As Leah Marcus has argued, James I quite consciously took festival pastimes, as he had taken the public theaters, under royal protection in order to allow a limited release of potentially seditious impulses within the ludic boundaries of dramatic fiction and holiday folly. Responding to Charles's continuation of this policy, Milton objects that current theater and public sports promote only license, not the liberty of expression that could further the progress of true reformation.[4]

---

4. Leah S. Marcus, *The Politics of Mirth: Jonson, Herrick, Milton, Marvell, and the Defense of Old Holiday Pastimes* (Chicago: University of Chicago Press, 1986), 1–23. For James I and the Stuart control of drama, see Margot Heinemann, *Puritanism and Theatre: Thomas Middleton and Opposition Drama under the Early Stuarts* (Cambridge: Cambridge University Press, 1980), 36–38. For arguments that Puritan objections to the public theater were often less ideological than practical and that Puritanism as an antitheatrical force

In deliberate contrast to both the "interludes of libidinous and ignorant Po-etasters" and the "festival pastimes . . . such as were autoriz'd a while since," Milton proposes three forms of recreation—one for the body and two for the mind (1:818–19). To "inure and harden our bodies . . . to all warlike skil and performance," he recommends "martial exercises" (1:819). To "civilize, adorn and make discreet our minds," he proposes that the magistrates "take into their care" first "the learned and affable meeting of frequent Academies" and second "the procurement of wise and artfull recitations sweetned with eloquent and gracefull inticements to the love and practice of justice, temperance and forti-tude," these recitations to be delivered perhaps in pulpits or "at set and solemn Peneguries, in Theaters, porches, or what other place, or way may win most upon the people to receiv at once both recreation, & instruction" (1:819–20). Although it has become a critical commonplace to claim that Milton here pro-poses a species of reformed drama, I am arguing that in these academies and public recitations, Milton imagines a recreative space markedly different from the London stage and the village green—a space he had experienced and ad-mired two and one-half years earlier in Italy.[5] In order to understand what Mil-ton envisioned transplanting to England at this revolutionary moment in 1642, let us turn our attention to the Italian academies and to Milton's academic ex-perience.

Undoubtedly, he was proud that the Florentine literati had invited him to their academic gatherings, and throughout his career as a pamphleteer, when he needs to establish his authority for learning or poetry, he recalls his academic experience. After the episcopal controversy had given way to civil war and regi-cide, Milton recounts his trip to Italy in his 1654 *Second Defence of the English People* and remembers his academic friends by name:

---

in the 1630s has been exaggerated, see Heinemann, *Puritanism and Theatre*, 31–36; and Martin Butler, *Theatre and Crisis, 1632–1642* (Cambridge: Cambridge University Press, 1984), 84–99.

5. According to the *Oxford English Dictionary*, in the seventeenth century *recitation* meant "the action of rehearsing, detailing, or enumerating; recital" or "an instance of this; an account, narrative." The passage from *The Reason of Church-government* is cited for the second meaning. None of the definitions connect recitation to theatrical perfor-mance. For arguments that Milton here proposes "a reformed drama," see William Haller, *Liberty and Reformation in the Puritan Revolution* (New York: Columbia University Press, 1955), 59–61; John F. Huntley, "The Images of Poet and Poetry in Milton's *The Reason of Church-Government*," in *Achievements of the Left Hand: Essays on the Prose of John Milton*, ed. Michael Lieb and John T. Shawcross (Amherst: University of Massachusetts Press, 1974), 108–9; Butler, *Theatre and Crisis*, 98; and David Loewenstein, *Milton and the Drama of History: Historical Vision, Iconoclasm, and the Literary Imagination* (Cam-bridge: Cambridge University Press, 1990), 27.

> In [Florence], which I have always admired above all others because of the
> elegance, not just of its tongue, but also of its wit, I lingered for about two
> months. There I at once became the friend of many gentlemen eminent in
> rank and learning, whose private academies I frequented—a Florentine in-
> stitution which deserves great praise not only for promoting humane stud-
> ies but also for encouraging friendly intercourse. Time will never destroy my
> recollection—ever welcome and delightful—of you, Jacopo Gaddi, Carlo
> Dati, Frescobaldi, Coltellini, Buonmattei, Chimentelli, Francini, and many
> others. (vol. 4, pt. 1: 615–17)

Defending England's actions before an international audience, Milton alludes
to his academic experience in order to represent England's defender as a cultured, learned, and cosmopolitan man of letters. But in his private correspondence, Milton voices a more personal longing for the society of learned friends.
In 1647 he wrote to Carlo Dati, lamenting,

> [W]henever I think that, reluctant and actually torn away, I left so many
> companions and at the same time such good friends, and such congenial
> ones in a single city—a city distant indeed but to me most dear . . . I could
> think of nothing pleasanter than to recall my dearest memory of you all, of
> you, Dati, especially. . . . Meanwhile, my Charles, farewell and give my best
> greeting to Coltellini, Francini, Frescobaldi, Malatesta, Chimentelli the
> younger, and any other of our group whom you know to be especially fond
> of me—in short to the whole Gaddian Academy." (2:763–65)

This community of learned friends is what Milton remembers most about Italy,
not the paintings, sculptures, palaces, ruins, and manners that impressed other Englishmen on the grand tour.[6] A space to foster such "learned and affable
meeting[s]" among friends is precisely what Milton calls for in *The Reason of
Church-government*. Throughout Italy, academies were the foci for such civilized
recreation.

In the sixteenth and seventeenth centuries, every Italian town of considerable
size had one and often many more academies devoted primarily to literary and
philosophical study, although some patronized the visual arts, while others
gambled, staged comedies, and sponsored carnival masques.[7] In seventeenth-

---

6. According to John Walter Stoye, Milton was the "almost solitary instance of an English traveller who assiduously attended Italian literary societies" (*English Travellers
Abroad, 1604–1667* [London: Jonathan Cape, 1952], 223–25).

7. Eric W. Cochrane, *Tradition and Enlightenment in the Tuscan Academies, 1690–1800*
(Chicago: University of Chicago Press, 1961), 1–34.

century Florence the most prominent were the Accademia Fiorentina, the Alterati (the changed or the spoiled), the Accademia della Crusca (the academy of chaff or the sifters), the Svogliati (the unwilling or the listless), and the Apatisti (the dispassionate or the indifferent). These academies differentiated themselves from one another by their names, imprese, and written constitutions.[8] Names were often witty, ambiguous, or fantastic. In addition to the sifters, the unwilling, and the dispassionate of Florence, there were the Oziosi (the leisured ones or the idlers) of Naples, the Addormentati (the sleeping or the benumbed) of Genoa, the Umoristi (the humorists or the moody) of Rome, and hundreds more. Individual members sometimes chose a comical academic name for themselves. For example, Milton's friend Benedetto Buonmattei, a priest and grammarian, was il Ripieno (the stuffed one or the tidbit) in the Accademia della Crusca, and among the Apatisti who delighted in anagrams he was Boemonte Battidente. Carlo Roberto Dati, the academic friend with whom Milton continued to correspond after his return to England, was a polymath whose expertise spanned Greek literature and modern mathematics; nevertheless, among fellow Cruscans he was known as Smarrito (the bewildered), and among the Apatisti he was Currado Bartoletti.[9] Each academy also had its own impresa, a mysterious emblem and motto signifying for the initiates the scope or intention of the organization. The impresa of the Incogniti of Venice, for example, depicted the Nile descending from the mountains, fertilizing Egypt, and flowing into the Mediterranean, with the motto "Ex ignoto notus," the known from the unknown.[10]

The more established and prestigious academies wrote elaborate procedures for electing leaders (presidents, censors, porters, and so on), regulating meetings and social events, judging members' literary compositions, and assessing fines for infractions of the rules. Ceremony, ritual, and pomp ordered all academic events. In the Accademia della Crusca, compositions were placed in an urn prior to reading in order to secure the approval of elected censors; formal proposals, speeches of thanks, odes, and lighted tapers marked the admission of a new member or the funeral of an old one; and amendment of the charter required a suspension of business, nomination of regents, and orations com-

8. Amedeo Quondam, "L'Accademia," in *Letteratura Italiana*, ed. Giulio Einaudi, 9 vols. (Turin: U. Panelli, 1982), 1:842–58.

9. Alessandro Lazzeri, *Intellettuali e consenso nella Toscana del Seicento: L'Accademia degli Apatisti* (Milan: A. Giuffré, 1983), 67, 69; A. M. Cinquemani, *Glad to Go for a Feast: Milton, Buonmattei, and the Florentine Accademici* (New York: Peter Lang, 1998), 23–27, 95.

10. Michele Maylender, *Storia delle Accademie d'Italia*, 5 vols. (Bologna: L. Cappelli, 1926–1930), 3:205.

paring the chosen officials to Solon or Lycurgus, those admired lawgivers of Athens and Sparta.[11]

By their often fantastic names, symbolic imprese, complicated rules, and insistence on ceremony, academicians located their discussions and entertainments in a time and space set apart from the world of work and mundane cares. In his dialogue *La civil conversatione* (1575), Stefano Guazzo makes this separation explicit: one of his interlocutors, a dedicated academician, claims, "Quando questo mio corpo è rinchiuso là dentro, sono esclusi da lui tutti i noiosi pensieri, i quali aspettandomi alla porta mi tornano nell'uscire a caricar la soma sopra le spalle" (When my body is enclosed there within [the academy], I have excluded from it all bothersome thoughts that, awaiting me at the door, return to burden my shoulders when I exit).[12] In fact, many academies began as informal groups of friends meeting to enjoy conversation, food, and wine in someone's home or garden. In these banquets, they sought to re-create the conviviality of ancient Greek symposia. Other groups originated in carnival fetes. Even after such irregular meetings evolved into formal institutions with regularized procedures, academies always retained a festal aura. With their arcane names and imprese understood by only initiates and their rituals and ceremonies of self-definition, they circumscribe a play space such as Johan Huizinga described in his now classic study of "the play-element in culture," *Homo Ludens.*[13]

A brief survey of the development of academies in Florence illustrates the potential always present, albeit often dormant, in the space of academic play. In 1540 a group of Florentine wits decided to meet regularly to discuss the Tuscan language; they called themselves Umidi because water is the element of fertility and growth, and members chose appropriate names, such as il Lasca (the roach, a freshwater fish). Their constitution, specifying elections and rules for reading and judging explications of Petrarch and other Tuscan writers, was perhaps the first codification of academic procedures in Florence. Despite this serious intent, the constitution makes clear that "questa nostra accademia degli Umidi è creata per passatempo" (our academy of the Umidi is created for amusement).[14] This declaration notwithstanding, three months after its creation, Cosimo I, the grand duke of Tuscany who was embroiled in bitter polit-

---

11. Cochrane, *Tradition and Enlightenment,* 4–6, 19.
12. Quoted in Quondam, "L'Accademia," 1:840.
13. Huizinga, *Homo Ludens: A Study of the Play-Element in Culture,* trans. Karl Mannheim (1949; reprint, Boston: Beacon, 1955), 12, 28.
14. Quoted in Maylender, *Storia delle Accademie d'Italia,* 5:365.

ical struggles, dissolved the Umidi as an organization extraneous to the court. Not all Florentines had forgotten their republican past, so Cosimo had reason to fear an independent organization that gathered together the intelligentsia, many of whom came from the powerful merchant families who had once dominated the republic. Their avowed purpose to pursue literary, linguistic, and jocular exercises did not wholly remove the danger that the Umidi might become a center of opposition to the court.

Instead of simply prohibiting meetings, and thus making them a cause célèbre, Duke Cosimo took the academy under his magnanimous patronage, renaming it the Accademia Fiorentina, with himself as "protettore," welcoming them into the ducal palace for meetings, encouraging them to perfect the Tuscan language, sponsoring public lectures about Dante, Petrarch, and Boccaccio, and including their *consoli* in state ceremonies and processions.[15] In fact, the Duke co-opted all academic activities, and while the Fiorentina remained the most prestigious Florentine academy and its members became known for upholding Dante and Petrarch as ideals of style and language, it also gained a reputation for stuffiness.

In 1582 some literati, rejecting the austerity and gravity of the Fiorentini, decided to form a new academy with more breathing room where they could read light literary exercises. Although many maintained their positions in the Accademia Fiorentina, they began to meet in private homes or gardens to dine, drink, and recite *cicalate* (literally "chats"). Calling themselves the Crusconi (the chaff), they forbade any priggishness or grave arguments at their meetings. As their gatherings evolved a form and purpose, they established themselves as the Accademia della Crusca, and eventually became the arbiters of Tuscan style and usage, sifting the wheat from the bran. They took as their impresa a flour sifter, chose individual names such as l'Infarinato (the floured), and signified in their motto a line from a Petrarchan sonnet, "Il più bel fior ne coglie," their goal to gather only the most beautiful flowers of language. In order to codify Tuscan and replace Latin as the language for intellectual discourse on the peninsula, they set out to compile a monumental dictionary, which during the seventeenth and eighteenth centuries went through four editions.[16]

Despite their prominence and their serious project, amusement remained the focus of Cruscan activity. As the tedious labor of dictionary making dragged on, the academy's diary records speech after speech as each new *arciconsolo* took

15. Ibid., 3:1–6; Cochrane, *Tradition and Enlightenment*, 29–32.
16. Maylender, *Storia delle Accademie d'Italia*, 2:123–35.

office, exhorting the members to eschew idleness and press on with the work of a new edition of the dictionary.[17] Nevertheless, during these years, there was no lack of energy to put on two lavish *stravizzi* (banquets or debauches) every year—complete with decorations so gorgeous that nonmembers came to gawk and were generously regaled with wine at the academy's expense. The members summoned the energy to compose celebratory and satirical poems for the occasion, speeches roasting the outgoing *arciconsolo*, speeches defending his tenure of office, speeches praising the new *arciconsolo*, acceptance speeches by the new *arciconsolo*, and, of course, *cicalate*. Milton's friends Dati and Chimentelli regaled fellow Cruscans with *cicalate* titled "Chi fosse prima, o la Galli[n]a, o l'Uovo?" (Which came first, the chicken or the egg?) and "Delle Lodi dell'Insalata" (In praise of salad).[18] What appears to us, more than three hundred years later, as the central significance of this academy, its monumental dictionary, was only a part of the activities of this fundamentally recreative society.

Other Florentine academies avoided the gravity of the Fiorentini and the collective labor of the Cruscans altogether. In the sixteenth century the Alterati signified by their impresa, a tub of grapes, and their motto alluding to wine and tippling that their aim was amusement, albeit cultured amusement. Like all literary academies, they recited, criticized, and defended their own disquisitions, many quite serious and technical, but they also staged regular symposia, wrote mock polemics, played practical jokes, and paid for infractions of academic rules by writing a sonnet to an imaginary lady or delivering an impromptu oration on a topic assigned by the regent.[19] In the seventeenth century the Apatisti continued this tradition of learned play. Many of its members were Fiorentini and Cruscans, but they also came to the Apatisti meetings to debate *dubbi*, doubtful propositions such as "Se in volto leggiadro sia più stimabile l'occhio nero, o l'azzurro" (Whether black or blue eyes are more to be esteemed in a beautiful face), and "Se il fuoco d'Amore si risvegli più dal vedere il Riso, o il

17. See, for example, Cesare Guasti, ed., *Scritti vari di Lorenzo Panciatichi* (Florence: Felice le Monnier, 1856), 53, 71.

18. Cartesio Marconcini, *L'Accademia della Crusca dalle origini alla prima edizione del vocabolario (1612)* (Pisa: Tipografia Valenti, 1910), 189–91, 197; Gaetano Imbert, *La Vita Fiorentina nel Seicento Secondo Memorie Sincrone, 1644–1670* (Florence: R. Bemporad and Figlio, 1906), 159–62; *Prose Fiorentine Raccolte dallo Smarrito Accademico della Crusca*, ed. Carlo Roberto Dati, 4 pts., 17 vols. (Florence: n.p., 1716–1745), 3.2.152, 3.2.83. Future citations from *Prose Fiorentine (PF)* appear parenthetically in the text by part, volume, and page. All translations from Italian are mine.

19. Maylender, *Storia delle Accademie d'Italia*, 1:154–55; Bernard Weinberg, "The Accademia degli Alterati and Literary Taste from 1570 to 1600," *Italica* 31 (1954): 207.

Pianto dell'amata" (If the fire of love is aroused more by seeing the beloved's smile or tears).[20] As trivial as these academic pastimes may seem, everyone who was anyone in Florence belonged to at least one, and preferably three, academies. They formed the city's social and intellectual elite.

Not coincidentally, the period of the greatest flowering of academic activity in Florence coincides with the reigns of the Medici dukes. Throughout these years of political docility, the intelligentsia sought organizations and activities independent of direct government control. Of course, the Medici "protected" and supported a number of these groups, even sponsoring public recitations on serious philosophical and literary topics. Indeed, by encouraging the Fiorentini and the Cruscans to uphold Tuscan as Italy's preeminent dialect, Cosimo I and his successors may have hoped to use the academy to further Medici political ambitions in the peninsula.[21] Nevertheless, by their names, imprese, rules, and conspicuously apolitical and often frivolous activities, these literary-philosophical academies marked off a space and time for intellectual activity separate from the state.

The pervasive jocularity and the nice refinements of wit cultivated in academic discourse have led some historians to judge academic play as but another indication of the decline of intellectual life in post-Renaissance Italy. In academic attention to apolitical literary topics, moral clichés, and conventional piety, they see a stifling of independent thought and open debate under the watchful eyes of the Inquisition. Absolutist rulers, these critics point out, deliberately diverted the talents of men of considerable erudition away from public affairs toward parlor games, empty speculations, and elaborate election procedures in politically impotent literary clubs.[22]

To dismiss academic theorizing and wit as signaling the exhaustion of Renaissance and humanist culture is, however, a partial judgment. The reinter-

20. Edoardo Benvenuti, *Agostino Coltellini e L'Accademia degli Apatisti a Firenze nel Secolo XVII* (Pistoia: Officina Tipografica Cooperativa, 1910), 273–76; Anton Maria Salvini, *Discorsi Accademici di Anton Maria Salvini . . . Sopra Alcuni Dubbi Proposti nell'Accademia degli Apatisti*, 2 vols. (Florence: n.p., 1695, 1712), 1.80.317, 2.16.103. Future citations to Salvini's *Discorsi* appear parenthetically in the text by volume, discourse, and page. Although the *dubbi* printed in Salvini's volumes postdate Milton's visit, the genre was widely practiced earlier, and Salvini's collection contains representative examples.

21. Maylender, *Storia delle Accademie d'Italia*, 2:144, 3:3.

22. Francesco de Sanctis, *History of Italian Literature*, trans. Joan Redfern, 2 vols. (New York: Barnes and Noble, 1968), 2:635–36, 709; Eric W. Cochrane, *Florence in the Forgotten Centuries, 1527–1800: A History of Florence and the Florentines in the Age of the Grand Dukes* (Chicago: University of Chicago Press, 1973), 124, 131; Gino Benzoni, "Per non smarrire l'identità: L'Accademia," in *Gli Affanni Della Cultura: Intellettuali e potere nell'Italia della Controriforma e barocca* (Milan: Feltrinelli Editore, 1978), 155, 172–73.

pretation of these academies, initiated by Eric Cochrane and continued by Gino Benzoni, Amedeo Quondam, and Allesandro Lazzeri, views them as not wholly symptoms of decadence and demoralization, but as significant cultural institutions. Cochrane argues that although the academies were politically impotent, they created a structure for dialogue among men (and in rare cases women) of letters—an institution based in cities, not courts, governed by constitutions and elections, with participation determined by talent, not birth. Their elections, charters, and rituals defined autonomous self-sufficient institutions. Thus, during these years of political repression, the heirs of the Salviati, Strozzi, Rucellai, and other powerful Florentine families sought institutions that were separate from the absolutist state and protected from ducal interference by their frame as mere play, academies in which they could play at republican self-governance, ruling over the matters left to them—literature, language, philosophical speculation, and learned conviviality.[23]

It is not likely that Milton knew the complicated history of the academies to which he was invited, and we are not wholly sure which ones actually extended invitations to this English Protestant poet. Minutes in the Biblioteca Nazionale in Florence show that Milton attended Svogliati meetings and read Latin poetry there. Scholars have speculated that he may also have visited the Florentine Apatisti, known for welcoming foreign visitors and frequented by many of his Italian friends; the Roman Fantastici, one of whose members, Giovanni Salzilli, Milton praised in *Ad Salsillum;* the Umoristi, the most prominent Roman academy, whose member Giovanni Battista Doni Milton mentions in a letter; the Neapolitan Oziosi, founded by Milton's host, Manso; and the Venetian Incogniti, whose membership included several of Milton's friends.[24] In any case, the language he uses in *The Reason of Church-government* to describe the effects of academies suggests that he understood much about their social functions—including their potential to promote the free play of ideas.

23. Cochrane, *Tradition and Enlightenment,* xiii–xiv, 52–54, 247. To Quondam, academicians played at being courtiers ("L'Accademia," 832–34, 842–43, 848–52), while Benzoni (*Gli Affanni,* 193, 198–99) and Lazzeri (*Intellettuali,* 30) emphasize their playing at self-governance and their creation of a new kind of identity for intellectuals.
24. See J. Milton French, ed., *The Life Records of John Milton,* 5 vols. (New Brunswick: Rutgers University Press, 1949- 1958), 1:389, 408–9, 414; John Arthos, *Milton and the Italian Cities* (New York: Barnes and Noble, 1968), 90 n. 24, 97, 115; Benvenuti, *Agostino Coltellini,* 240, 256–57; Edward Rosen, "A Friend of John Milton: Valerio Chimentelli," *Bulletin of the New York Public Library* 57 (1953): 159–74; Louise Schleiner, "Milton, G. B. Doni, and the Dating of Doni's Works," *Milton Quarterly* 16 (1982): 36–42; and James A. Freeman, "Milton's Roman Connection: Giovanni Salzilli," in *Milton Studies,* ed. James D. Simmonds (Pittsburgh: University of Pittsburgh Press, 1984), 19:87–104.

By classifying academies as a form of "recreating intermission of labour, and serious things," he locates these gatherings in a space set apart from the tumult of political discourse. By describing their learned meetings as "affable," he emphasizes the easy conversation among friends that he found so congenial in the "Gaddian Academy." And by identifying the goals of these meetings—to "civilize, adorn and make discreet our minds"—Milton gives a condensed survey of the central academic activities. In a letter to Buonmattei that he wrote while staying in Florence, Milton shows how highly he values the academic aim to purify the Tuscan language—a goal academicians pursued through both the compilation of a dictionary and the sponsorship of private disquisitions and public recitations about Dante, Boccaccio, Petrarch, Ariosto, and other vernacular authors. The man of letters, argues Milton, is second only to the good ruler because he "tries to fix by precepts and rules the order and pattern of writing and speaking received from a good age of the nation." Whereas the ruler protects the state from invading enemies, the literary scholar "undertakes to overcome and drive out Barbarism, that filthy civil enemy of character which attacks the spirits of men." And whereas the ruler "alone is able to effect an upright and holy society of Citizens," the man of letters "alone can make it truly noble, and splendid, and brilliant" (1:329). Thus, in *The Reason of Church-government*, Milton recommends creating a space in England for the kind of philological and interpretive activities practiced in Italian academies—activities that both "civilize, [and] adorn."[25]

But he also claims that academies can "make discreet our minds." By choosing the word *discreet*, with its connotations of discernment, judiciousness, and prudence, Milton emphasizes the mental exercise afforded participants in the practice of such academic genres as *lezioni*, *cicalate*, and *dubbi*.

Of all the academic genres, the *lezione* was perhaps the most serious. Academicians delivered *lezioni* with such titles as "Dell'Ordine dell'Universo" and "Se i Poeti abbiano contro al poetico decoro peccato, quando attribuirono agli Dei passioni indegne della divinità" (On the order of the universe and Whether the poets may have sinned against poetic decorum when they attributed to the gods passions unworthy of divinity) (*PF*, 2.2.34, 2.1.232). But during the seventeenth century more trivial topics became popular: for example, Milton's friend Dati read a *lezione* to the prestigious Accademia Fiorentina about the fashionable long hair worn by the Florentine nobility (*PF*, 2.5.263). Citing biblical and

25. See Cinquemani for a discussion of Milton's letter to Buonmattei (*Glad to Go for a Feast*, 15–16, 30–36).

classical authorities in extensive footnotes, and extending his argument for forty-nine pages in the printed version, Dati seems at points to take his subject seriously. With the requisite flattery, he cites the portraits "de' nostri Serenissimi Principi, nella quale rare volte incontreranno gli occhi vostri ritratti calvi, infiniti con zazzera mediocre, molti con lunghissima" (of our most serene princes, in which one's eyes will rarely encounter bald portraits, but infinite numbers with medium length hair, and many with quite long hair) (*PF,* 2.5.285–86); here, Dati is most surely not mocking his patrons. Furthermore, much of the *lezione* offers a history or ethnography of the custom of wearing long hair. Nevertheless, the entire disquisition is structured as a point-by-point refutation of a paradox in praise of baldness by Sinesio, bishop of Cirene. This *lezione* then becomes a paradox on a paradox; it pretends to take seriously what was originally intended as a joke, mere "alarums to truth," as John Donne called his own paradoxes.[26]

Although *lezioni* could be serious disquisitions, *cicalate* were overtly jocular "chats" that topped off an evening of academic banqueting. In one such after-dinner chat, Milton's friend Buonmattei divides his subject into logical categories—the natural (quality, form, origin, and virtues) and the accidental (choice, use, and quantity)—in order to argue that there is an astonishing similarity between pork and melon (*PF,* 3.1.91). In another, he fragments the definition of a poet as "un animale, che si fa uccellare in versi" (an animal who goes fowling in verse) to parody the kind of word-by-word explication practiced in sermons on biblical texts—dividing "animale," in good Aristotelian fashion, into those that walk, swim, and fly and into the tame, the wild, and those that can change natures. Each category applies to types of poets—as those who never get off the ground and those whose sharp teeth and fierce natures are best pacified by patronage (*PF,* 3.1.112–18). As Milton himself acknowledges in *The Reason of Church-government,* at academic meetings "the manner is that every one must give some proof of his wit and reading" (1:809)—even a Catholic priest and studious grammarian such as Buonmattei or an intense Protestant poet such as Milton.

Many academicians gave the requisite proof of their wit in *dubbi,* an academic genre of intermediate nature. Like *lezioni,* some *dubbi* required serious consideration, such as "Se l'invenzione dell'Arme da fuoco sia degna di lode o di biasimo" or "Se per ammaestrare la gioventù nella morale, abbia più forza

---

26. Helen Gardner and Timothy Healy, eds., *John Donne: Selected Prose* (London: Clarendon Press, 1967), 111.

la teorica de' precetti, o la pratica degli esempi" (Whether the invention of
firearms may be worthy of praise or blame, or Whether in the moral training
of youth the theory of rules or the practice of examples would have greater
force) (Salvini, 2.52.296, 1.19.68). These *dubbi* resemble the requisite exercises
in debate that Milton performed at Cambridge and later published as his prolusions.[27] Other *dubbi*, however, were frankly trivial and intended merely to exhibit the wit of the presenter, such as "Se sia più desiderabile il vedere l'Amata
senza poterle parlare, o il parlarle senza poterla vedere," "Qual sia più possente,
il Vino, o l'Amore" (Whether it may be more desirable to see the beloved without being able to speak to her or to speak to her without being able to see her,
or Which may be more powerful, wine or love) (Salvini, 2.31.194, 2.27.165).
By definition *dubbi* are doubtful, debatable, "academic" questions for which no
definitive answers are possible. Anton Maria Salvini, who published more than
two hundred of his own *dubbi*, describes them as untying intricate knots, and
defends the practice: "non è certo impresa da pigliare a gabbo, ma capace d'infinite, erudite, e dotte riflessioni, e campo amplissimo, e giocondissimo, per lo
quale i virtuosi, e spiritosi ingegni possano tuttora spaziare, e esercitarsi" (Certainly it is not an enterprise to make light of, but one capable of infinite, erudite, and learned reflections, providing a most spacious and mirthful ground
in which virtuosi and spirited wits can still range and exercise themselves)
(Salvini, 2.96.516). What Salvini says of *dubbi* applies equally well to *lezioni* and
cicalate: the primary function of all these academic genres was to fashion a witty gentleman, not to discover truth. In bravura performances of logical subtle-
ty, learned citations, and rhetorical flourishes, Dati, Buonmattei, Chimentelli,
and Milton's other academic friends thread their way through the nuances of
intricate arguments, creating elaborate tissues of nothingness. They become
what Richard Lanham has called *"homo rhetoricus,"* the man whose rhetorical
training prepared him to play any game and to avoid commitment to any single set of values or even to a central self.[28] Naturally, in the repressive political
and religious environment of sixteenth- and seventeenth-century Italy acquiring these skills of mental discretion could become a matter of life and death.

But, as Lazzeri has argued, these academic exercises have intellectual as well
as political significance. When disputants argue undecidable topics such as

27. See, for example, "Prolusion 1: Whether Day or Night Is the More Excellent." In
several of his prolusions, Milton seems bored with such trivial assignments and treats
them with playful irony (1:216–17).
28. Richard A. Lanham, *The Motives of Eloquence: Literary Rhetoric in the Renaissance*
(New Haven: Yale University Press, 1976), 1–35.

"Qual sia maggiore passione, l'amore, o l'odio" (Which may be the greater passion, love or hate) (Salvini, 1.10.34), discourse is removed to a rhetorical level; being becomes literary. Much of what these academicians debated had no immediate relevance to society, to politics, indeed to any life lived outside the academy, so the play of their debates created a space for theorization. Its very triviality helped create this privileged space, distancing it from political power and public use. Thus safely distanced, these academies formed autonomous, self-governing institutions that fostered intellectual exchange, even within the confines of an absolutist state.[29]

Milton's references to Italian academies in his prose treatises suggest he knew both the danger and the potential of academic discourse. In *The Reason of Church-government*, he announces his intent to imitate only those Italian writers who related "the best and sagest things . . . in the mother dialect," not those who seek to adorn their native tongue by creating only "verbal curiosities" (1:811–12). Two years later, in order to bolster *Areopagitica*'s argument for unlicensed printing, Milton describes his Italian friends as envying the "*Philosophic* freedom" of Englishmen, "while themselvs did nothing but bemoan the servil condition into which learning amongst them was brought; that this was it which had dampt the glory of Italian wits; that nothing had bin there writt'n now these many years but flattery and fustian" (2:537–38). Both Milton and his friends recognized that academic exercises participated in the literary decline of Counter Reformation Italy.

Nevertheless, in *The Reason of Church-government*, Milton emphasizes not the debasement, but the potential of academic discourse to "make discreet our minds." After all, his Catholic academic friends did invite him, a militant and vocal Protestant, to their private academies; confessed, he claims, their discontent with their state of repression; and probably took him to meet Galileo, who, he says in *Areopagitica*, had "grown old, a prisner to the Inquisition, for thinking in Astronomy otherwise then the Franciscan and Dominican licencers thought" (2:538). Friends such as Dati and Buonmattei had used a measure of freedom in dealing with this young Englishman whose poetry they so admired.[30] Thus, in the midst of his argument against what he sees as the tyranny of church government by bishops, Milton recommends replacing drama corrupted by decadent poets and public sports co-opted by royal control with the

---

29. Lazzeri, *Intellettuali*, 25–26.
30. For Florentine support of Galileo and the complex relations between Florentine and Roman Catholicism, see Cinquemani, *Glad to Go for a Feast*, 3–5, 26–27, 39, 57–58.

recreative space for performance, discussion, and debate that he knew from experience academies could offer.

In fact, this recommendation for reconfiguring recreative space comple-
ments Milton's larger proposal for reconfiguring church government. In arguing that there is no biblical warrant for exalting bishops above the lower clergy
and laity, Milton repeatedly contrasts the inclusiveness of church councils, in
which laity and clergy may participate, to the hierarchical organization of prelacy, which excludes laymen from discussion and administration in church matters. To emphasize this contrast, Milton calls attention to the Laudian attempts
to control ecclesiastical space, and he vehemently condemns "the scornfull
terme of Laick, the consecrating of Temples, carpets, and table-clothes, the rail-
ing in of a repugnant and contradictive Mount Sinai in the Gospell, as if the
touch of a lay Christian who is never the lesse Gods living temple, could profane dead judaisms, the exclusion of Christs people from the offices of holy dis-
cipline through the pride of a usurping Clergy" (1:843). Here Milton uses the
exclusion of the laity from sacred space—by the ceremonial reconsecrations of
church objects and the erection of altar rails—to image the far more pernicious
exclusion of the laity from the debate and discussion necessary to further reformation. "The reforming of a Church," Milton argues, "is never brought to effect without the fierce encounter of truth and falshood together," and inevitably
from the "splinters and shares of so violent a jousting" will fall "many fond er-
rors and fanatick opinions, which when truth has the upper hand, and the reformation shall be perfeted, will easily be rid out of the way, or kept so low, as
that they shall be only the exercise of our knowledge, not the disturbance, or
interruption of our faith" (1:796). Thus, Milton would replace the closed space
of Anglican worship and episcopal government, "under whose inquisitorius
and tyrannical duncery no free and splendid wit can flourish" (1:820), with an
open ecclesiastical space where dialogue even with fanatical opinion and error
can sharpen understanding and perfect the ongoing work of reformation.

Likewise, Milton's goal for English recreation is to replace decadent poetry,
corrupt drama, and festival license (all of which Milton will later associate with
the court) with a new kind of space that will foster the growth of the reformed
poet.[31] In Milton's catalog of subjects for future poetry, the career of Torquato

---

31. Early in his career, Milton does not necessarily associate festival pastimes, drama,
or lewd poetry with courts. See *A Mask Presented at Ludlow Castle* (performed 1634) and
Of Reformation (1641) (1:589). By the time he publishes *Paradise Lost* (1667), however,
he does associate debased love poetry, lewd masks, and mixed dancing with the court.
See Merritt Y. Hughes, ed., *John Milton: Complete Poems and Major Prose* (New York: Ody-

Tasso figures prominently. The epic poet of *Jerusalem Delivered*, whom Milton considered imitating, had belonged to ten academies, and Milton had made friends with his patron, Giovanni Battista Manso, himself a prominent academician, when he traveled to Naples.[32] Before he left Italy, in his Latin poem *Manso*, Milton had praised his host highly for nurturing the genius of great poets, and had imagined himself one day composing, as did Tasso, a heroic poem and enjoying the care of such "amicum / Phoebaeos decorasse viros qui tam bene norit" (a friend / who understands how to honor the devotees of Phoebus) (ll. 78–79). In the autobiographical digression from his antiprelatical argument, Milton ascribes to such academic friends as Manso a prominent role in having persuaded him to do "what the greatest and choycest wits of *Athens, Rome,* or modern *Italy,* and those Hebrews of old did for their country" (1:812)—that is, to write great English poetry in the vernacular. Milton imagines the academies he would transplant from Italy to England as nurturing that civic poetry that he covenants with the reader to pay as debt.

Thus, in *The Reason of Church-government*, Milton both describes social space as he experienced it in 1641–1642 and imagines an ideal reconfiguration of that space. Having been "Church-outed by the Prelats," he places himself in the "blamelesse silence" of retirement, separated from participation in church affairs by "the haughty distance of Prelaty," and from the recreative space of drama and festival by disdain for their lewdness (1:823, 826). Although preferring the privacy in which he prepares to become a poet, he represents himself as called by God into the marketplace of pamphlet warfare to champion the cause of reformation. Faced with a closed church, a tumultuous marketplace, decadent pastimes, and the option of virtuous but silent retirement, Milton proposes to remap English social space. In the pamphlet as a whole, he imagines an open ecclesiastical space of dialogue that would nurture the ongoing reformation, and in his autobiographical digression he imagines a space for recreative literary academies that would not only sponsor private disquisitions and public recitations, but also nurture the growth of the poet who will one day mount a public rostrum and exercise a "power beside the office of a pulpit, to imbreed and cherish in a great people the seeds of virtu, and publick civility" (1:816).[33]

---

ssey Press, 1957), 4:765–70. All quotations from Milton's poetry are taken from this edition.

32. Maylender, *Storia delle Accademie d'Italia*, 1:61; Arthos, *Milton and the Italian Cities*, 97–99.

33. For other treatments of the relationship between the autobiographical digression and the pamphlet as a whole, see Huntley, who emphasizes the poet's role in effecting the necessary interior reformation ("Images of Poet," 83–120), and Stanley E. Fish, who

Postscript

The dwindling of Milton's early hopes for reformation—in the church and in English cultural life—is a story familiar to us all. Civil war, government service, domestic discord, and blindness made the enjoyment of academic recreation seem a faraway dream.[34] Nevertheless, Milton continued in his later poetry to imagine scenes that recall the cultured leisure of the academies.[35] In one sonnet inviting his young friend Edward Lawrence to dinner, he asks,

> What neat repast shall feast us, light and choice,
>   Of Attic taste, with Wine, whence we may rise
>   To hear the Lute well toucht, or artful voice
> Warble immortal Notes and *Tuscan* Air?
> (Sonnet 20, ll. 9 – 12)

In another he invites Cyriack Skinner: "Today deep thoughts resolve with me to drench / In mirth, that after no repenting draws" (Sonnet 21, ll. 5 – 6). These sonnets (composed in the 1650s) offer a space set apart from "the hard Season," the hard study of Euclid and Archimedes, and the hard-to-fathom intentions of the Swedes and French—a space for poetry, good food, and wine among like-minded friends. At much greater length, in the dialogue between Adam and "Raphaël, / The affable Arch-angel" (7.40 – 41), which occupies five books of *Paradise Lost*, Milton imagines an ideal academic symposium where friends dine and discuss ethics, aesthetics, and metaphysics.

In both cases, however, Milton not only contrasts this privileged space to threats from without—winter, the workaday world of study and diplomacy, and the machinations of Satan—but also acknowledges the potential for debase-

---

argues that both treatise and digression demonstrate the dictum "those who have eyes will see" (*Self-Consuming Artifacts: The Experience of Seventeenth-Century Literature* [Berkeley: University of California Press, 1972], 298 – 300).

34. During the Restoration, John Evelyn, who had attended meetings of the Roman Umoristi, met with Cowley, Dryden, and Waller in an unsuccessful attempt to found an English academy on the Italian model (Stoye, *English Travellers Abroad*, 223; E. S. de Beer, ed., *The Diary of John Evelyn*, 6 vols. [Oxford: Clarendon, 1955], 2:364; William Bray, ed., *Diary and Correspondence of John Evelyn*, 4 vols. [London: Henry G. Bohn, 1863], 3:310 – 11). For Thomas Sprat's proposal in *The History of the Royal-Society of London* (1667) for erecting an English academy, see J. E. Spingarn, ed., *Critical Essays of the Seventeenth Century*, 3 vols. (Bloomington: Indiana University Press, 1957), 2:112 – 15.

35. Anna K. Nardo, "Milton and the Academic Sonnet," in *Milton in Italy: Contexts, Images, Contradictions*, ed. Mario A. Di Cesare (Binghamton, N.Y.: Medieval and Renaissance Texts and Studies, 1991), 489 – 503; and Anna K. Nardo, "Academic Interludes in *Paradise Lost*," in *Milton Studies*, ed. James D. Simmonds (Pittsburgh: University of Pittsburgh Press, 1991), 27:209 – 41.

ment inherent in the space of academic recreation. As the convivial sonnets persuade the friends to enjoy, they simultaneously remind Lawrence and Skinner that they will "waste" a day (Sonnet 20, l. 4), that they should "spare [refrain or afford?] / To interpose [such delights] oft" (ibid., ll. 13–14), and that sometimes mirth does draw "repenting" (Sonnet 21, l. 6). And each sonnet ends with words more appropriate to a warning than an invitation: *unwise* and *refrains*.[36] Likewise, before Raphael arrives for lunch in Eden, Milton has already introduced the reader to a debasement of academic discourse in the lesser devils' futile debates of false philosophy as they await Satan's return. I have argued elsewhere that to image their political impotence, acquiescence to Satan's tyranny, flattery of the powerful, and trivialization of philosophy into a pastime Milton concentrates and exaggerates the decadent aspects of academic discourse found in Italian academies.[37] Even during the Edenic symposium, Raphael must warn Adam against useless, obscure, and overly subtle knowledge that "soon turns / Wisdom to Folly, as Nourishment to Wind" (7.129–30). In sonnet and epic alike, Milton both affirms the academic ideal and reminds readers of its sometimes debased reality.

Then at the end of his career, in *Paradise Regained*, Milton stages what seems to be a forceful rejection of the academic ideal itself. Faced with the Son's refusal of "The Kingdoms of this world," Satan tempts his indomitable adversary with a vision of Athens:

> the eye of *Greece*, Mother of Arts
> And Eloquence, native to famous wits
> Or hospitable, in her sweet recess,
> City or Suburban, studious walks and shades;
> See there the Olive Grove of *Academe*,
> *Plato's* retirement, where the *Attic* Bird
> Trills her thick-warbl'd notes the summer long.
> (4.240–46)

Italian academicians, including Milton's friends Dati and Buonmattei, repeatedly cite as their origin and model Plato's Academy that met in the groves outside Athens.[38] Whereas in *The Reason of Church-government* Milton had hoped that English academicians such as Buonmattei, the grammarian and dictionary maker, might one day "civilize, adorn and make discreet our minds," here the Son of God must reject the temptation to become a mere bookman:

36. Stanley E. Fish, "Interpreting the *Variorum*," *Critical Inquiry* 2 (1976): 465–85.
37. Nardo, "Academic Interludes," 220.
38. See Buonmattei, "Sopra l'Ozio," and Dati, "Chi fosse prima, o la Galli[n]a, o l'Uovo?" (*Prose Fiorentine*, 2.4.276, 3.2.152–53).

many books
Wise men have said are wearisome; who reads
Incessantly, and to his reading brings not
A spirit and judgment equal or superior
(And what he brings, what needs he elsewhere seek)
Uncertain and unsettl'd still remains,
Deep verst in books and shallow in himself,
Crude or intoxicate, collecting toys,
And trifles for choice matters, worth a sponge;
As Children gathering pebbles on the shore.

(4.321–30)

This dismissal of academic bookishness as "toys, / And trifles . . . worth a sponge" recalls the triviality of much academic discourse and its parade of erudition for its own sake.

In the end, however, Milton's brief epic celebrates the Son's triumph with if not an academic symposium, then at least its pleasures of food and verse. After Satan's fall from the pinnacle of the temple, angels waft the victorious Son

through the blithe Air,
Then in a flow'ry valley set him down
On a green bank, and set before him spread.
A table of Celestial Food . . .
.   .   .   .
and as he fed, Angelic Choirs
Sung Heavenly Anthems of his victory
Over temptation and the Tempter proud.

(4.585–95)

Having learned his mission through the wilderness agon with Satan, the Son can, as the angels sing, "on thy glorious work / Now enter, and begin to save mankind" (4.634–35). But between the wilderness agon and a ministry that will lead to the cross, the Son—precisely because he is "enshrin'd / In fleshly Tabernacle, and human form"—must be "refresht" (4.598–99, 637), and his interim victory celebrated with such feasting, music, and song as Milton once offered his young friend Edward Lawrence during a "hard Season." Despite the failure of all Milton's hopes for reconfiguring England's church and cultural institutions, he did not forget in *Paradise Regained* (1671) what he had asserted in *The Reason of Church-government* (1641–1642): "the spirit of man cannot demean it selfe lively in this body without some recreating intermission of labour, and serious things" (1:818).

Stella P. Revard

Thomas Stanley and "A Register of Friends"

During the late 1640s in London a coterie—both poetic and political in nature—formed about the young poet Thomas Stanley. Newly returned from the Continent, Stanley was eager to establish a poetic reputation for himself, to offer support to royalist poets come upon hard times, and to comfort his king in the last troubled days of his life. For about five years, he lived in the Middle Temple and was at the center of a group of poet-scholars, having entered, as Anthony Wood reported, "into a near Communication of Friendship & Studies." During this period, Stanley and the poets in his circle brought forth collections of their own work, contributed commendatory poems affixed to the collections of their friends' works, and commented on literary and political matters. Many years later, Stanley composed a poem, "A Register of Friends," in which he remembered many of the poet-scholars with whom he associated during this period. Reflecting both on politics and on poetics, Stanley provides in this poem a retrospective view of the friends who formed his circle, of the literary pursuits that engaged them, individually and collectively, and of the difficult times during which they joined together in friendship and in studies.[1]

Stanley's circle included his kinsman Edward Sherburne, the dramatist James Shirley, his uncle William Hammond (the Greek scholar from Cambridge), his tutor William Fairfax (son of the translator of *Jerusalem Delivered*), the young poet John Hall from Durham, and the better-known poets Alexander Brome, Robert Herrick, and Richard Lovelace (another kinsman of Stanley on his moth-

---

1. Wood received his information from Edward Sherburne, who filled in information about not only Stanley, but also others in Stanley's group (Frans Jozef Van Beeck, ed., *The Poems and Translations of Sir Edward Sherburne* [Amsterdam: Stellingen, 1961], xxvii). The text of "A Register of Friends" as well as citations of Stanley's poetry (unless otherwise noted) are from Galbraith Miller Crump, ed., *Poems and Translations,* by Thomas Stanley (Oxford: Clarendon Press, 1962).

er's side).[2] With the exception of John Hall, all of the poets were, like Stanley, staunch royalists who expressed strong support for Charles I and were deeply distressed at the events of the late 1640s that led to his death. The group also shared similar literary interests and tastes; all of them were involved in translation of some sort, from Latin, from Greek, or from the Romance languages. So interconnected were their literary interests and their political allegiances that it is sometimes difficult to disengage the two or to pronounce positively whether the poets in Stanley's circle were more bound together by devotion to poetic pursuits or to the waning royalist cause.

The circle around Stanley formed at a crucial period in English history, at the point in 1645–1646 when it had become clear that the king's cause was lost and that the Parliament was now in control of the country's destiny. It is a curious moment for literary studies to revive—but so they did. Stanley himself was newly returned from the Continent where he had weathered, as had other expatriate royalists, the most intense period of the civil wars. Born in 1625, he had matriculated at Pembroke, his uncle's college at Cambridge, before attending Oxford and being admitted to the degree of master of arts in 1642 in the company of Prince Charles and the duke of Buckingham. He had left England in 1642 in the company of his tutor Fairfax and returned, probably in late 1645 or 1646, not long before the fall of Oxford and the flight of Charles I.[3] Stanley was only in his early twenties on his return.

Why should a literary circle have formed about so young a man and one who had not yet proved his poetic abilities? Stanley was an independently wealthy peer who had strong literary ambitions. Although loyal to the king, he had not actively served him and suffered in no way impoverishment or alienation because of his royalist allegiances. He seems to have drawn several types of men to his company: men allied by kinship and education, young men embarking (like himself) on literary careers, and needy royalists who in many cases had been men of established literary reputation, but were now without financial support. Necessarily, the types sometimes overlapped.

Probably the first members of the so-called coterie were Stanley's uncle Hammond and his tutor Fairfax, older men who had been responsible for his

2. For biographical information on Stanley and his coterie, see Crump, *Poems and Translations*. Also see Sandra A. Burner, *James Shirley: A Study of Literary Coteries and Patronage in Seventeenth-Century England* (Lanham, Md.: University Press of America, 1988), 160–61.

3. In "A Register of Friends," Stanley says he was driven to sea by the storm of the civil war.

education and for forming his literary tastes. In "A Register of Friends," Stanley describes his tutor Fairfax as "Learning's Hermitage," the "Guide" who informed his childhood, extended the same care to his youth, and "rais'd [him] at last to Manhood" (ll. 1, 18). In the lines to Fairfax we glimpse Stanley's zest for scholarly activity and also a nascent joy in collaborative enterprises:

> With scrutiny the Greeks we often vext,
> And disentangled oft the Romane Text;
> The old Philosophers we did excite
> To quarrell, whilst we smil'd to see the fight:
> Some serious hours Historians did divide,
> Our mirthfull by the Poets were supply'd.
> ("Fairfax," in "A Register of Friends," ll. 21–26)

In "A Register," Stanley also pays tribute to his uncle Hammond, the power of whose "Magnetick Letters" (ll. 8–13) and whose scholarly acumen he remembers during the "halcion-dayes" at Cambridge. Hammond was not only a Greek scholar but also a poet. Stanley gathered and printed his poetry in 1655 after Hammond's death. That Fairfax and Hammond were present when Stanley began to gather his circle about him is surely significant. They had been responsible for forming Stanley's literary tastes. Is it any wonder that the very tastes for ancient philosophers and poets that guided Stanley at Cambridge apparently also inspired the activities of his literary circle in the Middle Temple? Greek and Latin literature—as we shall see—were at the heart of the program of study and translation.

The next two men drawn to Stanley's circle were, like Hammond and Fairfax, also erudite classical scholars. But James Shirley and Edward Sherburne were also disfranchised royalists much in need of support from a wealthy peer. Although himself absent during the fighting, Stanley had deep sympathy with the royalists who had remained in England and had suffered dire consequences because of the king's defeat. We cannot ignore the force of this political sympathy. Shirley and Sherburne—both Catholics—had actively served Charles I. Shirley (1596–1666), the eldest poet in the circle, had been a well-known and successful playwright who was left without a profession with the closing of the playhouses in 1642. He relied first on the king's patronage and then with the failure of the royal cause took up teaching.[4]

Although impoverished, Shirley was not without literary influence and rep-

4. See Ruth K. Zimmer, *James Shirley, a Reference Guide* (Boston: G. K. Hall, 1980).

utation. The royalist printer Humphrey Moseley published Shirley's poems in 1646, and Shirley was engaged at the same time in writing a preface for Moseley's folio of the *Works of Beaumont and Fletcher* (1647). Shirley was likely the means for Stanley's introduction into Moseley's circle. Stanley became one among many Moseley poets to contribute verses to the Beaumont and Fletcher folio that Shirley was overseeing. One of the most prolific printers of the period, Moseley in the late 1640s and 1650s particularly smiled on out-of-favor Caroline poets. After the victory of the parliamentary forces at Naseby in 1645, the literary life in London began to revive, and poetry, rather than merely political pamphlets, issued from the presses. Moseley was one of the publishers who sought poets to publish. Edmund Waller was among the first, but Moseley also printed John Milton's first volume of verse in 1645/46—and Milton could hardly have been called a royalist poet.[5]

Stanley's first appearance in print was in a Moseley publication. Although without attribution, Stanley's epigram on Sir John Suckling appeared beneath the Marshall portrait of Suckling in the 1646 edition of *Fragmenta Aurea*. Moseley later became Stanley's regular publisher. Although Stanley himself printed his first volume by private means in 1647, Moseley published in the late 1640s Stanley's *Oronta* and later the second edition of Stanley's 1651 *Poems*.[6] If Stanley welcomed James Shirley into his circle as a dispossessed servant to the king and literally kept the wolf from his door in the 1640s and 1650s, Shirley richly repaid Stanley's patronage by helping the younger poet to a publisher and to the means of establishing a literary reputation. Certainly, one of the functions of the literary circle was mutual assistance. And older, more established poets such as Shirley seem to have helped younger poets make their way in the literary world.

5. Most of the poets whom Moseley published were royalists, the notable exception being John Milton, whose *Poems* were published by Moseley in 1645/46. A poem addressed by John Leigh "To the Stationer (Mr. Moseley)" in the 1651 edition of Cartwright's *Comedies and Tragi-Comedies, with Other Poems* lists with approval the poets whom Moseley had published, including Suckling, Carew, Waller, Denham, Stanley, Sherburne, Crashaw, Shirley, Quarles, Cleveland, Berkenhead, and Cowley ("The Mistress"). He asks Moseley for the royalist Cowley's later poems and something from Brome (presumably Alexander Brome). Milton is not on the list, and indeed when *Paradise Lost* came forth in 1667, it was not from Moseley.

6. Stanley reprinted the dedicatory poem to Suckling in 1651, when he also printed his dedicatory poems to Shirley and Hall, as well as the poem to Fletcher. Stanley published both his 1647 and his 1651 *Poems* privately. Apparently Moseley, however, was the actual publisher for the 1651 volume and its reprint in 1652. See *Oxford Bibliographical Society, Proceedings and Papers*, vol. 2 (1925–1927) (Oxford, 1930), which lists Moseley's publications for these years. My thanks to Peter Lindenbaum for pointing out this volume.

Edward Sherburne (1616–1702) also came into Stanley's circle as a needy royalist, but he had other and stronger claims for his place within it. He was probably the poet-scholar closest to Stanley in literary taste, and, as Anthony Wood notes, the most intimate member of his circle. Not surprisingly, Stanley devotes the longest poetic tribute in "A Register of Friends" to Sherburne. Distant cousins, they shared, as Stanley himself says, the "double Ty of Sympathy and Blood" (l. 10). Sherburne had been clerk of his Majesty's Ordnance and was turned out of his office in 1642. As a Catholic, his estates were later confiscated by Parliament. Both he and his brother served Charles I during the war and remained with him until the siege of Oxford. With the king's imprisonment at Carisbrooke, Sherburne was left without means of support. As he had assisted Shirley, Stanley also came to Sherburne's aid. Sherburne had come to London in 1646, residing first with Thomas Povey in the Middle Temple and then with Stanley.[7] It was a close association that bore fruit in what was, as we shall see, something very like literary collaboration.

We cannot be sure how closely associated with Stanley's circle were royalist poets such as Robert Herrick and Alexander Brome. But clearly in some way they were. It is easier to document Richard Lovelace's involvement. Here again ties of blood come into play, for Lovelace was also Stanley's cousin. Another accomplished classicist and translator, he too would have contributed to the circle's zest for classical translation. He was apparently connected to the group when he returned to England in late 1646, and continued to associate with it except for the ten months he spent in prison in 1648–1649.[8] Stanley pays tribute in "A Register of Friends" both to Lovelace's poetry and to his devotion to the royal cause: "There thy Love and Loyalty didst sing, / The Glories of thy Mistris, and thy King" (ll. 13–14). In Stanley's view poetry and politics are inextricably intertwined, and he affirms that Lovelace left to posterity a name "for Arts and Armes alike renown'd" (l. 24).[9]

Another accomplished translator in Stanley's circle was the young poet-essayist John Hall. Unlike the other members of the circle, however, Hall was a committed parliamentarian and antiroyalist. Stanley first met Hall in Durham

7. Sherburne's father had also been clerk of his Majesty's Ordnance. After his ejection from this post and imprisonment, Sherburne joined Charles I at Edgehill and was created by Charles commissionary general of the artillery, both he and his brother Henry serving Charles until the fall of Oxford. Sherburne was restored to his place in Ordnance after the Restoration to be ejected from it once more in 1688.

8. See C. H. Wilkinson, ed., *The Poems of Richard Lovelace* (Oxford: Clarendon Press, 1930), xlix.

9. Many poets contributed posthumous tributes to Lovelace that were added to the 1659 collection of his poems.

in 1641; the two became reacquainted in 1646 when Hall was at Cambridge. When Hall came to Gray's Inn in 1647, he became a member of Stanley's circle. The intimate nature of their friendship might be surmised by the warmth of Hall's dedicatory letter to Stanley in the first volume of his *Poems:* "What I was first indebted to you at Durham, I endeavour to acquit in part here at Cambridge." But if we conclude that Hall's presence within Stanley's group was determined only by youthful sympathy of two young poets, we mistake. Hammond and Shirley admired Hall and with Stanley contributed commendatory poems for Hall's book of essays, *Horae Vacivae.*[10] Hall inspired friendship in others of Stanley's circle. In "To his worthy friend M. John Hall" in *Hesperides* (1648), Herrick expressed admiration for Hall's precocious wit, remarking that Apollo had lent Hall his own lyre and made him "Master of the Quire":

> Tell me young man, or did the Muses bring
> Thee less to taste, then to drink up their spring;
> That none hereafter sho'd be thought, or be
> A Poet, or a Poet-like but thee.
> What was thy Birth, thy starre that makes thee knowne
> At twice ten yeares, a prime and publike one?
> Tell us thy Nation, kindred, or the whence
> Thou had'st, and hast thy *mighty influence,*
> That makes thee lov'd, and of the men desir'd,
> And no lesse prais'd, then of the maides admir'd.[11]

Lovelace was another admirer. Hall contributed a commendatory poem to Lovelace's *Lucasta* in 1649, and Lovelace returned the compliment with a poem for Hall's posthumously printed *Hierocles* (1657). Like Herrick, Lovelace commended Hall's genius and expressed particular admiration for his book *Paradoxes.* Other royalists apparently also admired Hall, including Thomas Urquhart who also exchanged commendatory poems with him.[12]

In the 1640s and 1650s in London—despite the turbulent times—a talent-

10. *Poems by John Hall* (Cambridge: Roger Daniel, 1646), 4. Stanley, Hammond, and Shirley wrote commendatory poems for the collection of essays *Horae Vacivae* that Hall published in 1646.

11. See "To his worthy friend M. John Hall, Student of Grayes-Inne," in *Hesperides; or, The Works Both Humane and Divine of Robert Herrick Esq.* (London: John Williams, 1648), 354.

12. See "To the Genius of Mr. John Hall. On his exact Translation of Hierocles his comment upon the golden Verses of Pythagoras" (Wilkinson, *Poems of Lovelace,* 190–92). Writing under the pen name J. de la Salle, Hall commends Thomas Urquhart in 1653 as the translator of Rabelais. Urquhart in 1650 had paid Hall the compliment of contributing verses to de la Salle's *Paradoxes* (see Wilkinson, *Poems of Lovelace,* 348).

ed writer could belong to more than one literary group. Such was the case with John Hall. He had written, while at Cambridge, a tract on education and on arriving in London affiliated himself not only with Stanley's circle but also with Samuel Hartlib's group, expressing a desire to meet the famous John Milton, author of another tract, "On Education."[13] In contrast, Stanley, on being approached in 1647 to join Hartlib's proposed academy, refused to join (according to John Hall) on the grounds that he belonged to the Order of the Black Ribband (a group professing sympathy for the captive Charles I) and would not be a renegade. Hall continued, however, to associate with parliamentarians and royalists alike, exchanging commendatory poems with Sherburne, Shirley, and others in the group.[14] He was soon writing pamphlets for the parliamentary side, eventually becoming one of the official apologists for Cromwell at a salary of one hundred pounds per year. He remained, however, on cordial terms with Stanley until the end of his life and dedicated a book, *Emblems*, to Stanley's wife, Dorothy.

Yet, not everyone in London was pleased with such easy double-dealing. In 1648 someone, probably Sir George Wharton, in the course of an attack on Hall questioned his membership in Stanley's group: "Art thou a fit *Associate* for such *Ingenious* and candid *soules* as Col. *Lovelace, captaine Sherburne*, Mr *Shirley*, or Mr *Stanley*? They shall kick thee out of their *acquaintance* and tel thee thou art no *legitimate* Son of the *Muses*, but a *Traytor* to *Ingenuity*, a meere *excrementitious scabb* of Learning."[15] What Lovelace, Herrick, Stanley, and Sherburne thought of Hall's antimonarchical tracts we can only guess. But clearly, they must have separated the politics from the person, for Hall remained among the intimate associates of the group. His talent as a translator and a wit obviously recommended him to a group in which classical translation was prized.

For many of the poets in Stanley's circle, however, loyalty to the king was a

13. For commentary on Hall's correspondence with Hartlib, see Don Cameron Allen, introduction to facsimile edition of *Paradoxes by John Hall* (Gainesville, Fla.: Scholars' Facsimiles and Reprints, 1956), viii. Hall shared many views about education not only with Hartlib but also with Milton.

14. "Mr. Stanley (who has been all this while in the country) though he was profered the second place (I mean Orator) will not accept it by reason himself hath a design Armilla nigra and forsooth will not be a riyatpi" (quoted in Crump, *Poems and Translations*, xxvi). On coming to London, Hall began to write tracts for *Mercurius Britannicus*, siding with the Independents against Presbytery and against the king. Soon Hall came to Cromwell's notice and was assigned the job of answering a tract by Prynne. He probably became acquainted with Milton at this time and he accompanied Cromwell to Scotland in 1651.

15. *Mercurius Elenticus*, No 27, May 24–31, 1648, 206; quoted in Wilkinson, *Poems of Lovelace*, 347.

central concern, one that provided them a sense of group identity. Stanley had
begun the practice of wearing a black armband to demonstrate support for
Charles I. The Order of the Black Ribband was a political subcircle of the literary group he sponsored. Its activities probably did not go beyond expressing
loyalty to the king and passive resistance to the revolutionaries. Yet, the order
was serious and commanded Stanley's allegiance, certainly enough to make
him refuse to join a literary group such as Hartlib's, made up mostly of parliamentarians. Further, the Order of the Black Ribband was not a silent circle. It
had a literary aspect and called forth poetic comment both from the republican John Hall and from the royalist James Shirley. In "To my honoured Noble
Friend, Thomas Stanley, Esq. on his Poems," Hall not only refers to Stanley's
wearing the black armband, but also commends the practice: "Nay, vestals
might as well such sonnets hear, / As keep their vows and thy black riband
wear." Shirley, who shared Stanley's royalist sympathies, makes an even more
positive statement about the order:

> All Orders have thir growth, and this, when sent
> To me, had somthing that was glorious meant,
> From One, whose blood writes noble, but his mind
> And Souls extraction leave that stream behind:
> And this who knowes in calmer time may thrive,
> And grow into a Name, if Arts survive?
> Till when, to this black Arme-let, it shall be
> My Honour to be call'd a Votary.[16]

Stanley reprinted Hall's and Shirley's poems on the black armband in the 1647
edition of his own poems. He expresses his loyalty to Charles I far more cogently, however. After the king's death, Stanley began in 1649 to compose a poetical paraphrase of *Eikon Basilike*, *Psalterium Carolinum*, which was set to music by John Wilson and published in 1657.[17]

Most of the poetry that Stanley and his group published during this period
was related only indirectly to their political convictions. Thus, the commendatory poems that they addressed to each other often became the medium for the
group to express views they might otherwise have suppressed. The commenda-

16. See "Armilla Nigra" and "To my honoured Noble Friend, Thomas Stanley, Esq.
on his Poems," in *Poems by John Hall*, 88–89, 63. Also Shirley, "On a black Ribband," in
his *Poems &c.* (London: Humphrey Moseley, 1646), 53.
17. "The Devotions of his Sacred Majestie in His Solicitudes and Sufferings, Rendered
in Verse, Set to Musick for 3 Verses and the Organ, of Theorbo, By John Wilson," in
Psalterium Carolinum (London: John Martin, 1657).

tory poems that Stanley, Sherburne, and Alexander Brome contributed for the Latin grammar that Shirley published in 1649 indicate not just their friendship for the erstwhile-popular Caroline dramatist, now turned teacher, but also their sympathy for the straitened circumstances Shirley was experiencing because of his loyalty to the royalist cause. In the dedicatory letter to Stanley that Shirley prefixed to his play *The Brothers* (1652), he expresses gratitude for Stanley's financial assistance as well as his friendship. These commendatory poems and dedicatory letters give us a notion just how difficult it was for royalist writers to survive during this period and how valuable the moral support that the group provided was to such writers.[18]

Sherburne offers a different perspective on the times in the poems and prefaces he published. In 1648 he dedicated to the king his translation, *Seneca's Answer to Lucilius His Quaere:* "Why Good Men suffer misfortunes seeing there is a Divine Providence?" In itself, translating Seneca might not be a political act, but Sherburne makes plain in the prefatory letter to Charles I just how much he intends it to be. Sherburne compares the king's suffering to Christ's, suggesting that Seneca's words offer in small part a consolation to the monarch: "I from thence assume the humble boldnesse to think that this Peece of *Seneca* of *The Sufferings of Good Men* might at this time be made *pardonable*, (I durst not thinke it a suitable) *Present* for Your *Majesties view;* wherein as by a weak *Reflex*, your Majesty may perceive a glympse of your own invincible *Patience*, and inimitable Magnanimity; in bearing and over-mastering Mis-fortunes."[19]

Inspired perhaps by Sherburne, Stanley himself versified a passage from Seneca (found among his unpublished poetry) that served both as a cheering philosophy and as a political commentary on the plight of the royalists in the 1640s and 1650s:

> No other refuge left to fly,
> The lawes of strict necessity
> Than cheerfully to entertaine

---

18. Shirley, *Via ad Latinam Linguam Complanata* (London: John Stephenson, 1649). Thomas Stanley contributed a commendatory poem in Latin, Sherburne poems in Latin and English (which he reprinted in his own *Poems* of 1651). Alexander Brome and John Ogilby also contributed poems. *The Brothers* was published in a single volume in 1652 and the next year (1653) in a collection, *Six New Plays,* both published by Humphrey Robinson and Humphrey Moseley (see Burner, *James Shirley,* 154–61). Another playwright, Richard Brome, dedicated *The Joviall Crew* to Stanley in 1652.

19. Sherburne, *Seneca's Answer to Lucilius His Quaere* (London, 1648), sigs. A2v–A3.

What she commands us to sustaine;
Beneath each crosse with joy to bow
As if thou wouldst it had bin so;
Nor canst thou wish it alterd be
Whats heavens immutable decree;
In miseries thus win the field,
They onely fate orecome that yield.
                                (Crump, 334–35)

Sherburne was one of the most outspoken members of the group. He expresses again and again in prefatory letters and poems his loyalty to the king and his discontent with parliamentary rule. In a poem affixed to Moseley's 1651 edition of William Cartwright's *Comedies and Poems*, Sherburne not only bemoans the defeat of the royalist cause, but also (with a sneer at the Levelers) deplores the standards of poetry that the new regime has brought in:

How subject to new Tumults is this Age?
With War lesse vex'd now, than Poetick Rage!
Were not State-Levellers enough! That yet
We must be plagu'd with Levellers of Wit.[20]

Sherburne's publication in 1648 of his translation of Seneca's *Medea* might not at first appear politically relevant. But Stanley in a commendatory poem suggests its hidden agenda and takes the occasion to make a comment on the times. Addressing Sherburne, he hints that Medea's revenge against Jason reflected in a peculiar way the bold acts of Parliament in the present age:

This Cruelty thou didst once more expresse,
Though in a strange, no lesse becoming dress,
And her [Medea's] Revenge did'st rob of half its pride
To see it selfe thus by it selfe out-vy'd;
Whil'st boldest Ages past might say, our Times
Could speak, as well as act their highest Crimes.[21]

20. "On the publication of the Posthume POEMS of Mr. William Cartwright," in *Comedies and Tragi-Comedies, with Other Poems by Mr. William Cartwright* (London: Humphrey Moseley, 1651).
21. "To my Honoured Friend, Edward Sherburne Esq., Upon his Translation," *Medea: A Tragedie. Written in Latine by Lucius Annaeus Seneca, Englished by E.S."* (London: Humphrey Moseley, 1648).

These kinds of intimate asides remind us that we are dealing with poets who shared political opinions and understood the subtleties of one another's work.

Nevertheless, to suggest that most of the publications of this period were politically motivated would be misleading. The late 1640s and early 1650s witnessed the printing of a great variety of writing from members of Stanley's circle. Stanley's own first publishing ventures were celebrated enthusiastically by the poets of his coterie. As he brought forth the first edition of his *Poems* in 1647, he enjoyed the support of older poets such as Shirley as well as the fellowship and camaraderie of younger poets such as Sherburne and Hall.[22] Ample testimony to this is the gathering of commendatory verses by Hammond, Sherburne, Hall, and Fairfax prefixed to the 1647 *Poems*. Moreover, affixed to the final pages of the Huntington Library copy of the 1647 *Poems* is a collection of epithalamiums composed by Shirley, Sherburne, Fairfax, and Hammond for Stanley's marriage in 1648.[23] Stanley's 1647 *Poems* was an ambitious debut for the young poet, containing amatory pieces as well as his first translations of writers as diverse as Theocritus, Catullus, Secundus, Marino, and Girolamo Preti. His lyric and amatory poetry won a certain amount of contemporary favor. It was praised by members of his coterie and was set to music. John Playford's *Select Musical Ayres and Dialogues*, Lawes's *Second Book of Ayres and Dialogues*, and John Gamble's *Ayres and Dialogues* (1657) all contain settings of Stanley's lyrics.

Stanley's translations were also much admired. He had undoubtedly determined early (under the tutelage of Fairfax and Hammond) on a literary career that would also include translation, classical scholarship, and imitation. After the publication of the 1647 *Poems*, he began almost immediately to work toward a second expanded volume, cutting from the earlier volume many of the love poems in the style of Donne and other Caroline poets and adding a number of important translations, including the first complete translation of the anacreontics in English and a translation of the majority of Joannes Secundus's *Basia*. Stanley's second volume of poetry, published in 1651, contains most of

22. Stanley warmly commended both Hall and Shirley, publishing prefatory poems in 1646 both in John Hall's *Essays* and in James Shirley's *Poems*.

23. See the reprinting of this group of poems (Gerald Eades Bentley, "James Shirley and a Group of Unnoted Poems on the Wedding of Thomas Stanley," *Huntington Library Quarterly* 2 [1938–1939]: 219–32). Shirley's epithalamium is a Spenserian celebration of the bridal day. In the following year Lovelace wrote an epithalamium (published posthumously in 1659) celebrating the anniversary of the marriage (see Wilkinson, *Poems of Lovelace*, 177–78).

the works for which we now remember him and was the culmination of his own achievement as the leader of the poetic circle.[24]

In looking at the range of Stanley's translations, we can learn something about the activities and interests of his poetic circle, for Stanley was not the only poet in his group who was translating classical and continental writers. In "A Register of Friends," Stanley bears witness to Sherburne's interest in these same texts.[25] Indeed, it would appear that Sherburne was closely associated with him in a program of study and translation. What the one translated during the late 1640s is not unrelated to what the other translated. Both had a taste for the outlandish poetic romances of Girolamo Preti. Stanley published his translation of Preti's *Oronta* in 1649, Sherburne his translation of Preti's *Salmacis* in 1651. We find a similar interest in Giovanni Battista Marino, an Italian poet much admired in the earlier part of the century. Stanley translated Marino's *Echo* as well as a group of his shorter lyrics; Sherburne contributed Marino's *Forsaken Lydia* together with a pair of Marino's epigrams. While Sherburne translated from the French St. Amant's longer work, *The Metamorphosis of Lyrian and Sylvia*, Stanley undertook his shorter poem, "The Enjoyment." Such complementary undertakings cannot be accidental, but have must been part of a deliberate program of collaboration.

Both Sherburne and Stanley published volumes of poetry in 1651. When we look at the classical poetry that Sherburne and Stanley included in their respective volumes, we find a similar pattern. While Sherburne was translating a group of Theocritus's idylls (nos. 15, 31, 21), Stanley was concentrating on Theocritus's pastoral successors, Bion and Moschus. Sherburne undertook Theocritus's lament for Adonis, Stanley Bion's lament for Adonis. Both were interested in the late Latin poet Ausonius with Stanley translating "Cupid Crucified" and Sherburne "The Seven Wise Men." Both also seem to have been determined to explore some unusual items in the wider classical pantheon. Stanley was the first translator of *Venus' Vigil*, Sherburne of Coluthus's "Rape of Helen." The overlapping is not absolute, however. Sherburne had a taste for Martial's epigrams that Stanley did not share.

---

24. Stanley translated most of the anacreontic odes for the 1651 volume, adding them to the volume of poetry that he had first published in 1647. For the 1651 volume Stanley removed both the prefatory material and the commendatory poems of his friends— William Hammond, Edward Sherburne, John Hall, and William Fairfax.

25. In "A Register of Friends," Stanley says that Sherburne's interest in continental writers continued in later years: "There thy retirement, suiting with their strain, / French and Italian poets entertain; / And lest such strangers should converse alone, / Didst Civilly mix with their Songs thy own" (ll. 45–48).

What is still more interesting, however, is that other members of Stanley's circle shared his interest in translating classical and continental works, sometimes turning to the same authors. At approximately the same time, Stanley and Hall undertook translations of the "Golden Verses of Pythagoras." Stanley printed his verse translation with notes in 1651. Hall reserved his translation to print with the commentary of Hierocles on Pythagoras that he was preparing for publication when he died in 1656. In his foreword "To the Reader," moreover, he not only commends Stanley's version of the Pythagoras, but also includes in his text Stanley's verses after his own. He explains that he would not have printed his own version of Pythagoras had his not been more literal than Stanley's and thus most suited to his purpose, that is, to introduce Hierocles' extensive commentary. Stanley's cousin Lovelace took an interest in Stanley's and Hall's versions of Pythagoras's verses, writing a poem in commendation of the commentary on Hierocles that is prefixed to Hall's translation. The translation of Hierocles, moreover, was not the only classical translation for the busy parliamentarian pamphleteer. Hall also translated Longinus's Περὶ ὕψους, publishing it in 1652 and dedicating it to Bulstrode Whitelocke, the keeper of the great seal and adviser to Cromwell.

How extensively Lovelace worked with Hall or with Stanley and Sherburne we cannot know. As his posthumous volume of poetry published in 1659 amply demonstrates, however, Lovelace was, like other members of the group, an accomplished translator of classical and continental verse. Like Stanley and Sherburne, he undertook Seneca, Catullus, Martial, as well as epigrams from Ausonius; he translated from the French both Theophile Viand and Voiture, writers Stanley had translated. He also dipped into Italian Renaissance authors, translating some of Sannazaro's *Hexasticks.*

Then there is the question of the anacreontics, the lyrics on love and wine that Renaissance writers attributed to Anacreon. In the 1640s Stanley began to work on the first complete English translation of the anacreontics, a translation that he published in 1651. The anacreontics had been extremely popular with Caroline poets such as Ben Jonson and continued to be imitated in the 1640s and 1650s by so-called Cavalier poets. It is not an idle question to ask why Stanley and other members of his circle devoted themselves to translating the lyrics of amorous, bibulous old Greek Anacreon during the last dark years of Charles I's reign. As I have argued elsewhere, many of these translations and imitations have definite royalist subtexts. Robert Herrick assumes Anacreon as his spokesman throughout *Hesperides* and challenges in this persona the Puritan distaste for love, wine, and roses. Other poets in Stanley's circle—Richard

Lovelace, Alexander Brome, and Edward Sherburne—also composed anacreontics. Sherburne includes a translation of anacreontic no. 2 in the notes to his "Rape of Helen." Brome did not publish his drinking songs until after the Restoration, but several of them, written during this period, are translations of the anacreontics and are interspersed among drinking songs that fiercely attack the Puritan establishment.[26]

Lovelace chose to imitate the anacreontic on the cicada, making the southern insect into an English grasshopper. "The Grasshopper" is one of his more tantalizing lyrics, beginning as a paraphrase of the ancient Greek lyric but ending with philosophical reflections on the winter of the civil war era that has frozen the aspirations of men and grasshoppers alike. The ode is addressed to Lovelace's friend Charles Cotton the elder, who introduced his poet son Charles (1630–1687) to Lovelace and other royalist poets.[27] When Stanley published in 1651 as part of his complete series his translation of the anacreontic on the cicada, he retained Lovelace's title, perhaps paying tribute to his cousin's earlier adaptation. But apart from this cautious glance at Lovelace's grasshopper, we find nothing of political moment in Stanley's anacreontics. Unlike the anacreontics of Brome and Lovelace and Herrick, and still more to the point the *Anacreontiques* that Abraham Cowley was to print in 1656, Stanley's anacreontics are straightforward translations of the Greek that would have raised no murmur from the Puritans. If the group that assembled in Stanley's rooms in the

26. See Revard, "The Politics of Cowley's *Anacreontiques,*" *Ben Jonson Journal* 4 (1997): 131–50. Although Stanley does not address any poems to Herrick, we know that Herrick was in London in the late 1640s, having been ejected from his living in Devon. He is named as a member of Stanley's circle, and like so many of the other poets in Stanley's group, he was also occupied at this time with putting together a miscellaneous volume of lyrics, translations, and imitations (*Hesperides* [1648]). For Sherburne's translation, see his *Miscellaneous Poems, Reprinted from the Edition of 1651* (London, 1819), p. 186. See Alexander Brome, *Songs and Other Poems* (London, 1661), 26–27, 67–68, 68–69. Charles Cotton the younger, friend to Brome and Lovelace, was also proficient at the "royalist" drinking song. He also translated some of the anacreontics and like Brome wrote anti-Puritan drinking songs, which were published posthumously (*Poems on Several Occasions* [London, 1689]). See the translation of the anacreontic "Εἰς τὸ δεῖν πίνειν" (John Beresford, ed., *Poems of Charles Cotton* [London: Richard Cobden-Sanderson, 1923], 357).

27. The younger Cotton may have been briefly a member of Stanley's circle; he certainly was acquainted with Alexander Brome and Richard Lovelace and shared many of their interests, being also expert in Latin, Greek, and continental languages. The younger Cotton was in London in the late 1640s and wrote an elegy on the death of Henry, Lord Hasting, printed in Richard Brome's *Lachrymae Musarum* (see Beresford, *Poems of Charles Cotton*, 246–47). Cotton wrote a commendatory poem to Alexander Brome printed in Brome's posthumous *Songs and Other Poems* (London, 1668), and several other poems for Brome and Lovelace (see Beresford, *Poems of Charles Cotton*, 240–41, 397–98, 361).

Middle Temple had a particular literary project of imitating Anacreon, it was Stanley's associates—rather than Stanley himself—who employed the anacreontic drinking songs as models for the Cavalier songs in which they toasted the fortunes of the king.

Another interest that the group obviously shared was the amatory lyric. Love lyrics form a prominent part of the collections of Stanley, Sherburne, Shirley, Lovelace, Herrick, and Hall. But of the group, only Herrick and Lovelace developed distinctive voices as love poets. The others tended to follow the prevailing styles of the period. We might even guess that their program of reading included Donne, Carew, and others of the best-known poets from the previous decade. The John Donne that Stanley and his circle imitated, however, was a much chastened version of the poet. When Stanley echoed Donne, he mimicked his plaintive voice and extravagant conceits, but avoided the sharp wit and obscene wordplay. His verses speak of sighs that transfuse the soul, mystic "wreath[s] of hair," and complain of tyrannical mistresses who provoke both idolatry and apostasy in love, key concepts of the Donnean canon. The titles of his love poetry also resemble Donne's—"Loves Heretick," "Divorce," "The Bracelet," and "The Parting."

As with the anacreontics, the love lyrics betray some hint also of collaborative composition. We might assume that lacking the wider audience of the court, the group itself might have assembled to provide an audience for the poetry that its members were composing. In "A Register of Friends," Stanley speaks of the friends forming the audience for Shirley that the poet-dramatist had lost with the close of the theaters:

> Then oft, withdrawne from the dull ears of those
> Who licenc'd nothing but rebellious Prose,
> Me with those pleasures thy kind Muse supply'd
> Which to it selfe the sullen Age deni'd.
>
> (ll. 13–16)

Compensating for the loss of other audiences, the circle of friends might well have listened to and read each other's poetry.

Certainly, on occasion the friends responded to one another's poems. In his 1647 *Poems*, Stanley included a poem written by Fairfax on the theme of one soul in two bodies, "The Union"; Fairfax's poem is followed by Stanley's response to it. It also appears more than likely that the verses written by Stanley and Sherburne on violets in the mistress's bosom were complementary lyrics. Stanley's is an elegant but sentimental piece. He congratulates the violets on finding a place in which they may revive and flourish: "Since thou from them dost borrow scent, / And they to thee lend ornament" (*Poems* [1647], 13). In contrast, Sherburne sarcastically remarks that the violets have found no refuge in his mistress's bosom: "What boots it to have escap'd winter's breath, / To find, like me, by flames a sudden death?" (*Poems* [1651], 22). As the two poets take these contrasting stances, they almost seem to have agreed (in advance) to disagree.

If collaboration and response are one part of the program that Stanley's circle engaged in, literary criticism is another. The friends describe, comment on, even dissect one another's poetry. Commendatory poetry seemed to encourage the practice, and the fact that the poets were part of a circle seemed to ensure that whatever commentary came forth, it would be friendly. Both Shirley and Hall comment on the polite manners of Stanley's love poetry—its purity, chastity, and innocence.[28] Shirley says, "Thy numbers carry height, yet clear, and terse, / And innocent, as becomes the soul of verse" (*Poems*, 31). Stanley's first volume of poetry celebrates his mistress Chariessa, whom he woos with soulful ardor. Substituting her name for Secundus's Neaera, he addresses to her "The hasty kiss," a literal translation of Secundus's *Basium* 3. Yet, as Hall expatiates, the love poets of the past—such as Anacreon or Secundus—might have learned proper decorum from Stanley:

> Thou noble soul! . . .
> Who lightest love's dying torch with pure fire,
> And breath'st new life into the Teian lyre,
> That love's best secretaries that are past,
> Lived they, might learn to love, and yet be chaste.
>
> . . . .
>
> So chaste is all, that though in each line lie
> More amorettoes than in Doris' eye,
> Yet so they're charm'd, that looked upon they prove
> Harmless as Chariessa's night love.
>
> (*Poems*, 63–64)

Stanley replies in kind, finding in the love poetry of his friends the innocence and chastity they had praised in his. Shirley, he contends in "A Register of

28. Even though he forswore love poetry after his first book of poems, the young John Hall as a love poet was often close to Stanley, particularly in the several Neoplatonic poems, such as his Donnean "Rapture" and "Platonic Love," in which he praises the union of souls (*Poems by John Hall*, 68–70, 57–58). But his poetry could also be satiric, as is evident in his opening, "A Satire."

Friends," infused into "dying Poetry" a new life (l. 41), reviving the conceits of the love poetry of the previous age, but purifying them into a diviner thing:

> Chaste as the kisses by the Morn bestowed
> Upon the Virgin-daughters of the year;
> Thy Lines and life alike unspotted were.
> ("Shirley," in "A Register of Friends," ll. 4–6)

He praises Shirley's idealized devotion to his mistress Odelia: "That Justice of all Ages must remit / To *Her* the prize of Beauty, *He* of Wit" (ll. 23–24).[29] Stanley in fact makes Shirley's Odelia next of kin to his own Chariessa or Lovelace's Lucasta or Amarantha—chaste ladies who (according to proper poetic decorum) inspire chaste flames.

We have remarked on how much of Stanley's poetry involved translation of continental and classical writers. He was the first English poet to translate into English Joannes Secundus's sequence, the *Basia,* including fourteen of Secundus's eighteen kisses.[30] The Dutch Neo-Latin poet Joannes Secundus (1511–1536) was immensely popular throughout Europe in the hundred years following his death. He had many imitators both on the Continent and in England; Elizabethan and Jacobean poets who had imitated or translated individual lyrics from Secundus's *Basia* include Jonson, Shakespeare, Drummond, and Carew.[31] Adjusting Secundus's sometimes earthly lyrics to his exacting Neoplatonic standards, Stanley determined to render the sequence more or less complete. Although he did not publish his "Kisses" until 1651, he had clearly been at work on the sequence for some time. A lyric in the 1647 *Poems* is a translation of *Basium* 3.

Interestingly enough, Stanley is not the only poet in his group who was imitating and translating Secundus. Several other members, prominent among

29. These lines were first printed in the poem prefixed to Shirley's *Poems* (1646), then reprinted in Stanley's *Poems,* before becoming part of "A Register of Friends."

30. See Stella P. Revard, "Translation and Imitation of Joannes Secundus' *Basia* during the Era of the Civil Wars in England," in *Acta Conventus Neo-Latini* (Avila), forthcoming.

31. Jonson's Celia poems, Carew's "Rapture," and Drummond's "Kisses Desired" are all imitations of Secundus. Antony's dying lines (when he imagines a lover's elysium for himself and Cleopatra) are probably drawn from Secundus (*Antony and Cleopatra,* 4.13.51–54). Charles Cotton the younger sent an imitation of Secundus to his tutor Rawson. Cotton's song "Join once again, my Celia" may also reflect the influence of Secundus (see Beresford, *Poems of Charles Cotton,* 17, 168–69). See Clifford Endres, *Joannes Secundus: The Latin Love Elegy in the Renaissance* (Hamden, Conn.: Archon Books, 1981), 32–33.

them Herrick, also modeled lyrics on Secundus's odes or on the *Basia*. In fact, Herrick includes throughout *Hesperides* poem after poem that imitates Secundus. Here again we have a hint that Stanley's circle was engaged in a collective—perhaps even a competitive—activity. The only evidence of collaboration or competition, however, is the poems themselves. Yet, it is possible to trace the permutations of one of Secundus's kisses in the works of three different members of the group, besides Stanley himself.

Several members of the group produced imitations of Secundus's *Basium* 6. By looking at the different versions of Secundus's lyric we may perhaps gain some understanding of how the group worked in responding to one another's poetry. In *Basium* 6, Secundus is asking his mistress Neaera for multiple kisses in exchange for his one (it is a kissing game, of course, in the tradition of Catullus):

> De meliore nota bis basia mille paciscens,
> > Basia mille dedi, basia mille tuli,
> Explesti numerum, fateor, iucunda Neaera,
> > Expleri numero sed nequit ullus amor.
>
> .   .   .   .
>
> Si numeras lachrymas, numeres licet oscula; sed si
> > Non numeras lachrymas, oscula ne numeres.
> Et mihi da, miseri solatia vana doloris,
> > Innumera innumeris basia pro lachrymis!
> > > (ll. 1–4, 23–26)[32]

Stanley translates Secundus in this way:

> Our Bargain for two thousand Kisses made,
> A thousand I receive'd, a thousand paid;
> The number I confess thou hast supply'd,
> But Love with Number is not satisfy'd
>
> .   .   .   .
>
> If thou wilt reckon, reckon both together;
> If both thou number not, ah, number neither;
> Give me (to ease the Pain my grieved Soul bears)
> Numberless Kisses, for unnumbred Tears.

This is a fairly straightforward version of Secundus's original, keeping quite exact the exchange of kisses in the opening lines and the juxtaposition of kisses

32. I quote from Scriverius's edition of Secundus (Leiden, 1619), which Stanley, according to Crump, probably had access to.

and tears in the finale of the poem. One thing, however, does not have a counterpart in Secundus; Stanley's lover—true to form—has a "grieved Soul."

When Herrick adapts Secundus's sixth kiss in "Kissing Usurie," it becomes a sportive kissing game. Herrick is teasing his mistress, who has given him only one kiss, and suggests that he will pay her back with interest:

> If thou will say,
> Ten will not pay
> For that so rich a one;
> Ile cleare the summe,
> If it will come
> Unto a Million.

The tears of Secundus's original are quite omitted, but the kisses multiply beyond the thousands to a million. In fact, Herrick likes the kissing game so much that he plays it also in "To Dianeme." There the poet coyly pleads for one kiss that he will "restore with two / Thousand score."[33]

Sherburne takes Secundus's lyric and turns it into a pastoral dialogue, "Love's Arithmetick." Sitting by the riverside, the shepherd Thirsis and his shepherdess Phillis enter into a competition. Thirsis protests, "Equal to these sandy Grains, / Is the Number of my Pains." Phillis replies in kind, "Many as the Earth hath leaves, / Are the Griefs my heart receives." The shepherd joyfully hears the declaration, and the "willing Shepheardess" has the last word:

> In Delight our Pains shall cease
> And our War be cur'd by Peace;
> We will count our Griefs with Blisses,
> Thousand Torments, Thousand Kisses.[34]

What is interesting here is not merely the dialogue form, but the fact that the lovers express a mutuality of desire. Each suffers the pangs of love, and each longs for kisses to requite the pain. Unlike Stanley's or Herrick's version, the lovers achieve a happy consummation.

But Sherburne's is not the last word on the multiplication of kisses. James Shirley also has something to say, which he too puts into a dramatic setting. His Ovidian narrative *Narcissus* is subtitled "The Self-Lover," which tells us that this is no amicable pair of lovers, but a discordant set. The hapless Echo is forced to

33. L. C. Martin, ed., *The Poems of Robert Herrick* (London: Oxford University Press, 1965), 29, 196.

34. Sherburne, *Miscellaneous Poems*, 100.

take the part of Secundus's lover to beg for the thousand kisses. She even echoes the witty language of John Donne, the group's favorite English poet, as she speaks of "loves warre" and "Lov's Exchequer":

67.

.   .   .   .

Thou wert unkinde Narcissus, to deny
Thy selfe the office of a courtesie.

68.

What was a kisse? the rape of such a Treasure
What Tyrant were he Judge, would call a sin?
Thou canst not loose thy lip, but finde pleasure:
Come let us now, though late, loves warre begin;
And meet me boldly, for one kisse of thine
Ile give a thousand: Lov's Exchequers mine.

69.

If thou bee'st scrupulous, I will not pay,
Thou shalt have halfe in earnest, if thou please:
Or if not so, I aske no longer day
To number the whole summe, before I cease:
And at the totall, if thy lip repine,
Ile trebble all, to have one more of thine.

70.

.   .   .   .

Be not too coy then to receive a Kisse,
Thou mightst have kist me twenty times 'ere this.[35]

The component of kisses and numbers is, of course, virtually the same as that in Secundus's original or Stanley's translation. But the reversing of the male to the female wooer has altered the dynamics of the exchange. Like the hapless Venus in another Ovidian poem, the woman takes the active role, even as she protests that the man ought to be doing the wooing. The manly pleading of Secundus's original takes on a plaintive female whine. Further, the shadow of Shakespeare's "Venus and Adonis" is not an accidental one. When we look back on the kissing scene in that poem, we find that Will Shakespeare has nicely set the scene for the younger dramatic poet James Shirley to follow. He himself has echoed Secundus, when his Venus repines:

"A thousand kisses buys my heart from me,
And pay them at thy leisure, one by one.

35. James Shirley, *Narcissus* (London, 1646), 18.

> What is ten hundred touches unto thee?
> Are not they quickly told and quickly gone?
> > Say for non-payment that the debt should double,
> > Is twenty hundred kisses such a trouble?"[36]

What are we to make of these different versions of Secundus's kissing game, rendered by poets who belong to the same poetic circle? Was Stanley the first to take up Secundus, or was it another member of the group? We cannot know for sure. The existence of different versions of the same poem by Secundus suggests that the poets of the circle were serving as audience and respondents to one another. Perhaps some kind of poetic competition within the circle sparked the composition. Although the resulting versions of *Basium* 6 are not close renderings either of Secundus or of each other, neither are they wholly independent productions. On the one hand, each version reflects the individual poet's personal taste. We would expect Stanley to make Secundus's kiss soulful, Herrick to make kissing into a country game, and Shirley and Sherburne to vie with Shakespeare and Donne in being witty and outrageous.[37] Thus, the imitations range from soulfulness to sensuality to flippancy. On the other hand, each seems deliberately not just to answer but also to echo the others. As Sherburne and Stanley gave us sentimental and caustic verses on violets that almost respond to one another, so each poet seems to respond to Secundus's original and at the same time to react to the versions of Secundus that his fellow poets have created. The spirit of playful competition reigns supreme. However, the imitations of Secundus, unlike those of Anacreon, do not comment on the times, other than perhaps to long for an era when a lover could salute his mistress or poets could compete in peace and tranquillity.

This kind of competition within the poetic circle perhaps enabled poets to retain a sense of community, a connection to older traditions of verse writing at a time when the Muses would seem to have been driven from their haunts. In a way the writing of witty and elegant love lyrics and polished translations may even have been a reaction to the very unruliness of the times. In their translations of Pico and of Seneca, Stanley and Sherburne perhaps make an effort to

---

36. "Venus and Adonis," in *The Riverside Shakespeare,* ed. G. Blakemore Evans et al. (Boston: Houghton Mifflin, 1974), p. 1711, ll. 517–22.

37. Although Stanley praised the chastity of Shirley's love poetry, the truth is that Shirley was often a rather "racy" poet. The opening love poem of Shirley's 1646 volume—"Cupids Call"—is a saucy carpe diem that invites country swains to reap willing maidenheads. Contrast this with Stanley's opener for his 1651 *Poems*—"To Love"—that is all Plato and divinity.

preserve classical and neoclassical virtues in an era they felt was inhospitable to them. By imitating the anacreontics and the *Basia*, poet-translators were also perhaps striving to keep alive the kind of poetry that had flowered in Charles I's time.

Stanley's circle was short-lived. After the king's execution, both Stanley and Sherburne left London for Stanley's Hertfordshire estates, probably in the company of Hammond and Fairfax.[38] Stanley apparently kept his rooms in the Middle Temple, however, and was in London from time to time throughout the 1650s. The circle was soon diminished further with the deaths of Hammond and Fairfax and Sherburne's departure abroad.[39] In his retirement Stanley produced an edition of Aeschylus and *A History of Philosophy*. After the Restoration he resumed his place as a patron of literature. He was a charter member of the Royal Society; he was acquainted with Ashmole, Browne, and Evelyn, and remained an intimate friend of Edward Sherburne. With Sherburne he encouraged Edward Phillips in the *Theatrum Poetarum*, and Phillips dedicated the work to them both. Stanley did not die until 1678, almost thirty years after his own circle had dissolved.

Stanley's most important years as poet and patron were those immediately preceding and immediately following Charles I's death. Such a retrospective piece as "A Register of Friends" (though written late) puts those years in perspective and gives us a sense of how Stanley was related to those poets he included in his coterie. "A Register of Friends" is divided into parts that celebrate consecutively those persons most important to Stanley, many now "drown'd in endless night" whom he remembers "with Greif and Joy" (ll. 1, 4).[40] The poem is partly made up from commendatory verses that Stanley had written in the

38. See Burner, *James Shirley*, 188.

39. In 1654 Sherburne became the tutor of Sir John Coventry and went abroad, returning in 1659 (see S. Fleming, "Biographical Sketch of Sir Edward Sherburne," in *Miscellaneous Poems*).

40. Besides Fairfax, Hammond, Shirley, Hall, Lovelace, and Sherburne, Stanley included in "A Register of Friends" Sir Justinian Iseham and Robert Bowman, citing them as men who remained faithful to the king during the hard times. He included only one other friend from a later period—Reverend Salmon. Stanley met the young royalist Robert Bowman on the Continent. In "A Register of Friends," he describes how they found each other "in a forreign Region" and enjoyed "sweet conversation" abroad until their return to England (ll. 5–8). There is no evidence, however, that Bowman was part of Stanley's poetic circle. Iseham was a later acquaintance whom he commends for attending the first Charles in war and the second in "peacefull Counsells" (ll. 15–16). "A Register of Friends" cannot be precisely dated, but since there are references to Hammond, Fairfax, Hall, and Lovelace as deceased and to the death of Shirley in 1666, it appears to be a piece written after the Restoration. For the account of the recovery of "A Register of Friends," see James M. Osborn, "Stanley's Lost 'Register of Friends,'" *Yale University Library Gazette* 32 (1958): 1–26.

late 1640s, some published in his own, some in other poets', volumes. To these he has added personal reminiscences, political reflections, and literary commentaries. Hence the poem is both a retrospective on the political times that the group weathered and a warm testimony of flowing conversation and joint scholarly endeavors. "A Register of Friends" begins—significantly—with addresses to those mentors most important to him as a young poet: Fairfax and Hammond. He interrupts this affectionate memoir of university days, however, to inveigh against the storm of civil war that ended them, separating uncle from nephew and leaving each to wail "the fury of unruly Times" (l. 16).

Writing after the Restoration, Stanley speaks more frankly than he could have in the late 1640s and 1650s. This late poem gives him the opportunity to express feelings that he had only hinted at in the commendatory verse of the 1640s and 1650s. He speaks of returning to England to find "Her face, disfigur'd so by Civill Wars" (l. 21) and with some bitterness inveighs against the "slavish peace" that followed the war:

> As Eastern Monarch's grant to Captiv'd foes,
> To servitude so miserable led
> That who remain'd alive envy'd the Dead.
>   (ll. 24–26)

Politics and political commentary assume a dominant role in "A Register."

For this reason we may wish to reassess the part politics played in holding Stanley's circle together. Stanley expresses his anger at the "barborous Times" that reduced poetry as well as men to a state of servitude. "A Register" gives Stanley the opportunity to speak candidly about how members of the group had suffered both political and literary oppression. He gives Shirley his due as the playwright who after Fletcher's death propped up the "sinking stage," a man whose conversation flowed "Smooth as [his] verse" (ll. 9–10, 3). At the same time he attacks those who suppressed the stage, depriving Shirley of a rightful audience for his verse. From a post-Restoration vantage, he can congratulate the Caroline dramatist on outliving his Puritan censors to see the stage and the monarchy restored. In old age Shirley received the applause he deserved:

> Thou didst live
> To see Dramatick Poesy revive,
> And haveing wellcom'd her return to day,
> Went'st off the stage, loaden with years and Bays.
>   (ll. 45–48)

Yet, even so, Stanley's praise of Shirley is mixed with regret at the heavy price paid merely to survive the time of national upheaval.

Stanley reserves the most extravagant denunciation of the interregnum for the sections on Hall and Lovelace. Instead of attacking the parliamentarian Hall as a regicide and deist, however, Stanley blames the abuses of the age, regretting that Hall ever left his home in the North:

> Ah! that thy innocent prodigious Youth
> Had never been transplanted to the South!
> Then had'st thou liv'd untainted with the Crimes
> Of those Rebellious Epecurian Times!
> Atheist and Theist then the Kingdome sway'd
> And, Rivall-like, each other did invade;
> Pernicious Twins of Hell, the elder brother
> Denyes a God, his providence the other.
>
> (ll. 7–14)[41]

Like Hall's biographer, John Davies of Kidwelly, Stanley tries to exonerate his friend, even indulging in the speculation that Hall in the end was "Repentant, Loyall, pious, at [his] death" (l. 38).[42]

Stanley portrays Lovelace, on the other hand, as a martyr to the "Rebel-Throng" (l. 6), even making praise of his cousin's poetry take second place to that of his bold loyalism. He pays tribute to Lovelace's soldiership at home and abroad, remembering how Lovelace had opposed the rebels when he represented Kent at the calling of the Long Parliament—and so "Wrought," as it were, his "own Chains" (l. 9), being imprisoned for the first time in 1642. While Lovelace was free, the "Usurpers" (l. 9), Stanley remarks, knew that they were not. He was harried and wasted by the "headlesse Rout" until he sank under the weight (l. 15).

Although much of "A Register of Friends" records the fervor of Stanley's royalism, the section on Sherburne moves beyond the troubles incurred by the band of friends to remark on the scholarly enterprises that absorbed them. The lines he addressed to Sherburne affirm how important classical and continental scholarship were to Stanley and his circle. As we have noted earlier, Stanley

41. Hall continued on friendly terms with Stanley and probably was in touch with him when he returned to the North before his death. Hall's posthumous *Hierocles upon the Golden Verses of Pythagoras* (London, 1657) also defers to Stanley and his superior classical scholarship.

42. John Davies of Kidwelly defends Hall against charges of atheism, attaching a life of Hall to the posthumously published *Hierocles* that he saw to press for his friend.

described Sherburne's translations of Seneca's prose and drama as acts of loyalty. But here he revises that view and praises for its own sake Sherburne's appreciation of Seneca's literary excellences:

> Next I remember well, thou didst distill
> The Prose of Seneca through thy smooth Quill
> Into soft Numbers, such as might preferre
> The Poet high as the Philosopher.
>
> (ll. 35–38)

Sherburne continued to be an active poet, translator, and critic long after Stanley had all but given up poetry. He outlived his cousin by a quarter of a century to become a respected scholar in the Restoration era. As Stanley's literary executor, Sherburne may even have corrected the verses Stanley wrote to him. Stanley sees Sherburne as one of the most successful members of the group. Rather than stressing the political conditions that restrained him, he emphasizes the quality of Sherburne's work. With Sherburne poetics would seem to have prevailed over politics.

Important as Stanley's post-Reformation memoir is to our assessment of the poetic circle he presided over in the late 1640s, it does not fully answer the question of why this particular group of poets came together during the years when monarchy was ending and republicanism thriving. Did the times create the necessity of the poetic circle, or would it have flourished quite as well outside of the era that birthed it? Did loyalty to the king hold the group together, or was poetry itself sufficient impetus to spark their delight in collaboration and competition? What we do know is that the friends in Stanley's circle supported each other's work, that they encouraged its publication in an era that was not outwardly congenial to their kind of poetry. Short-lived as it was, it served a particular function in its particular time. Stanley was to belong to other circles after the Restoration, but he was never at the center of so like-minded a group as he had been in the late 1640s. Stanley's circle, however, had a legacy, as it were. That Sherburne, Stanley's closest friend and collaborator, lived on to become part of other poetic circles after the Restoration, circles hospitable to the theories of translation and poetry that he and Stanley had espoused, is an indication of the far-reaching effect of the band of friends who had met in Stanley's rooms at the Middle Temple many years before.

Paul G. Stanwood

Community and Social Order
in the Great Tew Circle

Literary and critical fashions are tidal, moving like waves but often less predictably and sometimes with newly gathered force and unexpected strength. Such may be the special influence of Richard Hooker, the great apologist of the Elizabethan Settlement, on the intellectual and social culture of a significant group of early-seventeenth-century thinkers, many of whom were members of an informal circle that met in the years before the English civil war in a country house in Great Tew, Oxfordshire. I shall presently examine what constituted Hooker's appeal but first of all describe this fellowship that assimilated and advanced his ideas.

Great Tew is a small village that lies about sixteen miles northwest of Oxford, approached by "Taking the route you would be likely to take / From the place you would be likely to come from."[1] Little remains now to recall the importance that this place enjoyed as an intellectual center, the home once of the celebrated Lucius Cary, the second viscount Falkland (1610?–1643). Yet, Falkland himself would hardly be remembered except for the testimony of such admirers as Ben Jonson who wrote his Pindaric ode (composed about 1630) "To the Immortal Memory and Friendship of That Noble Pair, Sir Lucius Cary and Sir H. Morison." The poem serves as an elegy on Morison, who died in 1629, but most of all it exalts the transforming, nearly divine quality of friendship, for these young men "lived to be the great surnames / And titles by which all made claims / Unto the virtue" (ll. 113–15)—that virtue being "Friendship in deed . . . not in words" (l. 123). Jonson's praise reflects his own sense of classical and

---

1. Unlike Little Gidding, T. S. Eliot left no record of this place, but there is an ancient and pretty church at Great Tew and also a pub that carries the name of the most illustrious family of the village. The Falkland Arms annually celebrates the recent struggle over the famous islands, named after the fifth viscount.

humanist values, for he implies that these "twi- / Lights, the Dioscuri" (ll. 92–93) are noble Roman Englishmen.[2]

The Falkland family estates in Oxfordshire were small, but the house in Great Tew, now vanished, was ample—"a pleasant seat," notes John Aubrey, where Falkland lived in the early 1630s and entertained "the best Witts" of Oxford, turning his house into a kind of college, "full of Learned men."[3] These young men—for they were all young—met informally, coming and going as suited them, to discuss theology, politics, philosophy, and literature. But this was no easy seminar or idle gathering, and the Great Tew circle, as it came to be called, forged lasting and influential friendships. Edward Hyde (1609–1674), later first earl of Clarendon, the most renowned of the group, honored Lucius Cary in his *History* and again in his *Life*, recalling:

> [H]e contracted familiarity and friendship with the most polite and accu-rate men of that university [of Oxford]; who found such an immenseness of wit and such a solidity of judgment in him, so infinite a fancy bound in by a most logical ratiocination, such a vast knowledge that he was not ig-norant in any thing, yet such an excessive humility as if he had known noth-ing, that they frequently resorted and dwelt with him, as in a college situ-ated in a purer air; so that his house was a university bound in a lesser volume, whither they came not so much for repose as study, and to exam-ine and refine those grosser propositions which laziness and consent made current in vulgar conversation.[4]

Falkland obviously impressed Clarendon deeply, and the meetings and the brief years at Great Tew were for him the most formative of his life.

2. Jonson is quoted from the Oxford Authors edition of Ian Donaldson, ed., *Poems of Ben Jonson* (Oxford: Oxford University Press, 1985), 394–98, with excellent notes, 702–5. The ode is *Vnder-Wood* LXX. See also Jonson's epigram "To Sir Henry Cary" (no. 66, ed. Donaldson, 244), Lucius Cary's father (1575?–1633). Lucius Cary also wrote an el-egy for Morison, an "anniversary poem" addressed to his "Noble Father," Ben Jonson. As a "Son of Ben," Cary also wrote an elegy on Jonson's death. See A. B. Grosart, ed., *The Poems of Lucius Carey, Viscount Falkland*, vol. 3 of *Miscellanies of the Fuller Worthies' Library* (Blackburn, Lancashire: privately printed, 1871), 37–50; and see Kurt Weber's bio-graphical study, *Lucius Cary: Second Viscount Falkland* (New York: Columbia University Press, 1940), esp. app. 1, "Falkland's Verse."

3. See Oliver Lawson Dick, ed., *Aubrey's Brief Lives* (1949; reprint, Ann Arbor: Uni-versity of Michigan Press, 1957), 56. Aubrey claims that "Mr. William Chillingworth . . . was [Falkland's] most intimate and beloved favourite. . . . For learned Gentlemen of the Country, his acquaintance was Mr. Sandys, the Traveller and Translator; Ben. Johnson; Edmund Waller, Esq.; Mr. Thomas Hobbes, and all the excellent of that peacable time."

4. See W. Dunn Macray, ed., *The History of the Rebellion*, 6 vols. (1888; reprint, Oxford: Clarendon Press, 1969), 3:180 (book VII.220).

Moreover, Clarendon wrote in his *Life* of Falkland's generosity. In 1633, when he came into his inheritance on the death of his father, Clarendon says:

> He seemed to have his Estate in Trust, for all worthy Persons, who stood in Want of Supplies and Encouragement, as *Ben. Johnson,* and many others of that Time, whose Fortunes required, and whose Spirits made them superior to, ordinary Obligations; . . . He did all He could, that the Persons themselves who received them, should not know from what Fountain They flowed.
>
> Falkland was to leave London and retire to Great Tew for the next six or seven years, but his friends continued to visit him in the country. They were delighted with his company, and discovered that during their Stay with him, He looked upon no Book, except their very Conversation made an Appeal to some Book; and truly his whole Conversation was one continued *Convivium Philosophicum,* or *Convivium Theologicum,* enlivened, and refreshed with all the Facetiousness of Wit, and Good-Humour, and Pleasantness of Discourse, which made the Gravity of the Argument itself (whatever it was) very delectable. . . . His House . . . looked like the University itself, by the Company that was always found there. There were Dr. *Sheldon,* Dr. *Morley,* Dr. *Hammond,* Dr. *Earles,* Mr. *Chillingworth,* and indeed all Men of eminent Parts and Faculties in *Oxford,* besides those who resorted thither from *London;* who all found their Lodgings there, as ready as in the Colleges, nor did the Lord of the House know of their coming, or going, nor who were in his House, till He came to Dinner, or Supper, where all still met; otherwise, there was no troublesome Ceremony, or Constraint to forbid Men to come to the House, or to make them weary of staying there; so that many came thither to study in a better Air, finding all the Books They could desire, in his library, and all the Persons together, whose Company They could wish, and not find, in any other Society.[5]

The Great Tew circle has often been regarded as a kind of graduate reading group, yet its graduates formed bonds of lasting significance, and most remained faithful to the ideals that Falkland stimulated—of tolerance, irenicism, independence, critical reason, humanist scholarship, and active virtue. At the same time, this group included persons who would become notable,

5. See *The Life of Edward Earl of Clarendon, . . . Written by Himself,* 3 vols. (Oxford: Clarendon Printing-House, 1759), 1:41–43. The relationship between Clarendon's *History* and his *Life* is complicated. He began the *History* in 1646, and carried it down to 1644; but he began his *Life* in 1668, bringing it down to 1660. During his last years, he drew largely upon the *Life* in order to compose the *History,* but finally returned to his *Life,* extending it in the *Continuation,* from 1660 to 1668. A recent biographical study of Clarendon is Richard Ollard, *Clarendon and His Friends* (New York: Atheneum, 1988).

even able to shape the course of English politics and culture in the years ahead. In addition to Falkland himself and Clarendon, there were, besides those whose names have already been mentioned, Thomas Hobbes, George Sandys, Edmund Waller, Sidney Godolphin, the "ever memorable" John Hales, and more: theologians, political philosophers, poets, and scholars. Falkland's home and estate at Great Tew provided a unique place for these persons to meet, to talk, to exchange views, and to develop their ideas. Personal connections and influences are nearly always difficult to describe accurately, yet the importance of this circle of friends or near acquaintances to seventeenth-century literary and intellectual accomplishment is remarkable. Although we may not be sure that Ben Jonson visited Great Tew, we know that he was alive there in such "Sons" as Lucius Cary who offered accommodation and audience to a new generation of poets and writers—of whom Waller and Godolphin are exemplary figures.[6]

Relationships in earlier-seventeenth-century England are tangled and close, and I think Great Tew and its circle of friends and relatives provides an area for an unusually helpful and steady focus on one of the main currents of intellectual life in this period. Lord Dacre has written well of these men of Great Tew and of the philosophical tradition that informed them, naming their forebears from Erasmus through his descendants: Sebastian Castellio (1515–1563) urged religious toleration in his *Conseil à la France désolée* (1562); Jacobus Acontius (1500?–1566?), humanist scholar and theologian, the author of *Stratagemata Satanae* (1565), declared his belief in toleration, skepticism, and liberty of conscience; Bernardino Ochino (1487–1564), Italian Protestant reformer and preacher, was at one time prebendary of Canterbury and later pastor of Zurich; Georg Cassander (1513–1566) attempted to mediate between Catholics and Protestants, especially in his *De Officio Pii ac Publicae Tranquillitatis vere amantis Viri in hoc Religiones Dissido* (1561); "Socinus," uncle (1525–1562) and nephew (1539–1604), well known for reformist theology; Philippe du Plessis Mornay (1549–1623), French Huguenot scholar, author of *Traité de la verité de la religion chrétienne* (1581), insisted on "natural reason"; and, of course, there

---

6. Lucius Cary's mother, Elizabeth (1585?–1639), was herself a writer, the author of *The Tragedy of Mariam: The Fair Queen of Jewry*, written about 1608 but not published until 1613. There is a good modern edition with a useful introduction that includes also the fascinating contemporary biography: Barry Weller and Margaret W. Ferguson, eds., *The Lady Falkland: Her Life by One of Her Daughters* (Berkeley: University of California Press, 1994).

were the eminent figures Richard Hooker (1554–1600) and Hugo Grotius (1583–1645).[7]

Of all these, the last two were most influential, Grotius being "everywhere," known especially for his *De Veritate Religionis Christianae* (On the truth of Christian faith) (1622), and Hooker's influence was likewise predominant, for Hales was said to love "the very name of Hooker"; Earle translated the fifth book of the *Lawes of Ecclesiastical Polity;* Clarendon modeled the beginning of his *History of the Rebellion* on the opening of the *Lawes,* implicitly writing its secular counterpart; and William Chillingworth (1602–1644) appropriated Hooker's fundamental views in his *Religion of Protestants* (1637). Above all else, this catalog of names and works points to a common tradition that may be generally characterized by its insistence on toleration, detachment, reason, and the multiplicity of truth, and its unwillingness to force belief or to become preoccupied with systems and doctrines. B. H. G. Wormald has rightly urged that "the men of the Tew circle belonged to the Renaissance rather than to the Reformation," for they went beyond Calvin and Luther and the other magisterial reformers to Erasmus. Controversy was the symptom of disintegration, of the church and of the state. And if one might prove that controversy was unnecessary, then it could be hoped to put an end to the damage that it caused. The theological and political thinkers and writers of Great Tew wished to emphasize that essential concerns, especially of the church, were so simple and so few that no one should need to argue about them. They held, therefore, to a unity already present, and urged charity and accommodation above dispute.[8]

Religious and political concerns cannot readily be separated in this time, and

7. See Hugh Trevor-Roper (Lord Dacre of Glanton), *Catholics, Anglicans, and Puritans: Seventeenth-Century Essays* (London: Secker and Warburg, 1987), esp. chap. 4, "The Great Tew Circle." Richard Tuck, *Philosophy and Government, 1572–1651* (Cambridge: Cambridge University Press, 1993), examines European and English political theory, with chapters on Hugo Grotius and Thomas Hobbes (1588–1679), and a brief section on Richard Hooker. See also J. C. Hayward, "New Directions in Studies of the Falkland Circle," *Seventeenth Century* 2 (1987): 19–48, and also James Ellison, "George Sandys: Religious Toleration and Political Moderation in an Early Anglican" (D.Phil. thesis, University of Oxford, 1998), esp. chap. 3, "The Caroline Court and Great Tew: Panegyric and Admonition."

8. John Earle (or Earles) (circa 1601–1665), Restoration bishop successively of Worcester and of Salisbury, accompanied Charles II in his Paris exile where he translated a large portion of Hooker's *Lawes.* Only book 5 remains of this exercise, never published, and the autograph manuscript is in the Folger Library.

I quote from B. H. G. Wormald's indispensable work, *Clarendon: Politics, Historiography, and Religion, 1640–1660* (1951; reprint, Cambridge: Cambridge University Press, 1964), 255–56.

their inevitable connection is one of the cohering features of the Great Tew philosophy. I wish therefore to urge the enduring significance of Hooker's *Lawes* (1593, 1597), of central importance to the Great Tew circle because it blends a doctrine of the church with a polity of the state. Then we may be well situated to reflect on Chillingworth's response to this work. Beyond Chillingworth, I want to suggest the continuity of Hooker's influence by noticing Henry Hammond, and, at the Restoration, Gilbert Sheldon, and finally Izaak Walton. Although perhaps never present at any of Falkland's gatherings, Walton did know most of the people who assembled there, and he certainly conveyed their values through his *Life of Hooker.*

Of the eight books *Of the Lawes of Ecclesiastical Polity,* Hooker intends to set forth "generalities" of his subject in the first four books, and "particularities" in the remaining books. Throughout his work, he is dedicated to human reason— a gift given to mankind by God that might enable fallen human beings to discover their common fellowship and the construction of their intellectual being. Sometimes the polemical character of the *Lawes,* especially in the long preface, obscures the essential irenicism that is most pervasive, for Hooker aims to sound out the very depth of truth. Toward this end, he begins by analyzing the eternal law that is grounded upon reason, God himself being seen as a rational being who chooses to observe the law of his own inner nature. How, then, may civil disturbance be legitimately expressed when such rebellion is against the metaphysical and divine order? Thus, the eternal law guides all the operations by which God has chosen to govern the world, but this law must be conventionally or humanly understood as that order that God allows to his creatures, "according to the severall condition wherwith he hath indued them" (63.10). Herein lies the constitution of Christian community and authority, for in the best kind of political association, the well-being of all people derives from and participates in the life of God.[9]

The definition of authority is, of course, the principal theme that unites the whole of Hooker's vast work. He is careful to thread his way through scripture, reason, and tradition by rejecting biblical omnicompetence, and by urging the

---

9. See Arthur Stephen McGrade's commentary "The Adequacy of Hooker's Idea of a Christian Society," in *Richard Hooker: "Of the Laws of Ecclesiastical Polity,"* ed. W. Speed Hill, vol. 6, pt. 1 (Binghamton, N.Y.: Medieval and Renaissance Texts and Studies, 1993), 378–83; compare to Arthur Stephen McGrade, foreword to *Richard Hooker and the Construction of Christian Community,* ed. McGrade (Tempe, Ariz.: Medieval and Renaissance Texts and Studies, 1997). Hooker is quoted from W. Speed Hill, gen. ed., *Preface: Books I to IV,* ed. Georges Edelen, Folger Library edition, vol. 1 (Cambridge.: Harvard University Press, Belknap Press, 1977), 1.10–11.

dependence of human authority and tradition on the natural or revealed law. Tradition is useful—indeed, essential—and Hooker is obviously deeply learned in the historical and theological literature of many centuries, but he allows the sufficiency of scripture provided that it is understood with the important caution

> that the benefite of natures light be not thought excluded as unnecessarie, because the necessitie of a diviner light is magnifyed. There is in scripture therefore no defect, but that any man what place or calling soever hee holde in the Church of God, may have thereby the light of his naturall understanding so perfected, that the one being relieved by the other, there can want no part of needfull instruction unto any good worke which God himselfe requireth, be it naturall or supernaturall, belonging simplie unto men as men, or unto men as they are united in whatsover kinde of societie. (129.1–10)

"Nature," which we perceive through the eternal law, must buttress scripture, and these two—nature and scripture—"sufficeth": "wee neede not the knowledge of any thing more" (129.13).

Hooker's argument is weighty and complex, yet this slight glimpse must stand as a reminder of the ideas that formed the foundation of Great Tew and were to be taken up by its members: the emphasis upon natural law, reason, design, and harmony, and the desire to uncover the divine order in human affairs. In spite of its polemical origin in the midst of puritan and controversial attacks, the *Lawes* is a work ultimately of notable serenity and accommodation. Clarendon was moved by Hooker's *Lawes* to write of the consequences of faction in his *History of the Rebellion*. John Hales, having "bid John Calvin good-night" after the Synod of Dort (1619), was moved to write *A Tract Concerning Schisme and Schismatiques* (1642), in which he urges that "*Schisme* . . . is nothing else but an unneccessary separation of Christians from that part of the visible Church, of which they were once members."[10] Moreover, Chillingworth had left the English church in 1628, supposing that the Roman church would afford him some rest from dogmatic authoritarianism through its supposed liberal and rational outlook. Being disappointed, he migrated to Great Tew and with the help of Clarendon, Hales, and others (and incidentally of his godfather,

10. John Hales (1584–1656), the oldest member of the circle of Great Tew, wrote his treatise on schism in 1636, though it was not published until 1642. I give a summary review of the life and work of this man to whom his contemporaries gave the inalienable epithet "ever memorable," in *Dictionary of Literary Biography: British Prose Writers of the Early Seventeenth Century*, vol. 151.

William Laud) recovered the spirit of Hooker, whose ideas he transmuted into a "rational" system of comprehensive nonsectarianism that his enemies would style "Socinianism."

Chillingworth directed his *Religion of Protestants, a Safeway to Salvation* (1637) against the Jesuit Edward Knott and other Catholic controversialists. But like Hooker before him, Chillingworth needs an adversary in order to explain his own position and to discover a rhetorical situation. Like Hooker, Chillingworth allows that the Church of Rome is true though corrupted, but the English church may claim rationality, simplicity, and ecumenicity—Chillingworth indeed sees Rome as schismatic, inconstant, and unorthodox in its doctrine. The truths of Christianity are clear, and they are ascertainable through natural reason, a reason cultivated by charity, openness, a lack of sectarianism, and a deep skepticism—a skepticism, one should add, greatly stimulated by the work of the Huguenot pastor of Charenton, Jean Daillé (1594–1670), the learned author of *Traicté de l'employ des saincts père* (1632), a book well known at Great Tew that revealed the numerous incompatibilities in patristic writings and rejected the authority of the Fathers as irrelevant for his time. Daillé's book strengthened the Protestant cause and encouraged Chillingworth's own incertitude and return to the generous amplitude of Hooker. Chillingworth thus pleads for unity based implicitly on his understanding of Hooker's explication of the eternal law, and the primacy of scripture read through right reason.

Chillingworth's great book is long and difficult to extract, its progress full of interruptions and digressions. But one well-known passage from chapter 6 expresses the force and the substance of his argument. Chillingworth rejects the "Doctrine of *Bellarmin,* or *Baronius,*" or of any private man, or of any company, or of the Council of Trent. For his own part, "on the other Side, by the *Religion of Protestants,*"

> I do not understand the Doctrine of *Luther,* or *Calvin,* or *Melancthon;* nor the Confession of *Augusta* [Augustine], or *Geneva,* nor the Catechism of *Heidelberg,* nor the Articles of the Church of *England,* no nor the *Harmony* of Protestant Confessions; but that wherein they all agree, and which they all subscribe with a greater Harmony, as a perfect Rule of their Faith and Actions, that is, the BIBLE. The BIBLE, I say, the BIBLE only, is the Religion of Protestants! Whatsoever else they believe besides it, and the plain, irrefragable, indubitable Consequences of it, well may they hold it as a Matter of Opinion: But as matter of Faith and Religion, neither can they with coherence to their own Grounds believe it themselves, nor require the Belief of it of others, without most high and most schismatical presumption.

I for my Part, after a long and . . . impartial search of *the true way to Eternal happiness,* do profess plainly that I cannot find any Rest for the sole of my Foot, but upon this Rock only.[11]

Chillingworth speaks with the enthusiasm and the generous intensity of a member of Falkland's circle at Great Tew, here recommending the supposed clarity and simplicity of Christianity. Times have changed in the forty years and more since Hooker wrote his *Lawes,* but there remains the insistence on natural reason and its capacity to survey the scriptures with urgency, along with an underlying belief in the supreme (and sensible) ability of the English church to reveal the necessities—essential and simple—of faith.

During the first civil war, Chillingworth was a chaplain in the royalist army, and several of his sermons survive. One of the most interesting was preached before King Charles in 1643, on 2 Tim. 3:1–5: "This know also, that in the last Days perilous Times shall come. For Men shall be Lovers of their own selves, covetous, Boasters, proud, Blasphemers, disobedient to Parents, unthankful, unholy. Without natural Affection, Truce-breakers, False accusers, incontinent, fierce, Despisers of those that are good. Traitors, heady, high minded, Lovers of Pleasures more than Lovers of God; having a Form of Godliness, but denying the Power thereof." Here is a text (or texts) seemingly appropriate for condemning the enemies of the king, and after a long exposition of the hideous ills mentioned in the scriptural verses, Chillingworth does not disappoint the royalist side: "To come a little nearer to the Business of our Times, The chief Actors in the bloody Tragedy, which is now upon the Stage, who have robbed our Sovereign Lord the King of his Forts, Towns, Treasure, Ammunition, Houses, of the Persons of many of his Subjects, and (as much as lies in them) of the Hearts of all of them; is it credible they know, and remember, and consider the Example of *David,* recorded for their Instruction?" (2:170–71). But Chillingworth admonishes his own side with surprising openness: "They that maintain the King's righteous Cause with the hazard of their Lives and Fortunes, but by their Oaths and Curses, by their Drunkenness and Debauchery, by their Irreligion and Prophaneness, fight more powerfully against their Party, than by all other Means they do or can fight for it" (2:171). He urges reformation, repentance, amendment, "constant Piety toward God," loyalty toward the king, justice and charity toward neighbors, and temperance and sobriety toward ourselves. Otherwise, desolation awaits us all. Chillingworth is reaching for peace in the midst

11. Chillingworth is quoted from his *Works,* 2 vols. (Dublin: William Brien, 1752), 2:97. Future citations appear parenthetically in the text.

of destruction, for only in the right and reasonable ordering of royalist hearts can victory properly be achieved. He died in January 1644, not long after preaching this sermon, pursued to his grave by the intolerant Francis Cheynell who believed that Chillingworth's impartiality, comprehensiveness, and skeptical faith revealed weakness rather than strength.

The Great Tew circle was to last for only a brief time, and by the early 1640s its halcyon days were long past: Falkland himself had died in the battle of Newbury in 1643, leaving the group leaderless; Chillingworth's death robbed Great Tew of its prime apologist. But the ideals of Great Tew survived war and revolution. Clarendon continued as the political leader and genius in the place of Falkland and would become lord chancellor in the Restoration. And Henry Hammond (1605–1660) would succeed Chillingworth as the philosophic voice of rational theology, whom Lord Dacre of Glanton properly styles "the philosopher and propagandist of the underground Anglican Church."[12] Although Hammond died only weeks before Charles II returned from exile to rule in England, he had fashioned the way that Gilbert Sheldon, another friend of Great Tew, would be able, as archbishop of Canterbury, to follow. This was the way of "natures light," the eternal law that underlies knowledge, a knowledge that leads through skepticism to right reason and the maintenance of religion and government.

Hammond was an enormously active writer and polemicist on behalf of the English church, perhaps best known in his own time for *A Practical Catechism* (1644), a work that particularly appealed to the king, whom he attended as chaplain until the king's confinement at Carisbrooke in December 1647. But many of Hammond's publications were written to meet particular exigencies, none more compelling than the execution of the king and the apparent collapse of the church and of the royalist cause in 1649. Thus, Hammond published *Of the Reasonableness of Christian Religion* (1650), a tract that displays cogently the basis of Christianity as he understood it—and recalls the intellectual tradition of Hooker's *Lawes* as transmitted through Great Tew. Underlying his argument is the discussion in chapter 2 "concerning the use of reason in deciding controversies in religion." Hammond says, for example, that "the measure of man's natural power of knowing or judging of things is his participating of those

12. Clarendon records the lamentable death of Falkland in his *Life of Clarendon* in a fashion reminiscent of Jonson's ode to Cary and Morison: "[Falkland] was little more than thirty Years of Age when He was killed; in which Time He was very accomplished in all those Parts of Learning, and Knowledge, which most Men labour to attain, till They are very old; and in Wisdom, and the Practice of Virtue, to a wonderful Perfection" (1:166). Trevor-Roper, *Catholics, Anglicans, and Puritans*, 219.

things, in some degree, with God, in whom they are as in the fountain: so that the man may find, and behold them in himself as truly, though not as eminently, or in the same degree, as they are in God."[13]

Hammond followed this work with numerous treatises for promoting the sequestered church, and he worked tirelessly toward its restoration. Of particular interest is his treatise *Of Schism: A Defence of the Church of England against the Exceptions of the Romanists* (1645) that urges the visibility and continuation of the old and nonschismatic English church whose temper is "docile," felicitous, and dedicated to preserving "the unity of the apostolical faith and primitive practices as entire as we would have done Christ's body or garment." Hammond's *Of Schism* would join Falkland's posthumously published *Discourse of Infallibility* in which it is claimed that no grounds exist on which the Roman church can claim infallibility.[14] Hammond's was a wise and peaceable voice in difficult times, for he provided quiet but determined leadership, building up a theological house where the church of the Restoration could live. Accommodated within this structure was Richard Hooker, whose religious more than political form I have wished to emphasize, though both are certainly present; the Great Tew circle provided the principal means for conveying Hooker's ideas across the seventeenth century.

There remains one further testimony to Hooker's significance, now provided by Izaak Walton (1583–1683), his first and most influential biographer. Walton settled in London in about 1608, where, through good fortune and personal connections, he soon came to know Ben Jonson, Michael Drayton, and other literary figures. He lived in the parish of St. Dunstan's, to which John Donne had been preferred in 1624, and he came to regard himself as the great preacher's "convert." Meanwhile, through his first marriage in 1626 to Rachel

13. See Henry Hammond, *The Miscellaneous Theological Works*, ed. N[icholas]. P[ocock]., Library of Anglo-Catholic Theology, 3rd ed., 5 vols. (Oxford: John Henry Parker, 1849), 2:29.

14. See ibid., 281–82. Falkland's *Discourse* was published also in 1646; Hammond wrote a defense of it, which appeared along with a further edition of the *Discourse* in 1646 (2d ed., 1651). See Robert S. Bosher, *The Making of the Restoration Settlement: The Influence of the Laudians, 1649–1662* (1951; reprint, London: Dacre Press, A. and C. Black, 1957), esp. chap. 1. On Hammond's life and importance to the rational spirit of Great Tew, the vital work is John W. Packer, *The Transformation of Anglicanism, 1643–1660, with Special Reference to Henry Hammond* (Manchester: Manchester University Press, 1969). Packer glancingly but suggestively invokes Hooker: "Against [the] picture of a Church struggling to find her way of life, there is the vital and potent fact from Hooker onwards of a Church laying a foundation of theological and philosophical argument that was to survive the wars" (172–73). My argument urges the centrality and continuity of Hooker's thought throughout the seventeenth century. See Hayward, "New Directions," 32–33.

Floud, he could claim relationship to Thomas Cranmer, for Rachel's mother, Susannah, was a grandniece of the great archbishop and a sister of George Cranmer, who was a pupil of Richard Hooker at Corpus Christi, Oxford; Dorothy, a second Cranmer sister, was first married to John Spenser, who was president of Hooker's college, and later to Richard Field, friend of Hooker, dean of Gloucester, and author of the important, controversial work *Of the Church* (1606–1610). Walton's associations led him to know numerous persons of influence in church and government; through Donne, for example, he came to know Sir Henry Wotton, James's ambassador to Venice and in his last years provost of Eton College. Wotton's inability to finish (or perhaps even begin) his life of Donne led to Walton's own *Life of Donne* (1640) and later to his *Life of Wotton* (1651). The success of these two biographies, and the concurrent popularity of *The Compleat Angler* (1653, 1655, 1661, and onward), no doubt helped further to bind his old friendships with George Morley, who was to become bishop of Winchester, and Gilbert Sheldon, the powerful archbishop of Canterbury (1663–1677).[15]

Morley, Sheldon, Hammond, Chillingworth, and Clarendon were all familiar names at Falkland's country retreat. Although these and the other members of the Great Tew circle knew and evidently approved of Izaak Walton, we do not know whether Walton actually visited Great Tew itself. Yet, he must have been aware of the conversations that occurred there, and obviously he profited from them, particularly when he came to write many years later, at Sheldon's request, his *Life of Hooker* (1665).

The Restoration years were marked by the republication of a number of "orthodox" authors who had been overshadowed during the difficult years of the civil wars and the Commonwealth: Lancelot Andrewes's *XCVI Sermons* (1629; 6th ed., 1661) in the edition by William Laud and John Buckeridge, Laud's *Conference with Fisher* (1639, 1673, 1686), and most particularly, the first complete edition of Hooker's *Lawes of Ecclesiastical Polity* (1662), which included for the first time book 7, on the episcopacy. Archbishop Sheldon had evidently entrusted John Gauden, bishop of Exeter, with this edition and with the composition of a prefatory life. Dissatisfied with Gauden's *Life of Hooker*, though apparently not with the edition itself, Sheldon sought the help of his old friend Walton, perhaps through the advice of another mutual friend such as George Morley. In the new preface, Walton says little about the contents of Hooker's

15. For a more detailed discussion of how Walton came to write the biography of Hooker, see my *Izaak Walton*, Twayne's English Authors Series, 548 (New York: Twayne, 1998), 38–42.

work, except in rather large terms, but he does cast doubt on the authenticity of Hooker's previously unpublished book on bishops, in which Hooker sees them as traditional, useful, but not indispensable to the order of the church. Such a view surely did not accord well with the old clergy, now in positions of episcopal power in the restored English church. Nor had they satisfied the views of the Laudian clergy in the years that led up to the civil wars. Yet, these views had agreed well with the arguments of Great Tew whose members quite correctly saw difficulties in Laud's high sense of the episcopacy.[16]

In his speech to Parliament on February 9, 1640, on the "London Petition" that would see the diminution, even abolition, of bishops, Falkland, with Clarendon at his side, declared his belief in the traditional episcopacy, but not in its most extravagant claims. Like other members of Great Tew, he had little use for the seeming confinements of Laudian ritualism, order, and inflexibility. Of the bishops, Falkland considers them "not to be *Jure Divino; but neither do I believe them to be Injuria humana;* I neither consider them as necessary, nor as unlawful, but as *convenient* or inconvenient; But since all great Mutations in Government are dangerous . . . my Opinion is, That we should not root up this Ancient Tree."[17]

Had Falkland seen the last unpublished books of Hooker's *Lawes*, especially book 7? Evidence is only circumstantial, yet the intimate connections of the members of the Great Tew circle with Hooker, and probably with his surviving manuscripts, are extremely likely. In book 7, which "disappeared" after Hooker's death until Gauden edited it for publication in the Restoration, Hooker describes in detail the "conveniency" of the episcopal order, which has no more legitimacy than tradition has given to it:

> For what is there which doth let, but that from contrary occasions, contrary Laws may grow, and each be reasoned and disputed for by such as are subject thereunto, during the time they are in force; and yet neither so opposite to other, but that both may laudably continue, as long as the ages which keep them do see no necessary cause which may draw them unto alteration. Wherefore in these things, Canons, Constitutions, and Laws which have been at one time meet, do not prove that the Church should always be

16. There is no doubt that Hooker wrote the three last books of the *Lawes* (that is, books 6, 7, and 8), although he left them "imperfect" when he died in 1600. See *Works,* vol. 3, *Books VI, VII, VIII,* ed. Paul G. Stanwood, Folger Library edition (Cambridge: Harvard University Press, Belknap Press, 1981), xliv–li, where I discuss Hooker's autograph notes for these books (in Trinity College, Dublin).

17. I quote from John Rushworth, ed., *Historical Collections* (London, 1692), pt. 3, vol. 1, p. 186.

bound to follow them. . . . Herein therefore we must remember the axiome used in the Civil Laws, *That the Prince is always presumed to do that with reason, which is not against reason being done, although no reason of his deed be exprest.* Which being in every respect as true of the Church, and her Divine Authority in making Laws, it should be some bridle unto those malapert and proud spirits, whose wits not conceiving the reason of Laws that are established, they adore their own private fancy, as the supreme Law of all, and accordingly take upon them to judge that whereby they should be judged.[18]

Hooker's ideas might well have been alive at Great Tew, but suppressed by the Laudian regime, then discredited in the Restoration by those who had formerly approved its doctrines.

Walton's role in all of this activity was to fashion the record as Sheldon wished to read it during the time of his own episcopacy and in the years of Clarendon's ascendancy as lord chancellor—leaving us not quite to believe, but not really to deny, the integrity of Hooker's authorship of the last books, particularly his rather doleful account of the episcopacy in book 7. Walton wishes principally to emphasize Hooker's role as the most famous and capacious theological thinker of England, and as the preeminent expositor of community and social order whose thought continues to inform all of Europe. Hooker's studied uneasiness about the role of the episcopacy (in book 7) and also his reservations about the role of the monarchy, which begin to sound like constitutional or contractual republicanism (in book 8), must have worried Walton and his friends. Thus, he came to write his *Life,* which forever replaced Gauden's, and it appeared in the next edition of Hooker's *Works* in 1665, there to remain in all subsequent editions down to the present century. Walton's remarkable achievement was to canonize Hooker, which should have pleased Sheldon, for Hooker might continue to sustain the survivors of Great Tew, still determined in a different age to claim him as their own.

18. Hooker, *Works,* 241–42.

M. L. Donnelly

"The Great Difference of Time"

The Great Tew Circle and the Emergence
of the Neoclassical Mode

In writing of Great Tew we are dealing with an ethos,
and not with a social unit.
—J. C. Hayward,
"New Directions in Studies of the Falkland Circle"

The most substantial recent scholarly interest in the group that gathered around
Lucius Cary, second viscount Falkland, at Great Tew has centered on matters of
religion, philosophy, politics, and the history of toleration and freedom of
thought. In this essay I will argue instead a predominantly literary thesis: that
Falkland's circle and its extended later contacts contributed decisively to the construction of the neoclassical aesthetic that came to dominate the literary scene
through the last forty years of the seventeenth century and into the next age.

Purely aesthetic concerns may, indeed, have been marginal to the central intellectual interests of the group. However, the contributions of members and
their extended contacts, not only to the formal expression of neoclassical poetics, the heroic couplet, but also to the fundamental literary ethos of the
neoclassical age, were early and pivotal. Perhaps the most central and distinctive element contributing to the elaboration of that ethos was a rationalism
thoroughly grounded in an informed sense of historical difference. This rationalism based in historicism derived chiefly from classical and patristic historical and linguistic studies central to the dominant religious and philosophical
concerns of the leading members of the Great Tew circle.

In order to make this case, I will first review some of the principles articulated by Sir William Davenant and Thomas Hobbes in their critical discourses

prefixed to Davenant's heroic poem *Gondibert,* in 1651, highlighting their congruence with modern definitions of the neoclassical ethos. I will then examine the roots in Great Tew of Davenant's and Hobbes's circulation of ideas with Abraham Cowley and Edmund Waller in Paris at midcentury. As a connecting link with Great Tew, the origin of these principles in the social exchanges of elite conversation is no less important than the principles themselves. For the participants, this genesis in a polite, informed social context contrasts in a valued way with the other matrices from which literary texts conventionally arise, sources in books and traditional erudition on the one hand, or charismatic and egoistic individual inspiration on the other. Origin and refinement of ideas in social converse markedly inflects the style and tone of the discourses produced. Finally, I will relate a sense of historical difference, "the great difference of time," to both the Tevian ethos and the emergent neoclassical attitude, tracing its origin for Davenant and Hobbes's Paris circle to the humanist study of classical and especially patristic literature that was a central concern at Great Tew. Thus, the influence of Great Tew manifests itself both in a fundamental, determining historicist attitude and in the formal features and social tone of expression.[1]

1

Sir William Davenant wrote his "AUTHOR'S PREFACE *To his much Honour'd* FRIEND MR HOBS," to invite the philosopher's "censure" of "the Method" of his heroic poem. Davenant's account of that method begins with examination of what a heroic poem should be, grounded in a critical survey of his greatest predeces-

---

1. J. C. Hayward, "New Directions in Studies of the Falkland Circle," *Seventeenth Century* 2:1 (January 1987): 19–48, surveys the scholarship on Great Tew, but was too early to include Hugh Trevor-Roper, Lord Dacre's substantial essay "The Great Tew Circle," chapter 4 of *Catholics, Anglicans, and Puritans: Seventeenth-Century Essays* (London: Secker and Warburg, 1987; Chicago: University of Chicago Press, 1988). Important on the theological affiliations of the Falkland group is H. J. McLachlan, *Socinianism in Seventeenth-Century England* (London: Oxford University Press, 1951). I use the term *neoclassical* rather than *Augustan* in order to call attention to the implication of *difference,* implying an imitation or revival at an unbridgeable remove (according to the *Oxford English Dictionary,* "neo" is defined as "In combs. denoting a *new or modern form* of some doctrine, belief, practice, language, etc." [emphasis added]). I borrow the alternative sources of authority, namely, tradition, charisma, and rationalism, from J. G. A. Pocock, "Time, Institutions, and Action: An Essay on Traditions and Understanding," in *Politics, Language, and Time: Essays on Political Thought and History,* ed. Pocock (Chicago: University of Chicago Press, 1971), 233–72, an essay to whose stimulating ideas I acknowledge a much larger and more general indebtedness. In the same volume see Pocock's "Time, History, and Eschatology in the Thought of Thomas Hobbes" (148–201), which is relevant to the view of Hobbes's ideas on history that I relate below to roots in the classical and patristic readings and discussions at Great Tew.

sors in the genre. Statius closes this examen of the ancients, and is found "accomptable" for "follow[ing Vergil] there also where Nature never comes, even into Heaven and Hell." Statius thus undermines the function of heroic literature, which is to "prevail . . . on our manners" and like the dramatic poets to "make [the people] civill by an easie communication with reason (and familiar reason is that which is call'd the civility of the Stage)."[2]

Polite and rationalist language and attitudes such as these, which are characteristic of Davenant's preface throughout, have ensured a general scholarly recognition of the work as a radical critical document, a new departure voicing neoclassical critical canons. In neoclassical fashion Davenant invokes Nature as a criterion and object of imitation, emphasizes familiar and practical uses of literature to induce "civility," vests his hopes in "communication with reason" and "familiar reason," and assumes an audience characterized by "manliness" and the essentially social attribute of "discretion." And, of course, his act of criticism has begun by canvassing the ancients in a spirit of peculiarly qualified respect and admiration. Homer is "like an eminent Sea-mark by which they have in former Ages steer'd," and hence "ought not to be removed from that eminence, least Posterity should presumptuously mistake their course." But (in a particularly Baconian-sounding metaphoric argument) "Sea-marks are chiefly useful to Coasters, and serve not those who have the ambition of Discoverers, that love to sail in untry'd Seas." Likewise, while Vergil is "unimitable," "some" would say he follows Homer so dutifully into the supernatural as to "deprive us of those natural probabilities in Story which are instructive to humane life," and it may be that his "excellence consists more in the solemness then in the fancy" (Spingarn, 1–3). In their ambivalence here, Davenant's comments clearly echo a central tension in the neoclassic aesthetic: acutely aware of his historical distance from his classical models, the neoclassicist is torn between the admiring imitation of those models and a "modern" desire to bring everything to the test of nature and reason.[3]

2. J. E. Spingarn, *Critical Essays of the Seventeenth Century,* vol. 2 (1908–1909; reprint, Bloomington: Indiana University Press, 1957), 1–4. Future citations appear parenthetically in the text as "Spingarn."

3. For the neoclassicism of the "Preface," compare, for example, Albert C. Baugh, ed., *A Literary History of England,* vol. 2, by George Sherburn and Donald F. Bond (1948; New York: Appleton-Century-Crofts, 1967), 714; Arthur H. Nethercot, *Sir William D'Avenant: Poet Laureate and Playwright-Manager* (Chicago: University of Chicago Press, 1938), 241 ("his theories marked a new stage in English criticism"); J. W. H. Adkins, *English Literary Criticism: Seventeenth and Eighteenth Centuries* (London: Methuen, 1951), 33, 34–35; and David F. Gladish, ed., *Gondibert* (Oxford: Clarendon Press, 1971), xi. On Davenant's anxiety concerning the prestige of his ancient predecessors, and how far they are to be, or can be, imitated, see William McCarthy, "Davenant's Prefatory Rhetoric," *Criticism: A Quarterly for Literature and the Arts* 20:2 (spring 1978): 128–43.

Paul J. Korshin's outline of the *idea* of neoclassical poetics affords a useful template for evaluating the ethos that lies behind Davenant's language and attitudes here—the ethos of the wider circle of literati and intellectuals with whom I want to associate Davenant and Hobbes. Among other things, Korshin points to the prominent place given in neoclassical criticism to ideas of linguistic and imagistic propriety and correctness. Such ideas reflect the neoclassical insistence on congruity of style and subject. Generally speaking, "propriety" and "correctness" are essentially social criteria. Neoclassical theoretical concern with appropriate modes of representation through trope, analogy, and allusion values the representation that is "subtle without being obscure." Here the ultimate criterion in relation to that which is represented is truth of the representation to nature, but in relation to audience or reception the constraints are social, and unmistakably inflected with class values—the language, concerns, manners, and attitudes of "gentlemen." While plainness and comprehensibility are paramount values for their assurance of effective communication, clarity and the avoidance of obscurity are also linked with elegance, which is not a utilitarian value. This association of clarity and elegance derives, of course, from ancient oratorical theory, but from the mid-seventeenth century has the additional edge of connecting the reprehended "dialect of these fanatick times," which is to be avoided, both with what is "low" socially and with seditious agencies of religious and political disruption. Underlying the whole system of thought, then, is a congruence between poetics and politics. In a revealing phrase, Korshin speaks of Denham's "poetics of moderation." Of the famous Thames passage in *Cooper's Hill,* he asserts that "Denham's intention here, as it is throughout *Cooper's Hill,* is founded upon a poetic theory which insists upon clarity, naturalness, and the utilitarian view of metaphor as the bases of mimesis. The goal of his aesthetic philosophy is the establishment of a poetic mean which parallels, recalls, or prophesies a similar parity in the body politic." By and large these observations might equally well be applied to the aesthetic articulated by Davenant and Hobbes.[4]

Proclaiming that his ideal of a heroic poem is that it should "in a perfect glass of Nature [give] us a familiar and easie view of our selves," Davenant exemplifies the neoclassic criterion of nature as the standard of truth and object of im-

4. Paul J. Korshin, "The Evolution of Neoclassical Poetics: Cleveland, Denham, and Waller as Poetic Theorists," *Eighteenth-Century Studies* 2 (December 1968): 103, 128, 119, 122. The memorable phrase "dialect of these fanatick times" is from Jonathan Swift, *A Proposal for Correcting, Improving, and Ascertaining the English Tongue* (1711–1712), quoted and taken as the title of his essay by Bernard Harris, in *Restoration Theatre,* ed. John Russell Brown and Bernard Harris (London: Edward Arnold, 1965), 16.

itation (Spingarn, 1). It is the "natural probabilities in Story which are instructive to humane life" (Spingarn, 2). Davenant blames the introduction of the supernatural and invocation of the Muse "not as his rational Spirit, but as a *Familiar*" (Spingarn, 2, 5). It is "nobler to contemplate the general History of Nature then a selected Diary of Fortune" (Spingarn, 3). Considering Spenser among his antecedents, he reflects historically upon the career of the heroic poem and the vicissitudes of language in time, dutifully drawing his analogical illustration from the natural facts of husbandry:

> Language, which is the onely Creature of Man's creation, hath like a Plant seasons of flourishing and decay, like Plants is remov'd from one soile to another, and by being so transplanted doth often gather vigour and increase. But as it is false husbandry to graft old branches upon young stocks, so we may wonder that our Language (not long before his [Spenser's] time created out of a confusion of others, and then beginning to flourish like a new Plant) should as helps to its increase receive from his hand new grafts of old wither'd words. (Spingarn, 6)

In a sense it is Jonson's old criticism that "Spenser writ no language," but the vehicle by which the judgment is conveyed and the heightened consciousness of historical process (which is probably owed to Hobbes) anticipate the emerging aesthetic.

If Jonson is "classical," then Davenant is unmistakably "neoclassical," and the developed historical sense lies at the heart of the difference. Paradoxically, though, his familiarity with historical change teaches Davenant to reject history as the ground of his fable: the heroic poem will teach sound morals that accord with the reasonable conclusions of philosophy, not the random plots of history: "Truth narrative and past is the Idol of Historians, who worship a dead thing, and truth operative, and by effects continually alive, is the Mistris of Poets, who hath not her existence in matter but in reason" (Spingarn, 11). As it causes his rejection of history as plot, so Davenant's faith in fact and reason leads directly to his deep suspicion of inspiration, which he links by suggestion with the pretensions to power and influence of Puritan agitators (Spingarn, 25). Set against the charismatic appeal of such individualistic and egotistical inspiration, it is an implicit social credential of his poem that its genesis has been in a particular kind of appropriate polite matrix. He has been fortunate to find "Friends as ready as Books to *regulate* my conceptions, or make them more *correct, easie, and apparent*" (Spingarn, 27; emphasis added to terms that point to the criteria of neoclassic aesthetics identified by Korshin).[5] Davenant's rationalism even makes an argument for natural religion, and poesy as the best teacher of it: "And as Poesy is the best Expositor of Nature, Nature being misterious to such as use not to consider, so Nature is the best Interpreter of God, and more cannot be said of Religion" (Spingarn, 48). On the book of God's works versus the Book of God's Word, Davenant here sounds as "Socinian" as anything their enemies found in Chillingworth's *Religion of Protestants* or in Falkland's *Discourse of Infallibility.*

In his response to Davenant's preface and poem, Hobbes, too, voices principles anticipating the neoclassical idea of poetry. Even more crushingly than Davenant, Hobbes dismisses the idea of poetic inspiration, *furor poeticus,* or the invocation of a Muse: "But why a Christian should think it an ornament to his Poem, either to profane the true God or invoke a false one, I can imagin no cause but a reasonless imitation of Custom, of a foolish custome, by which a man, enabled to speak wisely from the principles of nature and his own meditation, loves rather to be thought to speak by inspiration, like a Bagpipe" (Spingarn, 59). Adjudicating the rival claims of judgment and fancy in the invention of a heroic poem, Hobbes strongly impresses the view that judgment had best be in the driver's seat. "Judgment begets the strength and structure, and Fancy begets the ornaments of a Poem" (Spingarn, 59). Indeed, Fancy is ultimately herself beholden to Judgment: she finds all her materials ready at hand in the ordered and systematized results of the activity of Judgment in searching out, examining, and disposing the materials presented by memory, that is, the mirrored images of the world (Spingarn, 59). As Quentin Skinner has shown, Hobbes expresses in his later work, including *Leviathan,* "even clearer endorsement of . . . classical values," insisting in a way that "serves to align him with the neoclassical movement in aesthetics" that "the virtue of discretion enables us to reconcile fancy and judgment." Skinner caps his argument by noting in Hobbes, on the one hand, the congruence with, indeed the virtual paraphrase of, Quintilian's ideas on the role of discretion in moderating excessive fancy, and on the other, the great similarity of the resulting expressions with Dryden's.[6]

5. Compare Clarendon's account of Falkland's "whole conversation [at Great Tew as] one continued *convivium philosophicum* or *convivium theologicum,* enlivened and refreshed with all the facetiousness of wit, and good humour, and pleasantness of discourse, which made the gravity of the argument itself (whatever it was) very delectable" (*Clarendon: Selections from "The History of the Rebellion and Civil Wars" and "The Life" by Himself,* ed. G. Huehns [London: Oxford University Press, 1955], 65. Future citations appear parenthetically in the text as "Clarendon").

6. Skinner, *Reason and Rhetoric in the Philosophy of Hobbes* (Cambridge: Cambridge University Press, 1996), 361–75, esp. 368ff.

The identification of a dominant strain of neoclassical ideas in the critical papers prefacing *Gondibert* is nothing new, of course. But I have recalled some of the salient features of those ideas because I want now to attempt to connect them to their background, the matrix from which the ideas emerged as a literary strategy, indeed as an intellectual ethos with social and political implications. Biographer Arthur H. Nethercot speaks of Davenant, in exile in Paris during the interregnum, "bubbling" with "epoch-making" plans for a new, modern kind of heroic poem, and finding "three converts": "a philosopher and two poets, whose opinions bore as much weight as any of the age." Hobbes, of course, was the philosopher, and the poets were Edmund Waller and Abraham Cowley. The peculiar diffidence and wavering assurance of assertion that is so frequent a feature in Davenant's rhetoric from the preface might in themselves suggest that the ideas and criticisms he floats are not all comfortably his own yet. And indeed, his generosity abundantly acknowledges deep indebtedness: in Nethercot's words, he was "effusively grateful; he was prompt to admit that his debts, unlike those of most poets, were to those friends—poets and thinkers— who had lent him their learning and wits in conversation, rather than to books and reading."[7] These acknowledgments in fact make up a significant portion of the social credentials of his poem's origins—an assertion of genesis in an appropriate social milieu.

Davenant's friends at first glance seem a singularly diverse group. However, one thing all three had in common was an association with Lucius Cary, viscount Falkland, either through the Great Tew circle or through later acquaintance at the king's headquarters in Oxford.

2

Falkland had been associated with the Sons of Ben in London before and apparently after establishing the famous semipermanent symposium at his inherited estate, Great Tew. He and his wife, Lettice, were in residence in Oxfordshire from about the early spring of 1631, at least. A cultivated and social being, Falkland had delighted in the cultural life and human contacts of the capital: biographer Kurt Weber draws a winning picture of his engagements and relaxations there when called back during the winter of 1633 by business associated with the death of his father in September of that year. His circle of acquain-

---

7. Nethercot, *Sir William D'Avenant,* 241, 242.

tance by that time probably included Selden and John Hales, as well as Clarendon and other friends from the Inns of Court.[8] His legal and filial obligations discharged, Falkland returned to his studious retirement in Oxfordshire, and to his friends and conversations there. This famous idyll was finally interrupted by the mobilization for the Bishops' War in early spring of 1639, which called away the host of that "one continued *convivium philosophicum* or *convivium theologicum*" to business of state; to the further acquaintances, friendships, and rivalries of the king's headquarters at Oxford; and all too soon to early death in battle.

Falkland certainly knew Abraham Cowley, "the Muses' Hannibal," and patronized him. Cowley's roommate at Trinity College, Cambridge, Robert Cresswell, apparently had been the means of introducing Cowley to Falkland. Cresswell shared the mind of the lord of Tew to the degree that, thanking Falkland in 1638 for the gift of the Fathers Cyril and Synesius in Greek, he credits his patron for inducing him to exchange the cultivation of the Muse of poetry for the serious study of divinity. Cresswell's letter, dated May 12, 1638, concludes with his assertion of his absent "ingenious chamber fellow['s]" "like obligation" to his generous patron's humanity and discrimination. As Weber remarks, if this late introduction were the only connection of Cowley with Falkland, it would be a meager thread, for Falkland departed Great Tew to take up arms in the Bishops' War within the year. However, Bishop Sprat's *Life of Cowley* declares that "though he was then very young, [Cowley] had the entire friendship of my Lord Falkland" at Oxford after Cowley's loyalism drew him to the king's headquarters there, and that "That affection was contracted by the agreement of their Learning and Manners." Cowley's patron in the factionalized royalist circles in exile after the king's execution was Henry Jermyn, the intimate of Henrietta Maria and patron to Sir William Davenant, as well.[9]

The second of Davenant's Paris friends, Edmund Waller, is unequivocally connected with Falkland and Great Tew in all contemporary and retrospective accounts. Waller was twenty-eight or twenty-nine years old when, his domestic circumstances altered by the death in the autumn of 1634 of his first wife, a

8. Weber, *Lucius Cary, Second Viscount Falkland* (New York: Columbia University Press, 1940), 65–67, 74–75, 157–58, 160–63.

9. See Arthur H. Nethercot, *Abraham Cowley: The Muses' Hannibal* (1931; reprint, New York: Russell and Russell, 1967), 58–60; Weber, *Lucius Cary,* 120–30, 146; G. C. Moore Smith, *Notes and Queries,* 12th ser., 9 (Oct. 15, 1921), 305, who also supplies a transcript of Cresswell's letter from Rawl. Poet. MS 246, fol. 27. Sprat's assertions reprinted in Spingarn, *Critical Essays,* 122. On Jermyn's connections with Cowley, see Nethercot, *Abraham Cowley,* 88, 90–96, chaps. 8 and 10; with D'avenant, see Nethercot, *Sir William D'Avenant,* 130–31, 144–45, 191–98, 217–18, 234–35, 245–48, 341ff.

wealthy heiress, he embarked on a course of mental improvement guided by George Morley, involving a more or less systematic study of the Greek and Latin classics. Morley was a member of Falkland's circle, and introduced Waller to the group of broadly philosophical and civic-minded clergy, courtiers, literati, lawyers, wits, and country gentlemen already gathering at Great Tew. Although he had been a member of Parliament since the age of sixteen or eighteen, the significant development of connected ideas about political virtue, history, and classical models seems to have taken place for Waller for the first time in the context of Great Tew. Not only did he blossom as a poet in those years, but he also absorbed an ideologically Erasmian ethos, strongly resistant to both the exclusive claims of the Roman church and the radical certainties of enthusiasm but otherwise tolerant and rationalist, venerating the stance of both Hugo Grotius and Richard Hooker. This ethos, the ethos of Great Tew, informed Waller's outlook throughout the rest of his life.[10]

Thomas Hobbes stands undoubtedly as the most powerful intellect and the most radical thinker among those friends to whose learning and wit in conversation Davenant so handsomely acknowledges his debt. Moreover, we have in Hobbes's *Answer* to Davenant's preface a textual record of Hobbes's actual thoughts on literary kinds, on the virtues and ends of a heroic poem, and even on its social utility. That Hobbes was a "Tevian," a participant in Falkland's circle at Great Tew in the 1630s, has usually been accepted on the authority of John Aubrey's testimony. Hobbes's career and thought seem superficially so obviously eccentric in comparison to those of other well-known members of the circle, however, that some enthusiasts of Great Tew have desired to wish him away. His connection is apparently strongly doubted by Weber—or at least, Weber *wants* to doubt. However, J. C. Hayward calls for "rather more [emphasis] on Thomas Hobbes" in accounts of members of the "circle" in the 1630s. Hugh Trevor-Roper, Lord Dacre, devotes considerable attention to Hobbes as a Tevian, and gives a relatively detailed account of what he calls Hobbes's "desertion" and "betrayal" of Tevian ideals, at least as seen from Clarendon's perspective. Richard Tuck, noting Ernest Sirluck's remarks on the circulation of Hobbes's manuscript of the comparatively early *Elements of Law* among his friends from

10. For Waller's neoclassicism, see Bishop Atterbury's preface to the 1690 edition of Waller's *Works*, and Alexander Ward Allison, *Toward an Augustan Poetic: Edmund Waller's "Reform" of English Poetry* (Lexington: University Press of Kentucky, 1962). On Hooker and Grotius in the political and ecclesiastical ethos of Great Tew, see Trevor-Roper, *Catholics, Anglicans, and Puritans,* 189–99; and Hayward, "New Directions," 32–33. On Waller's subscription to the Tew values, see *Dictionary of Literary Biography,* vol. 127, s.v. "Waller, Edmund."

Great Tew in April and May 1640, accepts that "the evidence for [Hobbes's] friendship [with many of the Tew circle] and the manuscript's circulation is good," and asserts that "it is clear that [Great Tew] is . . . just the *milieu* [in which] . . . Hobbes's theory was developed." Paul J. Johnson has even remarked that Hobbes's "treatment of religious matters is firmly grounded in his full acceptance of the simplified Christianity developed by moderate Anglicans like Hales and Chillingworth."[11]

The elements of the ethos that brought spirits as diverse as Hobbes and Hales, Chillingworth and Waller together at Great Tew, being so largely expressed in conversation and social intercourse, and so slenderly preserved in surviving texts (especially such texts as might appeal to modern readers' tastes), are best appreciated through Clarendon's famous and eloquent accounts written years later in *The History of the Rebellion* and *The Life*. Central to the whole enterprise were, of course, the personality and character of the host. Clarendon's characterization of Falkland is full of extraordinary anticipations of neoclassical canons of understanding, judgment, decorum, and politesse: "With . . . great advantages of industry, he had a memory retentive of all that he had ever read, and an *understanding* and *judgment to apply it seasonably and appositely*, with the most dexterity and address, and *the least pedantry and affectation*, that ever man, who knew so much, was possessed with, of what quality soever" (Clarendon, 66; emphasis added). To this magnetic figure were attracted

> the most polite and accurate men of [Oxford, eighteen to twenty modern
> English miles away by road]; who found such an immenseness of wit, and

11. Hobbes's Tevian connections may be reviewed in Oliver Lawson Dick, ed., *Aubrey's Brief Lives* (London: Secker and Warburg, 1950), 56, 157; Weber, *Lucius Cary,* 130–31; Hayward, "New Directions," 19, 31–39, 41. Kenneth Murdock, too, accepts Hobbes as a Tevian (*The Sun at Noon* [New York: Macmillan, 1939], 112), as does Trevor-Roper (*Catholics, Anglicans, and Puritans,* 167–68, 175, 213; on the "apostasy," see 182–86). On Clarendon's later diminution of the philosopher's role at Great Tew, see Martine Watson Brownley, *Clarendon and the Rhetoric of Historical Form* (Philadelphia: University of Pennsylvania Press, 1985), 120, who also notes Clarendon's contempt for the abstraction and philosophical avoidance of "Precedents" and "Rules of practice" of Hobbes's political writings (102–3). Richard Tuck, *Natural Rights Theories: Their Origin and Development* (Cambridge: Cambridge University Press, 1979), 119, citing Sirluck in John Milton, *Prose Works,* vol. 2, ed. Sirluck (New Haven: Yale University Press, 1959), 35; see Tuck, chaps. 5 and 6, for connections with the Great Tew circle. Johnson, "Hobbes's Anglican Doctrine of Salvation," in *Thomas Hobbes in His Time,* ed. Ralph Ross, Herbert W. Schneider, and Theodore Waldman (Minneapolis: University of Minnesota Press, 1974), 114–15. Hobbes's view is seen as "a variant of . . . advanced but orthodox religious thought" (Gerard Reedy, S.J., *The Bible and Reason: Anglicans and Scripture in Late-Seventeenth-Century England* [Philadelphia: University of Pennsylvania Press, 1985], 23).

such solidity of judgment in him, so infinite a fancy bound in by a most logical ratiocination, . . . that they frequently resorted, and dwelt with him, as in a college situated in a purer air; so that his house was a university in a less volume; whither they came not so much for repose as study; and to examine and refine those grosser propositions, which laziness and consent made current in vulgar conversation. (Clarendon, 51)

Conversely, to their host the company of his friends was "so grateful . . . , that during their stay with him, he looked upon no book, except their very conversation made an appeal to some book; and truly his whole conversation was one continued *convivium philosophicum* or *convivium theologicum*, enlivened and refreshed with all the facetiousness of wit, and good humour, and pleasantness of discourse, which made the gravity of the argument itself (whatever it was) very delectable" (Clarendon, 65). Certainly, Clarendon's recollections may be idealized through the haze of nostalgia. But the profound impress of Falkland's personality, the rare combination of earnest seriousness of mind graced by an unassuming courtesy and social ease, deeply affected others of the group besides the future lord chancellor, and many of the traits sketched in Clarendon's characterization of Falkland later manifested as powerfully influential elements in the shared ethos of members of the circle.

3

At least in the early years of the group, a number of the Tevians were still or had recently been interested in the challenge of translation from the great dead languages. In 1629 Hobbes had produced as his first published work a translation of Thucydides (many years later, he ended his literary career with a translation of Homer's *Odyssey*). In between, he "studied classical and preclassical civilization in the works of Tacitus, Diodorus, Strabo, Josephus, and other ancient historians." George Sandys had translated Ovid's *Metamorphoses,* as well as the Psalms, the Book of Job, and other scriptural texts. Clarendon testifies that John Earle, author of *Microcosmographie* (1628), itself an imitation and updating of the Theophrastian character, "was an excellent poet, both in Latin, Greek, and English, as appears by his many pieces yet abroad; though he suppressed many more himself, especially of English incomparably good, out of an austerity to those sallies of his youth" (Clarendon, 38). Waller and Sidney Godolphin both set their hands to translations of Vergil, Waller eventually finishing what Little

Sid left undone at his death on the civil war battlefield of Chagford in 1643 — "The Passion of Dido for Aeneas" from book 4 of the *Aeneid*. And though his connection with Falkland dates chiefly from the days after the continuing symposium at Great Tew had been disrupted by the civil war, Cowley's most lastingly valued poetic achievements were to be classical adaptations, especially his Pindarics and his anacreontics.[12]

An intense interest in the classics marked their host at Great Tew, as well. Clarendon asserts that Falkland "had made himself master of the Greek tongue, (in the Latin he was very well versed before,) and had read not only all the Greek historians, but Homer likewise, and such of the poets as were worthy to be perused" (Clarendon, 64). Falkland resolved to master Greek relatively late: in fact, after he had married, failed to secure a place that would have ensured him a military career, and come into his inheritance from his grandmother. Nevertheless, Clarendon declares, "He made so prodigious a progress in learning, that there were very few classic authors in the Greek or Latin tongue, that he had not read with great exactness." However, having attained proficiency in the languages, Falkland did not stop his studies with the pagan classics. Clarendon testifies that "he had read all the Greek and Latin fathers; all the most allowed and authentic ecclesiastical writers; and all the councils, with wonderful care and observation; for in religion he thought too careful and too curious an inquiry could not be made" (Clarendon, 66).

The master of Great Tew, like his guests and friends (particularly such men as the irenic and learned bibliophile John Hales and the stupendously learned John Selden, Falkland's and Clarendon's acquaintance from earlier London days), had in his linguistic skills and eager immersion in classical and patristic literature and history an extraordinary window into times and cultures remote from his own. Classicism and the doctrine of literary *imitatio* were, of course, the common currency of culture among the educated classes in seventeenth-century England. But at Tew in at least some members of the circle, partly from their cultivation of classical letters in the learned humanistic tradition of Erasmus and Grotius that pervades the group and partly from anxious researches into patristic materials and church history, motivated by the polemic contexts

12. Robert P. Kraynak, *History and Modernity in the Thought of Thomas Hobbes* (Ithaca: Cornell University Press, 1990), 3. Cowley's anacreontics were composed probably during the exile in Paris when he, Waller, Hobbes, and Davenant were often together; the Pindarics were begun after that time, while he was serving Jermyn and the queen on the Isle of Wight in 1651 (see Nethercot, *Abraham Cowley,* 107, chap. 9).

of controversies among the Church of Rome, the Church of England, and various Protestant confessions, there developed a particular kind of "modern" historical consciousness. With all his fervent classicism, Jonson, the contemplator of "his toe, about which he hath seen Tartars and Turks, Romans and Carthaginians, fight in his imagination," never attained this consciousness of historical difference in anything like the same degree.[13]

The patristic researches that were Falkland's particular obsession may have been most influential in the development of this consciousness, but Falkland was not alone in having a sense of the impassable gulf finally separating the classical world from his own. The ground on which members of the Great Tew circle rejected the Roman and Anglican appeal to "unwritten tradition and 'traditive interpretations of scripture,'" as B. H. G. Wormald has noted, was "not that the Tew circle repudiated the ancient maxim that a tradition universally and always held must be true. It was rather that it seemed to them that no tradition could survive the test. . . . Certain things which seemed to have been universally held in early times were now universally repudiated." In asserting *The Religion of Protestants: A Safe Way to Salvation* against his Catholic antagonist, William Chillingworth maintains that

> after a long (and as I verily believe & hope,) impartiall search of *the true way to eternall happinesse,* [I] doe professe plainly that I cannot find any rest for the sole of my foot, but upon this Rock only [in other words, "the BIBLE only is the Religion of Protestants!"]. I see plainly and with mine own eyes, that there are Popes against Popes, Councells against Councells, some Fathers against others, the same Fathers against themselves, a Consent of Fathers of one age against a Consent of Fathers of another age, the Church of one age against the Church of another age. Traditive interpretations of Scripture are pretended, but there are few or none to be found: No Tradition but only of Scripture [that is, no tradition but the tradition itself of what is

13. For the importance of a sense of historical anachronism that gives a peculiar poignancy to the writings and thoughts of so many Renaissance humanists, see Thomas M. Greene, *The Light in Troy: Imitation and Discovery in Renaissance Poetry* (New Haven: Yale University Press, 1982), esp. chaps. 3 and 11; and Greene, *The Vulnerable Text: Essays on Renaissance Literature* (New York: Columbia University Press, 1986). I differ with Greene in seeing the development of a fully historical consciousness of the uniqueness and untranslatability of other times and social formations as being separate from, though derived from, the awareness of anachronism in the humanist differentiation of "classical" times, the Dark Ages, and their own age of revival. On Jonson's lack of this fully developed historical sense, compare F. R. Leavis, *Revaluation* (1947; New York: W. W. Norton, 1963), 19.

canonical, and the canonical texts], can derive itself from the fountain, but may be plainly prov'd, either to have been brought in, in such an age after Christ; or that in such an age it was not in.[14]

In Wormald's summary, "It was difficult to discover what the Fathers taught, and their opinions even if they were discoverable did not necessarily bear upon the disputes of an age so different from their own." Hence, tradition as a cornerstone of belief and practice is rejected on scrupulously examined historical evidence of the alterations of times and opinions, and with it the apostolic succession espoused by Anglicans as well as the Church of Rome: "I doe beleeve the Gospell of Christ," Chillingworth affirms, "and yet in this, I doe not depend upon any Succession of men that have always beleeved it without any mixture of Errour; nay I am fully perswaded, there hath been no such Succession, and yet doe not find my self any way weakned in my faith by the want of it." Again, he refutes the Catholic claim that "[Apostolic] Succession requires two things, agreement with the Apostles doctrine, and an uninterrupted conveyance of it down to them that challenge it" by charging that Rome itself fails on both points, "that some things wherein you agree with the Apostles have not been held alwaies, . . . and that in many other things you agree not with them nor with the Church for many ages after."[15]

Falkland asserts a more radical and Baconian claim, rejecting a priori any rational ground for privileging the ancients. Aligning himself with the moderns against any imagined superiority of old times, Falkland cannot understand why the Fathers "should weigh more then so many of the now learned, who having more helps from Arts, and no fewer from Nature, are not worse searchers into what is Truth, though lesse capable of being witnesses to what was Tradition." Clarendon, criticizing attempts to build contemporary church doctrine on the

14. Wormald, *Clarendon: Politics, Historiography, and Religion, 1640–1660* (1951; reprint, Cambridge: Cambridge University Press, 1964), 250. Wormald emphasizes the importance of the French Protestant Jean Daillé's book, *Traicté de l'employ des saincts père, pour le jugment des differends, qui sont aujourd'hui en la religion* (1631), in providing a demonstration of the fallibility of the Fathers, and the virtual impossibility of arriving at a clear sense of their positions applicable to Counter Reformation controversy "driven home with such comprehensiveness and force that there was little left to be said provided the reader was predisposed to agree with the thesis" (251). Falkland's translation of Daillé is lost (Hayward, "New Directions," 20). Chillingworth, *The Religion of Protestants: A Safe Way to Salvation* (Oxford: printed by Leonard Lichfield, 1638), 376 (Wing C5138). Hyde, writing *Of the reverence due to Antiquity* more than forty years later, makes a similar point, observing that the Fathers contradicted one another, and even some points maintained in unity by the whole primitive church were denied or ignored by the whole modern church; see Wormald, *Clarendon*, 271.

15. Wormald, *Clarendon*, 253; Chillingworth, *Religion of Protestants*, 357, 363.

basis of what the Fathers taught, argued in historical analogy (which perhaps has an additional edge directed at some of the common-law theorists of his day) that the Fathers' sources for an understanding of the Gospel period and apostolic age were no better than his own contemporaries' sources for English history of the fifteenth century, which were poor enough.[16]

Strongly as they differed in their later years, Clarendon and Hobbes share common ground in their similar foundational use of comparative history and their awareness of historical *difference*—differences in times, in nation and folk, differences in context and problems. Both share a rudimentary concept of the progress of civilization. Clarendon believes that, under the patronage and fostering care of government, and thus human prudence and conduct, the arts and sciences have advanced, though "subject to vicissitudes." Hobbes on his part maps a historical progress from barbarism to civilization, using as chief exemplars of this development the ancient Germans and the prefeudal Saxons, for whom Tacitus's *Germania* and the early English chronicles provided historical sources sufficiently full to satisfy his critical standards. He follows the evolution of culture in England through several stages, some of which were characterized by retention of the forms of institutions while their substance was altered, so that common terms and offices in fact would mask cultural change.[17]

Consequently, Hobbes, too, contemptuously scorns arguments from custom or tradition:

> Ignorance of the causes . . . disposeth a man to make Custome and Example the rule of his actions; in such manner, as to think . . . that Just, of the impunity and approbation whereof they can produce an Example, or (as the Lawyers which onely use this false measure of Justice barbarously call it) a Precedent; like little children, that have no other rule of good and evill manners, but the correction they receive from their Parents, and Masters. (*Leviathan*, 67)

On the contrary:

---

16. *Sir Lucius Cary, Late Lord Viscount of Falkland, His Discourse of Infallibility,* . . . (1651), 294 (Wing F317); Clarendon cited in Wormald, *Clarendon*, 271.

17. Wormald, *Clarendon*, 276, citing Clarendon's *Essays*, 2:134; Kraynak, *History and Modernity*, 13; see A. R. Waller, ed., *Leviathan; or, The Matter, Forme, and Power of a Common-wealth Ecclesiasticall and Civil* (Cambridge: Cambridge University Press, 1904), chap. 10, esp. p. 61, on "Titles of *Honour*" (future citations appear parenthetically in text as *Leviathan*). See also Joseph Cropsey, ed., *A Dialogue between a Philosopher and a Student of the Common Laws of England* (Chicago: University of Chicago Press, 1971), for substantial discussions by Hobbes. On disguised cultural change, see Kraynak, *History and Modernity*, 14.

> These words of Good, Evill, and Contemptible, are ever used with relation to the person that useth them: There being nothing simply and absolutely so; nor any common Rule of Good and Evill, to be taken from the nature of the objects themselves; but from the Person of the man (where there is no Common-wealth;) or, (in a Common-wealth,) from the Person that representeth it; or from an Arbitrator or Judge, whom men disagreeing shall by consent set up, and make his sentence the Rule thereof. (*Leviathan*, 30)

The whole of Hobbes's account of his new philosophy, but particularly the portions concerned with refutation of Romanist claims, is grounded in an understanding of historical development and relativism. His expositions fully outline the specific differences between the ancient ethnic constitutions and their societies, and the various kinds of sovereignty and political arrangements among the ancient Hebrews, postexilic Jews, and pre- and post-Constantinian Christian churches. Central to his argument stands the more recent history of the encroaching power of the papacy through the Middle Ages, and of the developments that accompanied the Reformation.[18] At times Hobbes works from analyses of the etymologies, usages, and original and contextual meanings of words, in the manner of the humanists. At others, he relies simply on the reported acts and facts of Scripture, expressly avoiding the pedantic "Ornament of quoting ancient Poets, Orators, and Philosophers, contrary to the custome of late time." He gives eight reasons for this failure of citation. The fundamental one is that "all Truth of Doctrine dependeth either upon *Reason*, or upon *Scripture*; both which give credit to many, but never receive it from any Writer." However (sounding much like Falkland himself and Chillingworth), he further alleges that "there is scarce any of those old Writers, that contradicteth not sometimes both himself, and others." In a characteristic gibe he adds that "such Opinions as are taken onely upon Credit of Antiquity, are not intrinsecally the Judgment of those that cite them, but Words that passe (like gaping [yawning]) from mouth to mouth." Moreover, what was nourishing at another time and in another place may not be healthful when recycled under a new dispensation—which is at least one of the possible constructions to be put upon his sardonic assertion that "it is an argument of Indigestion; when Greek and Latine Sentences unchewed come up again, as they use to doe, unchanged" (*Leviathan*,

---

18. See Hobbes, particularly chap. 29, "Of those things that Weaken, or tend to the Dissolution of a Common-wealth," in pt. 2, "Of Common-wealth"; the 3d pt. of *Leviathan*, "Of a Christian Commonwealth"; and the 4th pt., "Of the Kingdom of Darkness."

526–27). He concludes with a turn on the controversy of ancients versus moderns like that he used in his reply to Davenant's "Preface" to *Gondibert:*

> Lastly, though I reverence those men of Ancient time, that either have written Truth perspicuously, or set us in a better way to find it out our selves; yet to the Antiquity it self I think nothing due: For if we will reverence the Age, the Present is the Oldest. If the Antiquity of the Writer, I am not sure, that generally they to whom such honor is given, were more Ancient when they wrote, than I am that am Writing. (*Leviathan,* 527)

Transformation of social hierarchies inevitably alters manners and morals. Robert P. Kraynak puts together Hobbes's observation on the historical origins of titles of honor on the battlefield with his dry remark that "the *vain-glory* which consisteth in the feigning or supposing of abilities in our selves, which we know are not, is most incident to young men, and nourished by the Histories, or Fictions of Gallant Persons; and is corrected oftentimes by Age, and Employment" (*Leviathan,* 61, 34) to attribute to Hobbes a caustic judgment on the court culture of his own age: that "in the evolution from warlords to gentry, the code of honorable conduct was also transformed, from one of military prowess and magnanimity, acquired on the battlefield, to one of gallantry and vanity, derived primarily from reading romances."[19]

Hobbes also observes in the ancient polities the cycle of politics described by Aristotle and Polybius. But he makes on his own the distinctive observation that although civilization has fostered the growth of the "practical arts" and, in doing so, bestowed upon civilized peoples a greater portion of the "commodities of mankind," civilization in giving leisure for intellectual development has also promoted the growth of speculation. Religion, philosophy, law, and other intellectual disciplines of abstraction and dogma have become growth industries. Some of the consequences are pernicious. "As a result, a new type of authority arose: the rule of patriarchs and conquerors was replaced by the authority of priests, philosophers, orators, lawyers, and intellectuals of all types who sought to rule not by natural force but by *opinion.*" A new ground of conflict and a new kind of warfare arose out of the clash and contest of opinion. Feudal and contemporary Europe might be called the "doctrinal age," and Kraynak summarizes Hobbes's exasperated conclusion that in the modern age, "everyone has become the owner of a doctrine and a pretender to scientific knowledge, so that it has become the most artificial and unstable period in hu-

19. Kraynak, *History and Modernity,* 25.

man history."[20] Hobbes's judgment here accords surprisingly with that of another luminary of the Great Tew circle; of "the ever-memorable John Hales of Eton," Clarendon remarks, "Nothing troubled him more than the brawls which were grown from religion. . . . He thought that pride, and passion, more than conscience, were the cause of all separation from each other's communion" (Clarendon, 40).

Hobbes sees in this proud contentiousness a historical difference between his age and the age of the classical philosophers: he realizes also that "university learning and the widespread diffusion of academic doctrines" mean in the age of "doctrinal politics" that "the opportunity exists for an altogether new kind of political science which would not merely permit the chosen few philosophers to ascend from the darkness of the cave to the light of true knowledge but would bring light to the cave itself—enlightening the whole of society by making everyone a practitioner of true philosophy." That philosophy—"Hobbes's science of enlightenment"[21]—and his sense that its moment had come are based on a comparative reading of history, and a conviction of the historical difference (or differences) of modern times, that is not only shared with other leading members of the Great Tew group, but evidentially also based on their classical and patristic researches and discussions. (Conceptually, and in the forms in which it is asserted, it often adopts in Hobbes and others to whom we shall turn in a moment a Baconian formulation.) At the same time, Tevian historicism constitutes a fundamental distinguishing element in the neoclassical episteme, undergirding the neoclassical reliance on nature and reason, rather than tradition or charisma, and the neoclassical ethos of moderation and propriety in the face of the historical record of so much human fanaticism, aggressive extremism, blind pride, and folly.[22]

Hobbes, Clarendon, Cowley, and even Waller all express at some point their possession of this relatively sophisticated critical historical sense. These mem-

---

20. Kraynak's summary (ibid., 16) of Hobbes's accounts in *De Corpore*, I.7; *Elements of the Laws*, I, 13.3. and II, 1.6.2.; *De Cive*, v.2. and x.9; *De Homine*, x.3; and *Leviathan* Chap. 17; Kraynak summarizing the preface to *De Cive* and chap. 46 of *Leviathan* (*History and Modernity*, 18).

21. Kraynak, *History and Modernity*, 30–31.

22. Compare: "Classicists of the late seventeenth and eighteenth centuries used ancient literature to throw their own age into perspective. . . . They used it as a standard of achievement, a model and warning the more effective for being remote, whole, and exhaustive" (James William Johnson, *The Formation of English Neo-Classical Thought* [Princeton: Princeton University Press, 1967], 68). Johnson also points out the mesmerizing power over the neoclassical mind of the decline and fall paradigm so prominent in classical historiography, another assertion of the differences of times (56–67).

bers of Falkland's circle developed from their reading and study a profound consciousness of historical process and temporal change, a sense of the past-ness of the past, of the historically situated particularism of ancient formulas and dogmatic settlements. Doubtless, for men already inclined to a critical skepticism, Clarendon's and Selden's legal training might also contribute to this heightened sense of historical process, of the differences of times, though in much common-law discourse of "the ancient constitution" it manifestly did not. From their readings and discussions with one another, from reflecting on these elements of their learned experience, the leading Tevians evolved a habit of comparative and historically grounded thinking that issued in a thorough-going rationalism and skepticism toward dogmatisms and enthusiasm in religion and politics. The famous rationalism and skepticism of the group's leading intellectuals were, then, intimately bound up with their historicism.

This critical consciousness as applied to the literary avocations of members of the Tew circle and their peripheral connections translates into a suspicion of unnatural flights of fancy, metaphoric excess, extreme conceits, and self-assertive "strong lines." It establishes the dominance of judgment over fancy and, while interested in traditions and classical antecedents, and profoundly informed about them and their history, appeals rather to nature and a kind of socially vindicated reason as final arbiters of truth outside the small body of "things essential to salvation" conveyed in Scripture.

The formative discourses of Falkland's circle were the intellectually strenuous but socially easy exchanges of learned and earnest minds in a country house, presided over by a gracious, intellectually curious, and receptive host, not the least of whose gifts seems to have been the ability to draw out and develop the interests and talents of each of his guests, and to set their minds into fruitful dialogue. The debt that Davenant acknowledges in the preface to *Gondibert*, to literary and intellectual conversation and the face-to-face circulation of ideas with his friends in Paris rather than to books read in the isolation of his study, replicates participants' accounts of the original milieu and influence of Lucius Cary's circle, which was a formative influence on all three of the poet laureate's coadjutors in designing his "modern" heroic poem.[23]

Appropriately enough, the literary expression of the ethos that emerges from the Tevian milieu corresponds greatly in both details and fundamental spirit to Davenant's critical articulation of his design. Both elevate a gentlemanly sense

23. Hobbes, preface to *Gondibert*, 24–27; see Nethercot, *Sir William D'Avenant*, 242, and compare Clarendon's paeans to the golden years at Great Tew, quoted in the text above.

of propriety and graceful simplicity that disdains pedantry, bombast, excess, and self-aggrandizing display in belles lettres no less than in the irenic handling of theological controversy and political theory. Both erect judgment and reason as arbiters of truth and expression, and both are quick to dismiss inspiration theories and the poet's charisma. While admiring of the ancients, indeed, in Davenant's case perhaps profoundly anxious about the attempt to rival them, both Davenant and the Tevian ethos align themselves firmly with the moderns, fully aware of the equality of wit between their contemporaries and the august figures of the past, and reliant on the superior means of knowledge afforded by the scholarship and discoveries of their own age. Significantly, the only disadvantage Hobbes attributes to *Gondibert* in comparison to the great ancient models, the *Aeneid* and *Iliad,* is that "the languages of the *Greeks* and *Romans,* by their Colonies and Conquests, have put off flesh and blood, and are becom immutable, which none of the modern tongues are like to be." But in a sense, what he is saying (given the fundamental Hobbesian metaphysic of motion) is that they are *dead,* and he adds immediately the Baconian-sounding assertion: "I honor Antiquity, but that which is commonly called *old time* is *young time.* The glory of Antiquity is due, not to the Dead, but to the Aged" (Spingarn, 65–66).

Less imbued with Baconian modern principles, more deeply invested in the classics (or, perhaps, in the melancholy of the historically aware poetic aspirant to undying fame won by immortal verse), Waller provides another side of this consciousness of history, the disparity of times and the mutability of language:

> But who can hope his lines should long
> Last in a daily changing tongue?
> While they are new, envy prevails;
> And as that dies, our language fails.
>
> .   .   .   .
>
> Poets that lasting marble seek,
> Must carve in Latin, or in Greek;
> We write in sand, our language grows,
> And, like the tide, our work o'erflows.[24]

In his "Preface to *Pindarique Odes,*" justifying his nonliteral translation, or rather *imitation,* of Pindar's poetic art, Cowley warns the reader:

---

24. G. Thorn Drury, ed., *The Poems of Edmund Waller* (London: A. H. Bullen, 1901), 2:69–70. Compare Dryden on time's influence on linguistic and cultural change: for example, the last paragraphs of his *Discourse concerning the original and progress of satire* and in his treatment of Chaucer in his preface to *Fables Ancient and Modern.*

[W]e must consider in *Pindar* the great difference of time betwixt his age and ours, which changes, as in *Pictures,* at least the *Colours* of *Poetry,* the no less difference betwixt the *Religions* and *Customs* of our Countrys, and a thousand particularities of places, persons, and manners, which do but confusedly appear to our Eyes at so great a distance. . . . And when we have considered all this, we must needs confess, that after all these losses sustained by *Pindar,* all we can adde to him by our wit or invention (not deserting still his subject) is not like to make him a *Richer man* than he was in his *own Country.*[25]

Nethercot comments on this venture that Cowley has "thus shown himself to be one of the first of English critics to grope toward the historical point of view in criticism." But as we have seen, Cowley's recognition of distance and difference from past ages is one with the historical consciousness of Hobbes, Clarendon, and Falkland himself. It is worth noting that the preface and the imitations it introduces, so unlike most of Cowley's earlier poetic endeavors in both style and content, were produced after the poet's closer acquaintance with Falkland at Oxford, and after his frequent conversations with Waller and Hobbes (and Davenant) in Paris. It is also worth noting that Dryden, the authoritative voice of the neoclassical aesthetic in the coming age, while complaining that Cowley's imitation of the manner of Donne vitiated his poetry, made it a point to except "his Pindarics and his latter compositions, which are undoubtedly the best of his poems, *and the most correct.*" These mature panegyrics are large-scale, serious poems celebrating the great endeavors of civilization and culture: "The Muse," "To Mr. Hobs," "Hymn. To Light," and "To the Royal Society." They are characterized by rationalism, common sense, a glorification of judgment over fancy, "modernity," and a sense of historical progress and change tinctured with Baconianism and the New Science. Their mode of expression exhibits a gentlemanly sense of propriety and graceful simplicity that avoids pedantry, bombast, and excess. These elements and attitudes in Cowley's Pindarics, articulated in his prose essays as well, share the ethos and manners of Falkland and the leading lights of the Great Tew circle. Dryden's singling out of the "Pindarics and his latter compositions," so historically con-

25. L. C. Martin, ed., *Abraham Cowley: Poetry and Prose* (Oxford: Clarendon Press, 1949), 73–74. On the imitation as an Augustan or neoclassical form, see Howard D. Weinbrot, *The Formal Strain: Studies in Augustan Imitation and Satire* (Chicago: University of Chicago Press, 1969). Weinbrot treats Cowley especially on 35–40; compare also his concluding remark: "The Imitation is thus not a restrictive but a liberating form which enlarges the poet's possibilities for metaphor *and insists that the reader be aware of his moment in history and its relationship to other moments*" (219; emphasis added).

scious of difference and the need for a supplement to bring the ancient work across the divide to modernity, is no less significant than the neoclassic phrase in which he articulates his judgment of praise: they are not only Cowley's best but also his "most correct."[26]

Another whole discourse could be devoted to the examination of the actual poetic practices of the Tew circle. While Falkland's own verse has been excessively praised by Ruth Wallerstein and her pupil William Bowman Piper, their works give useful consideration to the translations of George Sandys, and call attention to his association with Falkland's circle. When we reflect on Douglas Bush's summary remark in *English Literature in the Earlier Seventeenth Century* that "in the work of Sandys, Jonson, Denham, Godolphin, and Waller we can follow the further development of the Augustan manner in both metre and diction," we cannot escape the fact that all the names but one—Denham's—are those of men who have been linked more or less closely with Lucius Cary, viscount Falkland, and his circle, or circles, of friends. But the foundation of neoclassical prosodic practices is not merely a matter of technique. It is a matter of concordant convictions about history, culture, social relations, and ultimate criteria of truth and value. James Sutherland comments on Dryden's achievement in the *Heroic Stanzas to the memory of Oliver Cromwell* that "he has caught very successfully the poetic manner of Davenant, and adopted the four-line stanza of *Gondibert*. He is now *master of a controlled and balanced rhythm,* and he has arrived at that *precision of thought and expression,* and that characteristic mode of *definition by antithesis* which is to distinguish his mature work." Sutherland later characterizes the couplets of Dryden's *Astraea Redux* as having "that firm, confident movement—strength with mobility, measure with variety—which wins the willing assent of the reader." In describing those features— "controlled and balanced rhythm," "precision of thought and expression," "firm, confident movement," and "strength with mobility, measure with variety" (and perhaps even the more peculiarly Drydenian "definition by antithesis")—Sutherland sounds almost like an expanded paraphrase of the famous lines on Thames in *Cooper's Hill*. Yet all, however quintessentially Drydenian, are among the qualities and features toward which the chief poets of the Great Tew circle—George Sandys, Sidney Godolphin, and Edmund Waller—pressed. Even as the superficial metrical features of the dominant form of neoclassical poetics were those perhaps at first fallen into, but then polished, smoothed, and perfected by

26. Nethercot, *Abraham Cowley,* 137; Dryden, "Discourse of the Original and Progress of Satire," in *John Dryden: Of Dramatic Poesy and Other Critical Essays,* ed. George Watson (London and New York: Dent and Dutton, Everyman's Library, 1962), 2:76.

Sandys, Godolphin, Waller, so were many of the central values and attitudes carried on by the Augustans originally elements in the ethos of Great Tew, further developed and enunciated in new contexts by writers such as Davenant and Cowley, under the influence of members of Falkland's elite circle. Lord Dacre has forcefully argued that the restored Anglican establishment owed its form and outlook to Tevians such as Sheldon, Morley, Earle, and Barlow, who became bishops, and to Hammond and Hales, who kept the English church alive intellectually by their correspondence and contacts during the interregnum. The balanced constitution likewise owed its continued chance for development to Clarendon, one of Falkland's oldest friends and his colleague in the king's cabinet at Oxford in the early days of the civil war. But the influence of Great Tew extended also to the dominant literary mode of the Restoration age, which owes many of its internal and formative principles to the historical consciousness, social ethos, and rational, skeptical moderation of the poets and thinkers who were the chosen circle of friends of Lucius Cary, viscount Falkland.[27]

27. Wallerstein, "The Development of the Rhetoric and Metre of the Heroic Couplet, Especially in 1625–1645," *PMLA* 50 (1935): 166–209; Piper, *The Heroic Couplet* (Cleveland: Case Western Reserve University Press, 1969), 63, 69–78; Bush, *English Literature* (Oxford: Clarendon Press, 1962), 65; Sutherland, *Restoration Literature, 1660–1700* (1969; reprint, Oxford: Clarendon Press, 1990), 179, 180, emphasis added; Trevor-Roper, *Catholics, Anglicans, and Puritans*, 175–79, 227–30.

Achsah Guibbory

Conversation, Conversion, Messianic Redemption
Margaret Fell, Menasseh ben Israel, and the Jews

When we talk about literary circles, we tend to think of a group of people who know each other socially, even personally, who share their writings, reading each other's texts, responding to them with their own, engaging in textual conversation. Members of a literary circle have certain things in common that bind them—it might be shared education or school ties, class, gender (as in the Sons of Ben), or a shared geographical site (as in the Great Tew circle). Most crucial is the existence of a shared ethos—social, political, or religious values and concerns that members of the circle have in common and that help define the community.

We might, however, usefully extend the idea of literary circles to consider other ways writing created cultural communities in the seventeenth century. Recently, Andrew Shifflett has suggested that Stoicism, as a predominantly "literary" activity, fostered a kind of transnational community in the early modern period. Stoicism constituted a potentially cosmopolitan republic of letters, a community that could include people from different countries or even from different sides of political conflicts, such as England's civil war.[1] This Stoic community of letters differed from more narrowly defined, more exclusive English literary circles; its doors were open for others to enter. I would suggest that, in the mid-seventeenth century, with its social and cultural upheaval, there were numerous fluid "literary" communities—people who were connected by the efforts of a few individuals to create a community through the exchange of ideas through print. Our recently expanded sense of what constitutes "literature"

---

1. See Shifflett, *Stoicism, Politics, and Literature in the Age of Milton: War and Peace Reconciled* (Cambridge: Cambridge University Press, 1998).

(which now encompasses more than the traditional category of aesthetically interesting "imaginative" writing) also might stimulate an interest in writing communities other than the conventional "literary circle."

The idea of a literary circle is tied to more general issues of community. Literary circles, as we usually understand them, tend to be conservative, preserving and reinforcing a shared ethos in the face of socioeconomic, political, and cultural change (we might think of the Sons of Ben in the 1620s and 1630s or even of Katherine Philips's Society of Friendship during the 1650s, though the circle that evolved into the Royal Society might seem to be an exception). But it is possible to imagine that different kinds of writing communities could be created to serve radical, revolutionary needs during the unstable period of the civil war and its aftermath. This was a time of unprecedented circulation of ideas through polemical printed texts. During the mid-seventeenth century, with the emergence of religious radicalism and the explosion of print in the wake of the dissolution of official structures of censorship, we might expect an experimentation with circles or networks of communication as people sought to communicate their new visions. These circles—constituted through printed texts—were not meant to preserve traditional ideals, or to reconfirm established values of an already well-defined group, but rather to reach out to others in the aim of changing their beliefs, of drawing these people into their circle. Like traditional "literary circles," these circles also functioned—or at least hoped—to create a community.

I am particularly interested in the efforts by the Quakers to create such a new kind of circle of communication in the service of enlarging their religious community. Powerfully affected by the millennial thinking of the mid-seventeenth century, vilified and persecuted by normative Christians at home, the Quakers sought contact with the Jews abroad who were seeking readmission to England. Through the medium of print and an evolving network of communication, Quakers under the inspired but practical leadership of Margaret Fell hoped to convert the Jews to their distinctive vision of Christian truth and draw them into their community. Like the spiritual community that was its goal, this "literary circle" was essentially religious, the text of the Bible and its promises the glue that was to hold it together. As in conventional literary circles, there were certain shared values and experiences—a history of persecution, a commitment to the truth of the Bible, and a belief they were living in the end times. But Quakers and Jews were divided by important differences that made conversation difficult and that ultimately spelled the failure of Quaker efforts to construct through their discourse a "universal" community.

Mid-seventeenth-century England saw the flourishing of millenarianism and messianic thinking. Not only radical but even some mainstream Protestants expected that the revolution might usher in the second coming of Christ and the reign of the saints. Some religious radicals such as John Naylor and John Robbins during the 1650s actually claimed to be the Messiah or God. When Parliament attempted to restrain religious heterodoxy after the execution of Charles I, radical sects such as the Quakers saw in their persecution a sign of the imminence of Redemption.

This expectation of the "last days" and the reign of the Messiah was not limited to England or to Christians. Jews in Europe and especially Holland, which was home for many persecuted Jews, were also seized by messianic hopes. The devastating pogroms, which began in 1648 and resulted in the deaths of tens of thousands of Jews in Europe, Russia, and the Ukraine, were seen by the Jews as evidence that the Messiah would soon appear, since the disasters seemed to be those of the end times foretold by the Prophets. It was about this time that the (in)famous Jewish false messiah Sabbatai Sevi appeared in Smyrna. Before his apostasy and conversion to Islam in 1666, he attracted a huge following among Jews in Europe.[2] The expectation of messianic Redemption inspired the Amsterdam rabbi Menasseh ben Israel in his efforts to have the Jews readmitted to England in the 1650s.

Because seventeenth-century millenarianism was transnational and transcultural (linking England and Holland, Christians and Jews), it had the potential to bring together disparate people. Thus, some religious radicals, and especially the Quakers, became Menasseh ben Israel's allies as he sought to find a home for the Jews in England.[3] In the wake of the revolution, the liberation of the press from the strict control of censorship had created an arena where ideas could be exchanged and debated, where there was a potential for new alliances to be formed such as the one that briefly developed between

2. David S. Katz, *Philo-Semitism and the Readmission of the Jews to England, 1603–1655* (Oxford: Clarendon Press, 1982), 142. Joachim Prinz suggests a much higher estimate of five hundred thousand Jews killed (*The Secret Jews* [New York: Random House, 1973], 112). See Gershom Scholem, *Sabbatai Sevi: The Mystical Messiah, 1626–1676* (Princeton: Princeton University Press, 1973), 521; Prinz, *The Secret Jews,* 111–22. Scholem discusses Sabbatai Sevi's widespread appeal as well as the controversy he provoked. J. Wout von Bekkum, professor of modern Jewish history at the University of Amsterdam, told me in conversation that fully half of the large Jewish population of Amsterdam believed Sabbatai was the Messiah.

3. We see in this phenomenon what Gershom Scholem has described as the "mutual influence" or commerce between Judaism and Christianity in messianic thinking (*The Messianic Idea in Judaism* [New York: Schocken, 1971], 15–17). Shelley Perlove has dis-

Quakers and Jews. As the readmission of the Jews was debated in the 1650s, there emerged a sense of a special connection between Jews and Quakers. Quakers saw themselves like the Jews, persecuted, outcasts, yet chosen by God, on the brink of a glorious redemption; they appropriated Old Testament texts, tropes, and narratives to themselves. They supported Jewish readmission, in part on humanitarian grounds but especially because Quakers saw the conversion of the Jews as necessary to the fulfillment of messianic Redemption.[4]

In order to convert the Jews, however, one had to bring them to accept Christ. Hence the phenomenon of the Quaker pamphlets in the 1650s and early 1660s addressed to the Jews, which reveal much about the religious motivation of literary production in seventeenth-century England and the literary dimension of religious communities. The goal of this Quaker project was not, as in conventional literary circles, the sharing or preservation of shared cultural, traditional ideals but the radical transformation of history and society. These pamphlets

---

cussed Rembrandt's involvement in the millenarianism and pansophism of the 1650s and 1660s. Stressing the connections between millenarian Jews such as Menasseh and millenarian Christians in Holland and England, she shows how Rembrandt was involved in this circle and how his late works participate in the millenarian effort to hasten the arrival of the Messiah ("Awaiting the Messiah: Christians, Jews, and Muslims in the Late Work of Rembrandt," *Bulletin of the University of Michigan Museums of Art and Archaeology* 11 (1994): 84–113). On the range of attitudes, even among "philo-Semites," toward the readmission of the Jews, see Katz's important book, *Philo-Semitism.*

4. See, for example, Francis Howgill, *This is Onely to Goe amongst Friends* (London, 1656), 1, 10–13; and Edward Burroughs, *To the Camp of the Lord in England* (London, 1656), 15–16. Not only Quakers but also other religious radicals identified in certain ways with the Jews and supported Jewish readmission (such as Thomas Collier, the Baptist leader, and Roger Williams, the independent who defended religious liberty for all creeds). On the way in which the "calling" and conversion of the Jews was linked to the interest in readmission, see Katz, *Philo-Semitism,* 89–126, who argues that most millenarians believed "the Jews would be called to Christ before the Redemption" (100), and suggests that for most of those who supported readmission, "the prime purpose of Jewish immigration was conversion" (216–17). See also Christopher Hill's classic essay, "Till the Conversion of the Jews," in *The Collected Essays of Christopher Hill,* vol. 2, *Religion and Politics in Seventeenth-Century England* (Amherst: University of Massachusetts Press, 1986), 269–300, which shows how the conversion of the Jews was seen in the sixteenth and seventeenth centuries as part of the events ushering in the end of the world and the millennium. Hill concludes that by 1656 their conversion "seemed less urgently relevant" (290)—a conclusion that seems belied by the continued appearance of Margaret Fell's pamphlets after this date. James Shapiro has shown how England's fascination with the conversion of the Jews appears as early as the 1570s, and he discusses various conversion narratives (*Shakespeare and the Jews* [New York: Columbia University Press, 1996], 131–65). The ideology of Jewish conversion in nineteenth-century England is discussed in Michael Ragussis, *Figures of Conversion: "The Jewish Question" and English National Identity* (Durham: Duke University Press, 1995).

were published in the hope of drawing the Jews, with their messianic expectations, into the Quaker circle. These texts functioned as expressions of a particular religious community, with the aim of enlarging that community.

In the Quaker effort to establish contact with the Jews, print was the medium of choice. George Fox published two pamphlets addressed to the Jews in 1661: *A Declaration to the Jews* and *An Answer to the . . . Jewes*. But Margaret Fell, a Quaker preacher and prophet, began addressing the Jews even earlier. She was the leader in the effort to reach the Jews, and it is on her that I wish to focus. In her persistent attempts to engage the Jews in dialogue, we see a fascinating effort to open up lines of communication between Jewish and Christian communities. Margaret Fell hoped to establish a universal spiritual community through a transnational network of publication that was supposed to effect "conversion." To some extent, the conversation created by Margaret Fell was more "imagined" than "real," a vision of possibility rather than actuality. We see in this episode how conversation and "shared discourse" can be illusory— and how the notion of a community may itself have a restrictive dimension. Despite the shared messianic discourse and reliance on the Jewish Prophets, not only were Fell's and Menasseh's messianic desires at cross-purposes, but Fell's vigorous agenda of conversion also disabled dialogue as it sought to erase Jewish difference.

The conversation between Quakers and Jews in the mid-seventeenth century took place largely through pamphlets that were published, translated, and circulated. The participants did not write consciously "imaginative" literature; they were not concerned with aesthetic values or high, classical culture. They were, rather, concerned with religious truth, and their goals were to change the world, to bring about the last days foretold by the Prophets.

The conversation began in 1650 when Menasseh ben Israel published his *Hope of Israel* in England, a book first published in Amsterdam in Latin and Spanish. Translated by Milton's friend Moses Wall, *The Hope of Israel* was Menasseh's effort to reach an English Christian audience. Five years later, Menasseh came to England on his mission and on October 31, 1655, presented a petition for readmission to Oliver Cromwell and his council; his *Humble Addresses* was published five days later. With Menasseh's request not just for admission but for also toleration of Jewish worship, a request that would be debated in the famous Whitehall conference in December, this learned Amsterdam rabbi touched off an explosion of pamphlets in England. Some, such as William Prynne's *Short Demurrer to the Jewes*, attacked Menasseh's proposition and revived the old anti-Semitic myths, some defended it, but others, such as

Margaret Fell's, sought to engage in dialogue with the Jews in expectation of their return to England and conversion.[5]

Reading Menasseh's pamphlets as if they were addressed to her, inviting conversation, Margaret Fell responded with *For Menasseth Ben Israel: The Call of the Jewes Out of Babylon* (February 20, 1656). Enlarging her address beyond Menasseh to the Jews more largely, she would publish two more pamphlets addressed to the Jews within the next year or two: *A Loving Salutation to the Seed of Abraham among the Jewes* (October 31, 1656, or 1657; republished in 1660) and the brief *Certain Queries to the Teachers and Rabbi's among the Jews* (appended to *A Loving Salutation*).[6] Her fourth and last pamphlet to the Jews appeared in 1668, *A Call unto the Seed of Israel*. No other Quaker writer tried so hard to initiate discussions with the Jews.

Fell worked to have her pamphlets to the Jews published abroad, hoping to reach world Jewry and effect a mass conversion to her Quaker beliefs. At the end of her first pamphlet, she wrote: "I charge thee *Manasseth Ben Israell*, as thou wilt answer it before the living God, that thou let this be read and published among thy Brethren, and to goe abroad among them where they are scattered" (*For*, 20). Not waiting for a response, Fell took steps to have her writings disseminated to the Jews. A circle of disciples, members of her literary and spiritual community, worked for her. Her books were carried to Holland by the publishers William Caton and William Ames, leaders of the missionary effort to Holland, as well as by John Stubbs and Samuel Fisher. Wanting her pamphlets published in Dutch and Hebrew, she asked Fisher to translate the pamphlet *For Menasseth* into Hebrew. When he failed to, Ames himself did the Dutch translation, which was then translated into Hebrew, quite possibly by the Jewish

5. The fullest account of Menasseh ben Israel's mission to get the Jews readmitted to England, and of various issues involved, is in Katz, *Philo-Semitism*. See also Lucien Wolf, *Menasseh ben Israel's Mission to Oliver Cromwell* (London: Macmillan, for the Jewish Historical Society of England, 1901), which reprints Menasseh's tracts and has a long introduction. Shapiro, however, insists that "virtually all parties" in the debate over readmission were aware there were already Jews in England who practiced their religion privately; he argues that the Whitehall conference was thus not really about readmission but about "what rights should be granted them, and thus what their legal and social identity in England should be" (*Shakespeare and the Jews*, 58, 59). See William Prynne, *A Short Demurrer to the Jewes* (1656) and *The 2nd Part* (1656); *Anglo-Judaeus; or, The History of the Jews Whilst Here in England* (London, 1656), for example, p. 4. On the English fear that Christians would "turn" Jew, see Shapiro, *Shakespeare and the Jews*, 131–65, though his focus is on the period before the debate over Jewish readmission.

6. Isabel Ross says that a third bilingual English-Hebrew edition of *A Loving Salutation* also appeared in 1660, translated by a rabbi who had come from Poland and apparently attended a Quaker meeting (*Margaret Fell, Mother of Quakerism* [London: Longman's, 1949], 96).

philosopher Spinoza, who had just recently been excommunicated from the Jewish community in Amsterdam.[7] In the spring of 1658 a Hebrew translation of her second pamphlet, *A Loving Salutation*, was published in Holland.

Fell's pamphlets were not only translated into Hebrew but also disseminated to Jews by her evangelists. In 1661–1662 Caton distributed Fell's books in a synagogue in Frankfort. Fisher and Stubbs may have passed out the Hebrew translations of Fell's tracts to Jews throughout Europe as the two Quakers traveled from Holland to Rome and Constantinople on a mission to convert the pope and the sultan. In 1660, apparently trying to address a new Jewish audience in England, Stubbs prepared a bilingual English-Hebrew edition of Fell's *Loving Salutation*, employing as the translator a Polish rabbi who had recently come to England.[8] All of these people (a few Jews as well as Christians) were part of Fell's circle, her community of workers in the faith. We might even think of this writing community as including peripherally Menasseh ben Israel, who initiated the conversation, and to whom she wrote her first pamphlet. His pamphlets made her think he might be open to her spiritual vision, that he too might be drawn into the fold.

It is hard to know how effective these efforts were in converting Jews. Caton's and Stubbs's letters suggest that European Jews were interested and receptive: Stubbs says that the Polish rabbi who translated Fell's pamphlet attended a Quaker meeting, and Caton speaks of the Dutch Jews "hungering" for her book. But such comments may reflect mainly the desires of the missionary, for Caton also voices the familiar Christian complaint that the Jews are obstinate in their

7. Bonnelyn Young Kunze says, "She was the first Quaker whose message to world Jewry was translated into Dutch and Hebrew and exported to Holland" (*Margaret Fell and the Rise of Quakerism* [Stanford: Stanford University Press, 1994], 210). Ross, *Mother of Quakerism*, 89; see also Kunze, *Rise of Quakerism*, 211–16, on the Quaker missionary effort in Holland and the details of Fell's efforts to disseminate these tracts abroad. Both Ross, *Mother of Quakerism*, 93–94, and Kunze, *Rise of Quakerism*, 212–13, find Richard H. Popkin's argument in "Spinoza's Relations with the Quakers in Amsterdam," *Quaker History* 73 (spring 1984): 14–29, convincing.

8. On Caton's distribution of Fell's books, see Ross, *Mother of Quakerism*, 96; on Fisher and Stubbs, see Kunze, *Rise of Quakerism*, 215. This bilingual 1660 edition (presumably a third edition of *A Loving Salutation*) has columns of English and Hebrew on each page and is printed, as customary with Hebrew, from back to front. I have examined copies of both the bilingual 1660 edition and the Hebrew edition of 1658 at the Friends House (the Quaker library) in London. Richard Popkin, in *Spinoza's Earliest Publication? The Hebrew Translation of Margaret Fell: "A Loving Salutation,"* ed. Richard H. Popkin and Michael A. Singer (Assen/Maastricht, the Netherlands: Van Goraim, 1987), observes that the 1658 and 1660 Hebrew translations are the same except for some 1660 misprints, and thus suggests the Polish rabbi (Samuel Levi Asshur) had a more limited role than Ross claims (*Mother of Quakerism*, 8–9).

religion. We do not know whether Menasseh actually read the pamphlet she addressed to him.[9] He probably would not have recognized the authority of a woman to discuss the Bible, and he would not have been a likely convert, as he was from a family of Spanish Marrano Jews who could not practice their religion openly until they came to Amsterdam. What is remarkable, however, is Margaret Fell's extraordinary and persistent effort to reach the Jews in print, to initiate a conversation that would lead to conversion.

I want to examine Fell's addresses to the Jews, her attempts to create a new community through the printed word. I will pay particular attention to the ways Fell's and Menasseh's messianic expectations both converge and conflict—at once making possible and preventing conversation. Despite growing interest in Margaret Fell, her pamphlets—and particularly those addressed to the Jews— have not received extended analysis.[10] In part they reveal conventional strategies of Christian proselytizing, which are nonetheless worth analyzing for what they tell us about Christian-Jewish relations. But we also see her particular stance as a seventeenth-century Quaker woman, her distinctive prophetic self-presentation. Close attention to these texts illuminates not only the ongoing, complex process whereby seventeenth-century English Christian identities were defined in relation to Jews, but also the way in which Fell sought to construct her Quaker-Jewish community and her own authority as its center.

Accounts of Margaret Fell have somewhat secularized and modernized her, stressing that she was an educated gentlewoman, minister, writer of polemics (including a defense of women's preaching), agitator for the rights of Friends in prison, and organizer of a communications network among itinerant Friends.[11] But it is important to recover the strangeness of her Jewish tracts that, for all their conventional proselytizing strategies, reveal Fell's sense of her own

9. Kunze, *Rise of Quakerism*, 214. Caton wrote Fell that the Jews in Amsterdam "willingly and greedily received" her writings (quoted in Ross, *Mother of Quakerism*, 95). Kunze speculates it "was probably never read by Menasseh himself. He was deluged by books such as this one when he was in London in 1656–57" (*Rise of Quakerism*, 211).

10. Kunze's fine book reflects a historian's concerns and does not actually discuss the substance or strategies of Fell's pamphlets in detail. Phyllis Mack, *Visionary Women: Ecstatic Prophecy in Seventeenth-Century England* (Berkeley: University of California Press, 1992), does not have an extended discussion of her pamphlets. Nigel Smith, *Perfection Proclaimed: Language and Literature in English Radical Religion, 1640–1660* (Oxford: Clarendon Press, 1989), discusses Fell's texts only in passing (66, 69).

11. See Mack, *Visionary Women*, for example, 216–19. In fact, Mack dissociates Fell from prophecy, which she sees as the activity of women from the lower class (219). Even in Kunze's corrective study of Fell's devotion to Quakerism, Fell emerges not primarily as a prophet but as a "model of powerful female public ministry," "a shrewd, complex, fascinating, enormously energetic, and savvy woman who was moved by both high and low motives" (*Rise of Quakerism*, 229–30).

special authority as spiritual leader. In her pamphlet *For Menasseth* and her *Loving Salutation to the Seed of Abraham among the Jewes,* she adopted not just a prophetic but also a messianic identity. Inspired by a millenarian vision of (Christian) unity and community, which bore its own marks of intolerance, she addressed Jews who had their own different messianic desires but were seen as a more receptive audience than mainstream Christians at home. In addressing the Jews, Fell turns to the Hebrew Bible, particularly to the messianic, prophetic parts, which constitute the material of her "Jewish" tracts. She presents the Hebrew Bible as *her* text, one that she identifies with and appropriates but that also provides common ground with her hoped-for Jewish audience. But Fell reads the Hebrew Bible through a Pauline lens, converting Old Testament into New, Hebrew prophecy into her own, as she sought to turn Jews into Christians, believing she was chosen to bring about their gathering and conversion.

Because Margaret Fell was responding to Menasseh, it is necessary to begin with his pamphlets in order to understand the conversation. When Menasseh ben Israel presented his *Humble Addresses* to Cromwell "in behalf of the Jewish Nation," he was not simply seeking readmission. He wanted permission for the Jews to practice their religion openly, to establish *"a free and publick Synagogue"* in England.[12] This proposal was threatening to Christians, such as Prynne, who were convinced that toleration of Judaism would mean the conversion of English Christians, their relapse into the bondage of Jewish Law from which Christ's gospel had liberated them. But Menasseh insisted that the Jews do not "entice any man to professe their Law." If others wished to join them, that would be their own choice—and he cited the example of Ruth who decided to follow Naomi even though told to return to her own people (*HA,* 22, 23).

Behind Menasseh's desire to establish the Jews and their worship in England and Margaret Fell's desire to convert the Jews lay incommensurable messianic hopes. We should not underestimate the power of religious motivations at this time or the ardor with which both Jews and Christians, Menasseh and Fell, embraced messianism. Convinced he was living in the messianic age foretold by the Hebrew Prophets, Menasseh felt specially chosen by God to bring about the coming of the Messiah by finding the Jews a home in England.[13] His instru-

---

12. Menasseh ben Israel, *To His Highnesse the Lord Protector of the Common-wealth of England, Scotland, and Ireland. The Humble Addresses of Menasseh . . .* (London, 1655), "A Declaration to the Common-wealth of England." Future citations appear parenthetically in the text as *HA.*

13. Menasseh ben Israel, *Vindiciae Judaeorum* (London, 1656), 37–38; this tract was

ment was to be the printed, published text. As the *Humble Addresses* reminded his audience, the final Redemption was not to take place until "the dispersion of the Holy people shal be compleated in all places" ("Declaration"). In his earlier book, *The Hope of Israel*, whose title taken from Jer. 14:8 ("O the hope of Israel, the saviour thereof in time of trouble, why shouldest thou be as a stranger in the land") referred to the Messiah, Menasseh recounted the evidence that Jews had long been settled in Ethiopia, Medea, even China, where synagogues and secret Jewish communities had been confirmed by Jesuit accounts.[14] But he had also printed a startling new account by a Marrano Jew, Antonio de Montezinos (Aaron ha-Levi), who had recently returned from America where he claimed to have met Israelites of the tribe of Reuben living secretly in the interior of Peru. Montezinos told of being taken by an Indian guide up into the mountains of Quinto Province (Equador) to a group of Indians who greeted him in Hebrew with the fundamental Jewish statement of faith, the She'ma, "Hear O Israel, the Lord our God is one God" (*HI*, 9), and revealed themselves to be secret Jews, also with messianic expectations. Even in the most remote regions, it seems, Jews were expecting the coming of the Messiah. Montezinos's account confirmed that the ten "lost" tribes of Israel, taken in captivity by the Assyrians, were indeed scattered over the four corners of the world.[15]

The worldwide dispersal of the Jews was the necessary prelude to the coming of the Messiah. Throughout *The Hope of Israel*, Menasseh cited verses from the Hebrew Prophets (Isaiah, Daniel, Jeremiah, and Hosea) and from the end of Deuteronomy that describe the scattering and the subsequent gathering of the Jews from all the parts of the earth. Montezinos's "discovery" that there were Jews in America confirmed that virtually all those things foretold by the Prophets had been accomplished (Epistle Dedicatory, *HI*). Menasseh's English translator, Moses Wall, shared his messianic excitement and assimilated it to Christian imperatives, suggesting that Menasseh's unusual address to England itself signified that the time was near when the Jews would be gathered and "their and our Prince, Jesus Christ the Messiah," would finally "triumph glori-

---

written to refute the anti-Semitic charges of William Prynne's *Short Demurrer* and Alexander Ross's *View of the Jewish Religion* (1656).

14. Menasseh told how the Jesuit Riccuis sent a Jew to China, who compared the books the Chinese Jews kept in their synagogue with "our Pentateuch, and saw no difference" (*The Hope of Israel* [London, 1650], 40). Future citations appear parenthetically in the text as *HI*.

15. Menasseh supplemented Montezino's account with a description of the similarity of laws and customs of Indians and Hebrews, both of whom practiced circumcision, rent garments in mourning, observed the Sabbath, kept purity codes as in Leviticus, divorced adulterous wives, and so on (*HI*, 25–26). On Montezinos and the debate in England over the lost ten tribes of Israel, see Katz, *Rise of Quakerism*, 127–57.

ously" ("Translator to the Reader," *HI*). Though Menasseh insisted that the exact time of the gathering, the Redemption, is a mystery not even "revealed to *Rabbi Simeon ben Johay,* the Author of the Zo[h]ar" (*HI,* 67), he suggested the Messiah might even at this moment be among us. "ALTHOUGH THE MESSIAH WERE LAME, HE MIGHT HAVE COME BY THIS TIME. Though we cannot exactly shew the time of our redemption, yet we judge it to be neer" (*HI,* 69). All the misfortunes foretold at the end of Deuteronomy have happened to the Jews—this is the point of Menasseh's recounting of the Jews' suffering in the latter part of his *Hope*—so it must be time for their redemption (*HI,* 73).

The only obstacle to fulfillment of Messianic prophecies was the absence of a synagogue in England: "this remains onely in my judgement, before the MESSIA come and restore our Nation, that first we must have our seat here" ("Declaration," *HA*).[16] A secret Jewish community in England was not enough; there had to be public worship. Menasseh's goal in the petition he published was messianic Redemption; religious toleration was only the means.

Margaret Fell thought the Messiah was already revealed, and set out to convince Menasseh and his fellow Jews through her pamphlets. *For Menasseth Ben Israel: The Call of the Jewes Out of Babylon* is written from the perspective of a Christian who believes that the Jews have only to accept Christ as Messiah in order to bring about the final Redemption. Where Menasseh had praised the Jews' constancy in their faithfulness to the God of Israel, despite persecution, Fell suggests their sufferings have been divine punishment for their rejection of Christ—a view expressed more harshly by George Fox in his pamphlets to the Jews.[17] Then she turns directly to address Menasseh in the peremptory tone of a person convinced she has the purchase on truth: "Therefore heare the word of the Lord, thou who art called *Mannasseth Ben Israel,* (who art come into this

16. Menasseh must have known there was already a well-established secret Jewish community in London (Shapiro, *Shakespeare and the Jews,* documents its existence). Katz speculates he could have attended or presided over High Holiday services in the autumn of 1655 in London (*Philo-Semitism,* 198). Still, Menasseh insists on the importance of a "publick Synagogue" in England where the Jews can pray for the messianic redemption "whiles we expect with you *the hope of Israel* [that is, the Messiah] to be revealed" ("Declaration," *HA*). Katz describes how the Jewish community pulled back from Menasseh, perhaps alienated by his messianic zeal (*Philo-Semitism,* 240–41).

17. Margaret Fell, *For Menasseth Ben Israel: The Call of the Jewes Out of Babylon* (London, 1656), 3. Future citations will appear parenthetically in the text as *For.* Compare George Fox, *A Visitation to the Jewes* (London, 1656), 1–2. Fell is critical of the Jews' supposed apostasy, though she avoids the harshly confrontational approach of George Fox, who in his proselytizing tract to the Jews described their afflictions as the punishment for putting Christ to death (1). Kunze points out that Fell is more "gentle and positive in tone" than Fox and that she does not emphasize the guilt of the Jews for Christ's death (*Rise of Quakerism,* 218).

English Nation with *all the rest of thy Brethren*) which is a Land of gathering, where the Lord God is fulfiling his promise, *for a small moment have I forsaken thee, but with great mercy will I gather thee, Isa: 54.7,8.* And this is fulfilled in our day" (*For,* 3). In Margaret Fell's version of the messianic Redemption, England is the Jerusalem to which God is returning the Jews. This is the end time where the Jews will be gathered to the promised land—England—and to the true worship of God, which, for Fell, is the embrace of Christ. The solution to the Jewish misery is Christian conversion.

Rhetorically tactful, much more tactful than George Fox in his addresses to the Jews, Margaret Fell never mentions Christ by name or cites the New Testament in either the pamphlet *For Menasseth* or *A Loving Salutation.* Rather, she quotes and discusses only Jewish texts, the Hebrew Prophets—demonstrating her knowledge of the same prophets Menasseh had invoked and creating the illusion of a shared discourse.[18] Fell quotes only the verses most amenable to Christianizing and reads them through Pauline eyes as texts announcing the need for the Jews to embrace God's New (Christian) Covenant of the spirit. Employing a familiar strategy of Christian missionaries who seek to convert Jews, she mines the Hebrew Bible for proof texts that "show" Christian truths. The idea is to convince Jews that the prophetic part of the Hebrew Bible actually refers to Christ and the "truth" of the gospel, that Christ is, in a sense, already there in the Old Testament and has only to be recognized. Margaret Fell refers to "the Law and to the Testimony written in your hearts . . . which *Moses* speaks of" in Deut. 30:14 (*For,* 7–8). She quotes Jer. 31:33—"*I will make a new Covenant with the house of Israel. . . . I will put my Law in their inward parts, and write it in their hearts*" (*For,* 6)—and the opening verses of Isaiah: "*To what purpose is the multitude of your sacrifices unto me saith the Lord. I am full of burnt Offerings of Rams, and the fat of beasts, and I delight not in the blood of Bullicks, or of Lambs, or of hee Goats. . . . [Y]our appointed feasts my soule hateth, they are a trouble unto me, I am weary to beare them*" (*For,* 4).

When Moses at the end of Deuteronomy warned the Israelites to keep the Law and God's words in their hearts, he saw the Law given at Sinai (inscribed on tablets) and the internalization of the Law in the heart as necessarily linked. To keep the Law in the heart was to perform all the commandments and statutes—Deuteronomy presumes a connection between outward and inward that would be severed in the New Testament Gospels. When Isaiah castigated

18. Kunze sees Fell's quotation of Hebrew Prophets and omission of New Testament verses as an effort to create a "religious affinity between the Jews and her special type of Christianity" (*Rise of Quakerism,* 217).

Israel for idolatry and empty ceremonial observances, he was bemoaning a state in which religion had degenerated into mere formal observances. Though there is a movement toward a more spiritualized understanding of religion, Isaiah still assumed an ideal where the observance of Law expressed the spirit, where outward worship of God expressed a heart in tune with God, and thus in the fifty-sixth chapter he prophesied that after the Redemption of Israel their "burnt offerings" will again be accepted.

But Margaret Fell interprets these Hebrew Prophets from a distinctly Christian perspective that contrasts the Law (identified with the outward and carnal) with the gospel (identified with the inward and spiritual). She assumes, as Calvin expressed it in his *Institutes,* that the Hebrew Scriptures actually contain the revelation of Christ, and that Moses and the other Hebrew Prophets in some sense knew that revelation, which later Jews who rejected Christ denied.[19] Reading the Hebrew Prophets through Paul, she sees the Prophets (and even Moses) as condemning adherence to Mosaic Law and expressing a distinctly Christian spirituality—an inward spirituality that Christ was presumed to have taught, but that also is seen as preceding the giving of the Law at Sinai. To turn to the "light within" is to embrace Christ, who was available to Abraham and the Jews long before the Covenant at Sinai. She tells Menasseh and his fellow Jews that the "inward" Law "written in the heart" is "the Covenant which the Lord made with *Abraham*" (*For,* 20). Only by "turning" to Christ, who dwells within, will the Jews fulfill the words of the Hebrew Prophets that promise that when the "remnant" "returns" to God, God will turn to them in compassion and save them.

But to turn to God is to convert, to renounce Judaism, to give up the very worship that Menasseh ben Israel wanted established in England. Margaret Fell brings the weight of all the Hebrew Prophets to bear against the Jews. "Heare the Lord God testifies against you, and the abomination of your worship" (*For,* 4). Just as "the Lord testified against *Israel,* and against *Judah* by all the Prophets" (*For,* 2), castigating their relapses into idolatry, so Fell uses the words of the Jewish Prophets, from Moses on, to indict the Jewish religion as idolatry.

The pamphlets of both Menasseh ben Israel and Margaret Fell are rooted in the Hebrew Bible, the common text shared by Quaker and Jew, Christian and Jew, the thing that unites them. Both Christian and Jew embrace it as their Bible,

19. Calvin, *Institutes of the Christian Religion,* trans. John Allen, 2 vols. (Philadelphia: Presbyterian Board of Publication, n.d.), vol. 1, bk. 2, chaps. 6, 7, 9, 10; see esp. pp. 384–87.

though Christians following Paul's supersessionism call it the Old Testament. But the Hebrew Bible is also contested ground, the site of interpretive struggle between religious and cultural communities that read it differently. Fell's pamphlets, with their mass of quotations from the Hebrew Prophets, show her vigorous struggle for control of the text. As we shall see, they also announce a claim of interpretive authority that she hopes will convince and convert the Jews.

Both Christian and Jewish messianism looked forward to a time when all would worship the same God. In the end time, according to Jewish tradition, the temple would be rebuilt and the sacrificial observances restored (Isa. 56; Ezek. 37, 40–44; Amos 9:11; Mal. 3:1–4); peace would rule over the earth, and all nations would be united in serving the one God of Israel (Isa. 56, 60; Zech. 14:16). Menasseh looked forward to this time of messianic peace when "all" will be brought to knowledge and fear of God, noting that this is part of the Jewish daily prayers. He assumed, but did not stress in his pamphlet to English Christians, that the Jewish temple worship would be restored. Conversion of the nations was to be the *result* of Redemption, and Menasseh vigorously denied having any design to convert Christians. For Margaret Fell, however, messianic Redemption can happen only after the Jews are converted and accept Christ who is within.[20]

Fell's understanding of the conversion of the Jews comes from Paul, the paradigmatic Christian convert from Judaism, whose own reinterpretation of the Prophets guides Fell's. In Rom. 9, Paul distinguished between the Jews as "children of the flesh" (8), the "seed of Abraham" (7) according to the "flesh," and "the children of God" (8), the true "children of the promise" (that is, Christians), who would inherit God's blessings of Abraham in Genesis. Having rejected the Jews as carnal, cut off from God's promise of Redemption, Paul in Rom. 11 held out the promise that some of them may yet be saved: "I say then, Hath God cast away his people? God forbid. . . . Even so then at this present time also there is a remnant according to the election of grace. . . . And

20. Menasseh Ben Israel, *Vindiciae Judaeorum,* 26. Traditional Jews in their daily prayers still include this hope in their "Aleynu," the prayer Menasseh cites. Modern Judaism, however, has virtually abandoned the idea of the restoration of the sacrificial temple worship. Replying to a letter criticizing him for believing that the Jews as a nation will be converted, Moses Wall, Menasseh's translator, insisted that he did not endorse any program to convert the Jews: "For my part, I pretend not to any way to convert them, for I verily thinke that when it shall be done it will be Gods worke, and not mans"—a position much closer to Menasseh's than Fell's (see Wall, "The answer to the Letter," appended to the 1651 ed. of *Hope of Israel,* 58).

they also, if they abide not still in unbelief, shall be graffed in: for God is able to graff them in again" (1, 5, 23).[21] Rom. 11 is Paul's revisionist interpretation of the end of Deuteronomy, Isaiah, and the other Hebrew Prophets, which speak of the "remnant" that will be saved after all the desolation. For Paul, the "remnant" of Israel that Moses, Isaiah, Ezekiel, and Micah speak of—the remnant that will turn back to God from their idolatrous ways and be redeemed—becomes the "remnant" who have "the election of grace," who turn to Christ and thus will be "grafted in again." In Paul's strong (mis)reading of the Hebrew texts, Christian "conversion" replaces the "turn" to God (in Hebrew, *teshuvah*), which in Deuteronomy and the Jewish Prophets meant a return to the Mosaic commandments. With Paul, the Jews' rejection of Christ, their very obedience to Mosaic Law that the Prophets counseled, is now understood as the idolatry for which the Jews are punished by dispersion, exile, and suffering.

It is this Pauline revision of the Hebrew Bible, which powerfully defined Christianity's relation to the Jews, that Margaret Fell adopts, as she uses Isaiah to castigate the Jews, seeking to convert them with Jewish texts that Christians and Jews understand in completely different ways. Menasseh ben Israel's and Margaret Fell's messianic hopes are thus at cross-purposes, for all their shared goals of peace and unity. Believing that religion must be inward and spiritual, Fell attacks Jewish worship as merely "outward." In order to "escape" the "fierce wrath" of God in the Day of the Lord, Jews must abandon their "Covenant with Hell and Death" (*For,* 7). It is not only the sacrifices of the ancient Jewish temple that are "abominations" to God (*For,* 18) but also their entire religion, the religion that Menasseh wants to practice openly.

Fell tells Menasseh: "[G]ive over your outward washings, your outward observances and Ceremonies, and carnall ordinances, they are beggarly and filthy, the Lord abhorres them; your Temple, and your Synagogues, that is outward, your Circumcision that is outward, your Sabbath, that is outward, . . . your calling of assemblyes and solemne Feasts; For all those things saith the Lord, doth my soule hate" (*For,* 19). The worship Menasseh described with pride as an example of their peaceableness and faithfulness here is denounced as "Synagogues of Satan" (*For,* 20), a phrase that recalls Prynne's overtly anti-Semitic

---

21. Jason Rosenblatt has an excellent discussion of the Christian understanding of "the seed of Abraham," which distinguished between the children of faith (Christians, the true "seed") and the children of the flesh (Jews)—a distinction that disinherited the Jews, though Paul left open the possibility of some Jews being regrafted (*Torah and Law in "Paradise Lost"* [Princeton: Princeton University Press, 1994], 228–33).

fear that the Jews have a "design" to "set up their Synagogues of Satan" in England.[22] Fell's "loving" approach to the Jews is compromised by her deep hostility to Judaism. The supposed "universalism" of her community, its inclusiveness, turns out to be exclusive as it rejects Jewish difference.

Echoing the passage in John 8:41–44 (the source of so much anti-Semitism) where Jesus tells the Jews, "Ye are of your father the devil, and the lusts of your father ye will do," Fell reveals, for all her Quaker sympathy for the Jews and her desire to welcome them into England, an underlying antipathy toward the Jew that can be alleviated only by the erasure of Jewish difference. Thus, she insists toward the end of *For Menasseth ben Israel* that Jews should stop practicing circumcision and should instead circumcise the heart (15–16, 19).[23] Fell's vision of unity requires the erasure of difference, a difference signified not only by Jewish worship (considered outward, corporeal, material) but also by the physical mark of circumcision.

Insofar as Menasseh's pamphlet had initiated the conversation between Quakers and Jews, he becomes someone she can address, his text a crucial part of the dialogue. Yet, he remains outside her circle, on its margins. In order for Menasseh and the Jews to be part of her community, they must be divested of the religious and ethnic differences that constitute their identity.

Like Menasseh, Fell presents herself as having been specially chosen, albeit for a different purpose. Believing she has been specially "appoynted" by God to convert the Jews, Fell transmits "the word of the Lord" (*For*, 10, 3). In her pamphlets, she quotes Deuteronomy, Daniel, Psalms, Ezekiel, Jeremiah, Hosea, and especially Isaiah. As she intersperses these quotations with her own biblically resonant sentences, she makes it seem that she and the ancient Hebrew Prophets are all participating in the same enterprise of conversion. Her spiritual community that manifests itself in the written word extends back into the remote past, transcending temporal as well as geographical distances. She appropriates the words of the Prophets as her own (sometimes without citations), converting them so that Isaiah and even Moses are good Christians, in the attempt to give herself prophetic authority to the Jews, preaching a Christian gospel in Jewish garb.[24]

22. Prynne, "To the Christian Reader," in *Short Demurrer*, sig. B2v. The phrase "the synagogue of Satan" invoked by both Fell and Prynne is from Rev. 2:9, which Prynne cites in the margin.

23. Fell takes much the same tactic in trying to convert the Jews in her *Loving Salutation*, which ends with a quotation from Deut. 30:6: "the Lord thy God will circumcize thine heart." Future citations will appear parenthetically in the text as *LS*.

24. This strategy of presenting a Christian message under a Jewish guise is not un-

> Therefore feare the Lord God, and give over looking outward, for now the
> Lord is gone forth as a mighty man, and his Jelousie is stirring up like a man
> of warre. . . . Heare yee deafe, and looke yee blind, that yee may see, this day
> is this Scripture fulfilled in your eares. The Spirit of the Lord God is upon
> mee, because the Lord hath appoynted mee, to preach good tyding to the
> meeke; hee hath sent mee to bind up the broken-hearted, to proclaime lib-
> ertie to the captives, and the opening of the prison to them that are bound,
> to proclaime the acceptable yeare of the Lord, and the day of vengeance of
> our God: and to comfort all that mourne. (*For,* 9 – 10)

Seamlessly moving from her words of warning to the words of Isa. 60:1, she offers the truth (the light of Christ within) that will liberate the Jews from the state
of captivity and exile that symbolizes their bondage under Mosaic Law.

Not only does Fell present the gospel as actually "in" the Hebrew Bible, but
I would argue that she also takes yet a further step in her effort to bring the Jews
in, to create her newly expanded community. Going beyond the conventional
stance of the Christian proselytizer, she implicitly suggests she is the Messiah
the Jews are expecting.

Menasseh had mentioned that, according to the Prophets, the ten tribes of
Israel will all come to Jerusalem "under the leading of a Prince, whom some
Rabbins . . . do call *Messiah* the son of Joseph; and elsewhere *Messiah* the son of
Ephraim; . . . who shall be, as *Ezekiel,* and *Hosea* say, *The Everlasting Prince of all
the twelve Tribes*" (*HI,* 64). In her pamphlets to the Jews written in the late 1650s,
Margaret Fell, I would argue, assumes the role of this princely Messiah, as she
"call[s]" the Jews out of Babylon (as in the subtitle of her tract to Menasseh)
and tries to reach those ten scattered tribes by having her words translated into
Hebrew and disseminated to world Jewry.[25] Margaret Fell, that is, presents herself as the Messiah, as Jews understand him — the charismatic figure who would

---

common, as a recent incident makes clear. On the weekend of March 24, 2000, a made-
for-television film titled *The Rabbi* aired in a number of cities throughout the United
States. Produced by Morris Cerullo, a San Diego–based Christian missionary, the film
presented itself as a Jewish film; its promoters infiltrated the Jewish press with adver-
tisements for what was supposedly an "unforgettable story of an Israeli rabbi and his
struggles in modern society." In fact, the film was about a "messianic Jew" who, using
texts from the Hebrew Bible, gradually convinces his Orthodox family (including his
rabbi father) and an atheist uncle who is a Holocaust survivor that Jesus is the Messiah — and that one can be a Jew and accept Jesus. See the article by Julie Wiener, "Jewish
Papers Duped by Ad for Jesus Movie," <http://jta.virtualjerusalem.com/index.exe?000
32610>.

25. Scholem has noted an essential difference between messianism in Judaism and
in Christianity: "Judaism, in all of its forms and manifestations, has always maintained
a concept of redemption as an event which takes place publicly, on the stage of history

gather and lead the Jews back from captivity and diaspora. In the spiritual community she is constructing, she is its messianic center.

The radicalness of Fell's stance becomes clear when we recognize that she identifies not just with the Prophets, but also with the messianic figures they announce. Her claim of messianic authority is extraordinary, even more so when we remember the strongly patriarchal basis of English society—evident even among the religious radicals, despite the transgression of gender roles by female prophets and preachers. An educated woman whose father and husband were of gentry status, Fell may well have brought a sense of class privilege to her religious mission. But it is also Paul's teaching that "there is neither male nor female; for ye are all one in Christ Jesus" (Gal. 3:28) that empowers her as a woman to make this claim. In Jewish tradition, the Messiah was not God but a human being—variously priest, prophet, and prince, but, as far as I know, always a man, albeit with extraordinary powers.[26] At once fulfilling and breaking with tradition, Margaret Fell takes on this mantle herself, not only as a kind of female Elijah ("I will send you Elijah the prophet before the coming of the great and dreadful day of the Lord" [Mal. 4:5]) but also as the redeemer who will return the Jews to the Lord and to Jerusalem, which turns out to be England. "This is the day of your visitation," she says, announcing the last days to the Jews, "wherein the Lord God hath visited you, and called you, and shewed you the way of peace" (*For*, 19). Fell is the instrument through whom God has called the Jews; she has shown them "the way" in her pamphlets, has shown them how

and within the community. . . . In contrast, Christianity conceives of redemption as an event in the spiritual and unseen realm, an event which is reflected in the soul, in the private world of each individual" (*Messianic Idea in Judaism*, 1). We see in Fell both the radical inwardness of Christian messianism and the influence of the public, activist aspect of Jewish messianism that, Scholem notes, influenced "the radical wing of the Puritans" (16).

In her last pamphlet to the Jews, Margaret Fell claims the Messiah has already come: "gloriously is the Lord risen, and shining in the consciences of men" (*A Call unto the Seed of Israel That they may come out of Egypt's Darkness and House of Bondage unto the Land of Rest* [London, 1668], 1). Such a spiritualized, egalitarian understanding of the Messiah and messianic Redemption would seem to work against the notion that there is a special, unique Messiah who is coming at a particular point in time to redeem his people. Maybe by 1668 she, like Milton, had lost the millenarian faith. Yet, her pamphlets in the 1650s express the early Quaker belief that "the moment of confrontation and decision was at hand for the kingdom of God to break into human history" (Kunze, *Rise of Quakerism*, 216).

26. On her family's status, see Kunze, *Rise of Quakerism*, chap. 2. The Messiah is essentially a postbiblical concept, though it has a prehistory in the Hebrew Bible and the Prophets. In rabbinic thinking, the Messiah is a human being, a king who will redeem and rule Israel and establish the kingdom of God (see *Encyclopedia Judaica*, vol. 11 [Jerusalem: Keter Publishing, 1971], 1407–12).

to worship God (in the heart and "the inward man," not in "outward Temples" [*For,* 14]).

In the opening of *A Loving Salutation to the Seed of Abraham among the Jewes,* she uses Isaiah's words foretelling the redeemer of Israel to declare her own messianic role. Isaiah's words are presented as referring to *her,* as she is the person who is bringing light to the world and restoring the remnant of Israel to true worship:

> It is a light thing that thou mightest be my servant to raise up the tribes of *Jacob,* and to restore the preserved of *Israel,* I will also give thee for a light to the *Gentiles,* that thou mayest be my salvation unto the ends of the Earth, Thus saith the Lord the Redeemer of *Israel,* and his holy one, to him whom man despiseth, to him whom the Nation abhorreth, to a servant of rulers: Kings shall see and arise, Princes also shall worship. (1–2)

These verses from Isaiah (49:6–7) are used both to refer to Christ (in the conventional Christian interpretation) and to give Fell divine authority as the person sent by God to restore Israel and to be a "light" to the world, the person (devalued as a woman and despised as a Quaker) who will nevertheless rule princes and kings.[27]

Margaret Fell's self-proclaimed messianic role, so rhetorically powerful, explains her remarkable identification with Moses in these pamphlets. Moses is the prophet with whom Fell most regularly and insistently identifies. Moses not only delivered the Israelites from Egyptian bondage but was also prophetically associated with the Jewish Messiah who would redeem the Jews after their period of desolation and exile. Deuteronomy foretold that a prophet "like unto Moses" would herald the final restoration of the Jews in the "last days" (18:18, 15). Even his Hebrew name, Moshe, linked him with the Messiah (Meshiach), the second Moses who would restore their happiness and the true worship of God.

In her efforts to create a discourse that would effect Jewish conversion, making them part of the Quaker fold, Margaret Fell repeatedly cites Deuteronomy, addressing the Jews as Moses had addressed the Israelites. Echoing Moses, she

---

27. Compare *A Loving Salutation,* 7, where again she appropriates a passage from Isaiah that Christians saw as referring to Jesus, using it to claim that God has chosen her as his agent for Redemption: "Behold my servant which I uphold, mine Elect in whom my soule delighteth, I have put my spirit upon him, he shall bring forth judgement to the Gentiles: I the Lord have called thee in righteousnesse, I will hold thine hand, and will keep thee, and give thee for a Covenant of the people, for a light to the Gentiles" (Isa. 42:1, 6–7).

tells them to "hearken to the voyce of the Lord thy God, to keepe his Commandements and his Statutes" (*For*, 4; compare Deut. 30:10, 28:1, 15), and she, too, offers them a "Covenant" (*LS*, 27). She appropriates Deuteronomy as she had Isaiah, telling the Jews: "God . . . said unto *Moses*, . . . I will raise them up a prophet, from among their brethren, like unto thee, and will put my words in his mouth, he shall speake unto them, all that I command him" (*LS*, 21). Though the Jews "have not hearkened yet" to "this prophet" (that is, they have not yet accepted Christ), "now is the prophet speaking unto you in the Spirit, which is light, which is in the midst of thee" (*LS*, 21). The "prophet speaking," of course, is Margaret Fell, in whom Moses and Christ have merged.

Perhaps it might be objected that Fell was too sophisticated and educated to have adopted a prophetic, messianic identity. But such an objection projects, I think, modern attitudes onto the seventeenth century. We might recall another highly cultivated and educated person, John Milton, who regularly compared himself to Moses and in his polemical prose presented himself as a second (Christian) Moses, offering the English deliverance from the bondage of prelacy, bad marriage, and tyranny.

Fell's adoption of a messianic posture links her with other Christian religious radicals of the 1650s whose transgressive claims of divinity the Blasphemy Ordinance of 1650 sought to repress. Some women believed they were like Mary, carrying the Messiah in their womb, but it was apparently only men who claimed the status of Messiah, sometimes attracting male and female followers.[28] The belief that God dwelled within the spirit of each believer encouraged messianic fantasies—fantasies that often incorporated Jewish elements. The most notorious messianic radical was Margaret Fell's acquaintance, the Quaker James Naylor, whose entry into Bristol in October 1656 on a donkey, with three men and three women disciples waving branches and singing "Holy, holy, holy, Lord God of Sabaoth," not only reenacted Christ's entrance into Jerusalem but also recalled the figure of the Jewish Messiah entering Jerusalem on a donkey, a familiar woodcut in Jewish Haggadahs, itself based on a comment in Zech. 9:9: "Rejoice greatly, O daughter of Zion: shout, O daughter of Jerusalem: behold, thy King cometh unto thee; he is just, and having salvation; lowly, and riding upon an ass, and upon a colt the foal of an ass."[29]

Fell never explicitly identified herself as Christ as Naylor did. Indeed, she

28. See *A List of some of the Grand Blasphemers and Blasphemies, which was given in to the Committee for Religion* (London, 1652–1653).

29. See figs. 1 (from a *Haggadah*, Munich, fifteenth century) and 2 (from the *Venice Haggadah*, 1609) in *Encyclopedia Judaica*, 11:1410.

wrote Naylor on October 15, 1656, just before his infamous entry into Bristol, warning him that he was improperly claiming divinity and being influenced by "unclean spirits" (namely, Martha Simmonds and Hannah Strange) who were encouraging him in his fantasy that he was the risen Christ.[30] Yet, Margaret Fell was at this very time obliquely but powerfully presenting herself in her pamphlets to the Jews as their Messiah—not as Christians understood him to be Christ, but as the Jews understood the Messiah, as a second Moses, the person who would lead the Jews back from captivity, restore the true worship of the Lord, and finally be accepted by all the nations as their prince. Seeking to bring the Jews out of darkness so they will inherit along with Christian believers the "promise" made to the "seed" of Abraham in Genesis (18:8, 12:3; compare Gal. 3:6–16 and Rom. 9:6–8), she calls to "the JEWISH NATION, *Greekes* and *Hebrewes*" who are "scattered" throughout the world (*For,* 1), calling them to return to God and to England, the promised land. Her identification with Moses as messianic redeemer is evident in the full title of her pamphlet to Menasseh, *The Call of the Jewes Out of Babylon,* which collapses several points of Jewish history (slavery in Egypt, captivity in Babylon after the destruction of the first temple, and the present diaspora) as she offers them deliverance from a condition of unfreedom understood in Christian Pauline terms as bondage to the Law. Blurring the distinction between herself and Christ, narrowly avoiding the charge that she is arrogating divine powers to herself, she suggests that she is "the Prophet, that the Lord is raising, like unto *Moses* (which is light) to which if ye will be obedient, it will gather you from all nations whither you are scattered, and bring you into the good land" (*LS,* 27).

The most powerful evidence of Fell's Mosaic-messianic identification comes at the end of her *Loving Salutation,* where we find three startling lines of Hebrew, standing alone, without citation or translation.

אללי הרבום ל   ומל יהוה אלהיך את-לבבך

לאהבה את-קה אלהיך

The first line (Aleh ha-Devarim, translated "these are the words") is the opening of Deuteronomy ("These are the words which Moses spake unto all Israel on this side Jordan in the wilderness" [1:1]). The other Hebrew lines are from Deut. 30:6, a favorite verse of Christian proselytizers: "And the Lord thy God will circumcize thine heart, . . . to love the Lord thy God." Fell uses these two Hebrew quotations from the Bible as the seal of her pamphlet, its final stamp of authority. But she also presents these Hebrew words (which are, significantly, *not* given a biblical citation) as if they are an extension of her text, written by

30. Ross, *Mother of Quakerism,* 98–114; Ross prints Fell's letter to Naylor in appendix 9 (pp. 396–97).

her, thus collapsing and identifying Moses' words and hers—an effect that would be even more pronounced in the Hebrew edition of this pamphlet. These Hebrew words, from the last Book of Moses that recapitulates the Law, retrospectively give Fell's entire text a Mosaic authority.

With these final words, Fell attempts to gain legitimacy with a Jewish audience, quoting their Bible in the original (albeit with an error), giving the illusion—or raising the possibility—that she knew some Hebrew. She suggests through her use of Hebrew biblical language a common ground, as she seeks to convert the Jews and create a new community that might usher in the hoped-for millennium. But, read through Paul, Moses' words are here turned against the Jewish religion, so that the great Hebrew prophet Moses becomes the spokesman for Christianity and Hebrew the language of the gospel, even as Fell presents herself as a second Moses.

Perhaps Margaret Fell's messianic identification was simply a clever way of appealing to the messianic preoccupations of her Jewish audience, a rhetorical strategy for authorizing her as the powerful center of a spiritual community that could draw them in. But I think it is possible that, for a time, Fell actually believed she was the divinely appointed Messiah of the Jews, that she believed she had more than the common share of the divine spirit that Quakers thought dwelled within all believers. At least one of her devoted Quaker followers thought of her in such elevated terms.

In August 1658, William Ames (the person who had translated Fell's pamphlet *For Menasseth* into Dutch and helped get it translated into Hebrew) wrote Margaret Fell from Holland, where he had been active in her missionary effort. Ames addressed her in the passionate, eroticized language of devotion derived from Psalms and Song of Songs that was traditionally reserved for addressing God. Hannah Strange and Martha Simmonds had used similar language to address James Naylor when they believed him to be the Messiah. "Thou knowest I love thee and great cause I have to love thee above all others that ever I yet saw . . . for in weakness thou has strengthened me, and in affliction thou has comforted me, and has borne my infirmities in patience and wisdom, and when other friends (of great account) have been no small trial to me, even then have I felt thy love supporting, therefore my soul loves thee."[31] To Ames, Margaret Fell was a person exalted "above all others," the source of his strength and comfort, the one to whom (as to God) he looked in his trials.

The Jews certainly did not embrace Fell as their Messiah; they turned instead,

31. The letter is printed in ibid., 97.

for a time, to their own Jewish "Messiah," Sabbatai Sevi, until his apostasy disappointed their messianic hopes. It is hard to know whether Margaret Fell had any success in drawing Jews into her circle, whether any Jews actually converted, though it would seem some were interested in her "universalizing" message from the fact that Jews translated her tracts into Hebrew. Nevertheless, it is unlikely that many Jewish men would have listened to the teachings of a woman prophet, since rabbinic tradition had long held that only men were permitted to study the Torah and the Hebrew Bible. For all Fell's dreams of an expanded community, ultimately her circle remained those few committed to her Quaker cause.

The role of Margaret Fell in the Quaker-Jewish dialogue of the mid-seventeenth century and the failure to achieve her goal of massive Jewish conversion show that the desire to communicate a spiritual message and to enlarge the community of faith is not in itself enough to ensure success. For all the commonality of the Quakers' and Jews' belief in the truth of the Bible and its promises, their suffering for their faith, their messianic hopes for an imminent happy ending to history, irreconcilable religious differences stood in the way. Fell's distinctly Christian perspective, her position of superior authority, and her desire to convert the Jews made productive conversation impossible as it denied integrity to their belief. Her rhetoric placed the Jews outside her circle even as she invited them to enter it.

Nonetheless, in writing pamphlets addressed to the Jews and establishing a network to ensure that her writings reached her intended Jewish audience, Fell was doing something remarkable. She was trying, like the early Christians, to form a community that was multicultural, that did not depend on a prior ethnic, religious, and cultural sameness. She thus had a vision of inclusivity that challenged the normative notion of community in England. We see in her pamphlets the dream of a more inclusive community, the desire to break down the boundaries between Christian and Jew and between different countries and ethnicities, at a time in history when such divisions seemed to be getting firmer.

Fell's goal of conversion inevitably compromised her inclusivity, turning a model of diversity into a model of sameness and thus reenacting the "exclusive universalism" of the traditional Pauline model of community.[32] Nevertheless, the most important thing Menasseh the Jew and Margaret the Quaker shared—the belief that bound them, however tentatively and loosely, and inspired their

---

32. The term is Paul Stevens's, who discusses the Pauline "exclusive universality" in his paper, "Milton's Janus-Faced Nationalism: Soliloquy, Subject, and the Modern Nation State," forthcoming in *JEGP* 100 (April 2001).

actions and writing—was the Hebrew Bible with its messianic ideal of a unified humanity, its vision of one humanity united in the worship of one God. As we have seen, the Hebrew Bible was both common ground and a site for struggle between different religious communities that interpreted the text differently. It had the potential both to bring together and to divide Quaker (or Christian) and Jew. There is more than a little irony in the fact that for two millennia this interpretive struggle has been waged over the meaning of Hebrew texts that envision a time when all of humanity will be united in the worship of one God.

It is often said that Christianity defined itself in contrast to Judaism as a universal religion, offering a universal, inclusive community transcending national, genealogical, and racial boundaries, though one might say that Christianity substituted a different marker for inclusion within the community of God's chosen people, the acceptance of Christ. However, long before the Christian gospel, the Hebrew Prophets of the Old Testament had offered a vision of universality that countered the narrower, restrictive sense of community defined by the worship and purity laws of Leviticus. The Hebrew Prophets' forecasts of catastrophic destruction were redeemed by their vision of peaceful community, of a time when religion would no longer be a divisive force. This is the vision of Isa. 2:2, which inspired Menasseh's hopes for a unified humanity and was printed on the title page of Fell's *Loving Salutation:* "It shall come to passe, that the mountaine of the Lords house shall be established in the top of the mountaines, and it shall be exalted above the hills; and all nations shall flow unto it."

The Hebrew Prophets envision a special kind of community, purged of the repressive or exclusionary qualities one sees in other parts of the Bible, Christian as well as Jewish. Isaiah says that when God "redeems" Israel, "the sons of the stranger" will also "join themselves to the Lord, to serve him": "[M]ine house shall be called an house of prayer for all peoples"; the "gates" of God's city will be "open continually" (56:6, 57:7, 60:11). In Isaiah's final chapter, God says, "I will gather all nations and tongues; and they shall come, and see my glory. . . . And I will also take of them for priests and for Levites. . . . [A]ll flesh [shall] come to worship before me" (66:18, 21, 23). In this inclusive worship, the distinction between the "chosen" people and the "nations" (the meaning of *goyim*) disappears, as "all nations" and "all flesh" come to worship God. Micah has a similar vision: "[M]any nations shall come, and say, Come and let us go up to the mountain of the Lord, and to the house of the God of Jacob; and he will teach us of his ways, and we will walk in his paths. . . . [A]nd they shall beat their swords into plowshares, and their spears into pruninghooks: nation shall not lift up a sword against nation, neither shall they learn war any more" (4:2–3). The next verses, though less familiar, are at least as important, for perhaps they give the condition for universal peace: "But they shall sit every man under his vine and under his fig tree, and none shall make them afraid: for the mouth of the Lord of hosts hath spoken it. For all people will walk every one in the name of his god, and we will walk in the name of the Lord our God for ever and ever" (4:4–5). Not only will the nations (as in Isaiah) come of their own free will (exactly the point Menasseh makes), but what seems most startling (in both the influential King James Version and the 1917 JPS translation) is the suggestion that they will also still remain distinct peoples, each having their different "names" for God even as they come together to worship the same deity.[33]

These Hebrew Prophets, of course, write from the position of a shared monotheism, which always constructs its identity in relation to polytheistic or atheistic "others" who are excluded from the community. Perhaps one might say that these Prophets simply envision all the "other" people becoming Jews. But what is striking in these passages is that the exclusivity and the traditionally firm boundaries of monotheism are softened and even dissolved (no longer will there be distinctions between "the chosen" and "the nations"), even as monotheism is maintained. Micah envisions a messianic age in which all peoples will be united in the recognition that, for all their differences, they worship the same divine being even though they may call God by different names. Though these passages might express only wishful thinking, they continue to be important, now as they were for Margaret Fell and Menasseh ben Israel, as they suggest an alternative model and goal for human community in which there is enlightenment without compulsion, difference without enmity, and harmony in diversity.

33. I have quoted the King James or Authorized Version of the Bible. The modern JPS translation is more problematic as it perhaps suggests a distinction between "we" and "the peoples," though such a distinction seems at odds with the universalism of the previous verse: "Though all the peoples walk / Each in the names of its gods, / We will walk / In the name of the Lord our God / Forever and ever" (*The Prophets, A new translation* . . . , 2d ed. [Philadelphia: Jewish Publication Society of America, 1978]).

Notes on the Contributors

John Considine teaches English at the University of Alberta and is a consultant to the *New Oxford English Dictionary* project. He has written about Sir Thomas Overbury for the *New Dictionary of National Biography* and is preparing further studies of Overbury's life and writings, both genuine and apocryphal. He also works on other aspects of language and culture in early modern England and on the history of scholarship, with a special interest in dictionaries.

M. L. Donnelly is Associate Professor of English at Kansas State University. His research and teaching interests center on classical humanities and seventeenth-century literature and culture. His publications include essays on Bacon, Cavalier amatory lyrics, Caroline panegyric, Milton, and Marvell.

Robert C. Evans is University Alumni Professor at Auburn University at Montgomery. He has published essays on many Renaissance topics; books on Ben Jonson, Martha Moulsworth, and Frank O'Connor; as well as short fiction. He serves on the editorial boards of the *Ben Jonson Journal* and *Comparative Literature*. He is general editor of the forthcoming *Ben Jonson Encyclopedia*.

Achsah Guibbory is author of *The Map of Time: Seventeenth-Century English Literature and Ideas of Pattern in History* and *Ceremony and Community from Herbert to Milton: Literature, Religion, and Cultural Conflict in Seventeenth-Century England,* as well as numerous articles on seventeenth-century literature from Bacon to Behn and Dryden. Her essay on Donne's *Elegies* received the John Donne Society's Distinguished Publication Award. She is Professor of English and Religious Studies at the University of Illinois at Urbana-Champaign.

Judith Scherer Herz is Professor of English at Concordia University, Montreal. She has written on a wide range of seventeenth-century and twentieth-century topics. She is the author of *The Short Narratives of E. M. Forster* and *A Passage to India: Nation and Narration.* She is a past president of the Association of College and University Teachers of English and is currently president of the John Donne Society.

M. Thomas Hester, Alumni Distinguished Professor at North Carolina State University, is founding coeditor of the *John Donne Journal.* The author and editor of numerous volumes of literary criticism, including *Kind Pity and Brave Scorn: Donne's Satyres* and *John Donne's 'Desire of More': The Subject of Anne More Donne in His Poetry,* and a recipient of the John Donne Society's Distinguished Publication Award, he is presently coediting the prose letters of Donne, editing a volume of the *Donne Variorum,* and completing a book on Donne's epigrams, elegies, lyrics, and Holy Sonnets.

Anna K. Nardo is Major Morris and De'Ette Anderson Alumni Professor of English Literature at Louisiana State University. In addition to the essay in this volume, she has published two other studies of Milton's experiences in Italian academies, as well as *Milton's Sonnets and the Ideal Community* and studies of Shakespeare, Jonson, Milton, Browne, Walton, fantasy literature, and the ludic self.

Paul A. Parrish is Professor of English at Texas A&M University, where he teaches courses in Renaissance and early modern literature. He is author of *Richard Crashaw* and other studies of seventeenth-century poetry and is chief editor of the commentary for *The Variorum Edition of the Poetry of John Donne.*

Ted-Larry Pebworth is William E. Stirton Professor in the Humanities and Professor Emeritus of English at the University of Michigan–Dearborn. He is author of *Owen Felltham,* coauthor of *Ben Jonson* and *Ben Jonson Revised,* coeditor of *The Poems of Owen Felltham* and *Selected Poems of Ben Jonson,* and coeditor of collections of essays on a variety of Renaissance and seventeenth-century figures and topics. A senior textual editor and member of the advisory board of *The Variorum Edition of the Poetry of John Donne,* he has served as president of the John Donne Society.

Timothy Raylor is Associate Professor of English at Carleton College. His published work on intellectual and literary circles of the seventeenth century includes *Cavaliers, Clubs, and Literary Culture.* He is currently preparing an edition of the poems of Edmund Waller.

Stella P. Revard is Professor of English Emerita at Southern Illinois University, Edwardsville. She holds degrees in English from Yale University and in classics from Washington University, St. Louis. An honored scholar of the Milton Society of America, she is president of the International Association for Neo-Latin Studies. She is the author of *The War in Heaven: Paradise Lost and the Tradition of Satan's Rebellion; Milton and the Tangles of Neaera's Hair: The Making of the 1645 "Poems"; Pindar and Renaissance Hymn-Ode,* as well as numerous essays on Renaissance poetry.

Sharon Cadman Seelig is Professor of English at Smith College. She is the author of *Generating Texts: The Progeny of Seventeenth-Century Prose; The Shadow of Eternity: Belief and Structure in Herbert, Vaughan, and Traherne;* and essays on Shakespeare, Milton, and other seventeenth-century authors. Her current project is a study of self-representation in texts by early modern women writers.

Paul G. Stanwood is Professor Emeritus of English at the University of British Columbia. He has edited a number of seventeenth-century religious and literary texts, including three books of Hooker's *Of the Laws of Ecclesiastical Polity* and Jeremy Taylor's *Holy Living and Holy Dying.* He has coedited *John Donne and the Theory of Language* and *The Selected Prose of Christina Rosetti.* He is author of a book-length study of Izaak Walton and *The Sempiternal Season: Studies in Seventeenth-Century Devotional Literature,* a collection of his own essays. He is a past president of the John Donne Society and serves on the executive council of the International Association of University Professors of English.

Claude J. Summers, William E. Stirton Professor in the Humanities and Professor of English at the University of Michigan–Dearborn, has published widely on Renaissance and modern literature. Coeditor of collections of essays on a wide variety of Renaissance and seventeenth-century topics and figures and author or coauthor of book-length studies of Marlowe, Jonson, Isherwood, Forster, and twentieth-century English and American gay fiction, he has recently published an edition of the *Selected Poems of Ben Jonson* and the Lambda Award–winning *Gay and Lesbian Literary Heritage.* He is a past president of the John Donne Society.

Index of Works Cited

This index includes only primary works. Lengthy titles are silently abbreviated, and anonymous works are alphabetized by title.